Lloyds TSB

Tax Guide
2000/2001

Lloyds TSB

Tax Guide 2000/2001

SARA WILLIAMS AND JOHN WILLMAN

P

PROFILE BOOKS

Published by Profile Books Limited
58A Hatton Garden, London EC1N 8LX

This edition published 2000

Printed in Great Britain by The Bath Press

A CIP catalogue record for this book is available
from the British Library

ISBN 1 86197 215 6

The Authors

Sara Williams is the CEO of e-Vitesse plc, owner of Growth Company Investor Ltd, which publishes a range of online publications on www.growthcompany.co.uk and a range of print publications such as *Growth Company Investor*, *Off Exchange* and *The AIM Guide*. She writes a weekly column in the *Express* and has contributed many articles on tax, finance and business for national newspapers, including the *Daily Mail*, *The Times* and the *Independent*. For a number of years she wrote for *Which?*, including the *Which? Tax Saving Guide* and the *Which? Book of Tax*. She is the author of the *Lloyds TSB Small Business Guide*. Sara Williams is a former investment analyst and lecturer in finance. She has been a public interest member for LAUTRO, Institute of Actuaries and Mortgage Code Register of Intermediaries, and a council member of the Consumers' Association.

John Willman is Consumer Industries Editor of the *Financial Times*. He has written extensively on personal finance and tax for *Which?*, including the *Which? Tax Saving Guide* and the *Which? Book of Tax*. Formerly publications editor at Peat Marwick McLintock (a firm of accountants which is now part of KPMG), he was the editor of *Assessment and Taxes*, published by the Inland Revenue Staff Federation. He is the author of *Make Your Will, How to Sort Out Someone's Will* and *A Better State of Health: A Prescription For The NHS*.

CONTENTS

A MESSAGE FROM SIR BRIAN PITMAN LLOYDS TSB GROUP CHAIRMAN

It is now four years since the Inland Revenue introduced the Self Assessment Tax Return and, once again, changes have been made to the taxes we pay.

Although Self Assessment should make things more straightforward, it is crucial that you take great care when you complete your tax return – and that you complete it by the deadlines set by the Revenue. Each year the Inland Revenue claims as much as £80 million from people who have either filled in the forms incorrectly or have sent them in too late.

Our Tax Guide, which is now in its 15th year, will help you to understand the complexities of personal taxation and the changes the Chancellor has introduced in his most recent budget. It is a valuable aid, providing clear, simple and accurate information, and detailed guidance on completing a tax return. Indeed, over the years it has earned a reputation for being one of the best personal tax guides available.

In addition to the Tax Guide, we can offer you support through our Personal Tax Management Service and our broad range of financial services. All of these are designed to help you manage your business and personal affairs in a complex financial world.

Meanwhile, I hope you find this Lloyds TSB Tax Guide a great help.

ACKNOWLEDGEMENTS

A tax guide of this type cannot appear without the help and hard work of a multitude of people. For this edition, Brian Clutterbuck has as usual helped us to avoid some mistakes. We are especially grateful to Jonquil Lowe for updating several of the chapters for us this year. On the production side, Jonathan Harley, Penny Williams and Frances Worlock have worked long hours to perfect the guide. Moira Greenhalgh has again produced a very useful index. In addition, Stephen Brough and Andrew Franklin at Profile Books and Stephen Page and his team at Fourth Estate have shown determination and commitment to bring the guide to as wide an audience as possible.

Thank you

Sara Williams and John Willman

NOTE
Both of us – along with everyone at Lloyds TSB and Profile Books Ltd – have made strenuous efforts to check the accuracy of the information. If by chance a mistake or omission has occurred, we are sorry that neither we, Lloyds TSB nor the Publisher can take responsibility if you suffer any loss or problem as a result of it. But please write to us at 9 Harley Street, London W1N 1DA if you have any suggestions about how we can improve the content of the guide.

Dear Reader

The Lloyds TSB Tax Guide went to press shortly after the 2000 Budget on March 21 – and much may change before the chancellor's proposals become law. If you want to keep abreast of developments, there are two ways to do it:

- send for our free update, which will be issued in the autumn – see below for instructions on what to do

- log on to the TaxGuide website – at www.taxguide.co.uk

To get the paper version send an A4-sized self-addressed envelope with a 41p stamp on it to: Sara Williams and John Willman, Lloyds TSB Tax Guide, 9 Harley Street, London W1N 1DA.

Yours sincerely

Sara Williams
John Willman

HOW INCOME TAX WORKS

Under self-assessment you operate the tax collection system in part or fully. You provide the records, fill in the tax return, and you may also work out the tax bill. You must pay what you owe by sending a cheque, along with your tax return and your tax calculation, to the Inland Revenue by 31 January. If you prefer, you can send in your tax return to the Inland Revenue by 30 September. The tax you owe will be worked out by your tax inspector and you must pay it by 31 January.

However, around one in 10 taxpayers fail to get to grips with self-assessment and end up paying a penalty for late delivery of their tax return. Remember that there are :

- dates by which you have to fill in your tax return (p. 16)
- penalties you have to pay if you don't stick to all the rules (p. 20)
- rules about records which you must keep (p. 14)
- dates to pay your tax bill (p. 17)
- rules about which income you will pay tax on (p. 3)
- dates for reporting income (p. 14)
- obligations which taxpayers must stick to (p. 14).

The taxes you might pay
There are a number of different ways in which the government raises money from taxpayers. Some of the taxes are as follows:

- income tax – some of your income is taxed at varying rates
- capital gains tax – some of the gains you make on investments or possessions may be taxed at varying rates
- inheritance tax – when you die, some of the money you leave to others could be taxed
- National Insurance – this is paid only by people who are earning, employees, employers, the self-employed or partners.

Other taxes include council tax, corporation tax, value added tax, stamp duty and excise duties.

The tax returns for the tax year ending 5 April 2000 should land on your doorstep during April 2000. These will cover your income and gains, reliefs and allowances. The information you provide will be used by you or your tax inspector to work out your income tax and capital gains tax bills.

How tax rules are changed
Parliament is responsible for changing the tax rules. The government produces a Budget to suggest changes from the start of the next tax year, which runs from 6 April to the following 5 April. The Finance Bill with the changes suggested in the Budget will be published in May, debated in Parliament and the Finance Act passed before 5 July.

What is in this guide?
This tax guide explains the rules for income tax, capital gains tax, inheritance tax and national insurance. It covers most of the rules which the majority of taxpayers need to know, but it may not cover very specialised cases.

In Part I, the guide gives a broad outline of the rules and helps you to plan your affairs to minimise your tax bills. It covers what you need to know for the coming tax year (ending 5 April 2001). It includes the changes proposed in the March 2000 Budget. By following its advice you should be able to save tax in the current and future tax years.

The guide went to the printers at the beginning of April 2000 and its advice is based on what was proposed in the Budget. Proposals are sometimes changed by debate in Parliament. You can receive notice of later changes in two different ways:

- contact our web site, www.taxguide.co.uk
- send an A4 stamped (41p), self-addressed envelope to Sara Williams, Lloyds TSB Tax Guide, 9 Harley Street, London W1N 1DA

In Part II, the guide helps you to fill in your tax return and has the information and figures for the tax year ending 5 April 2000. It includes lots of tax-saving tips which help you to cut your tax bill for the last tax year.

A simple guide to income tax
There are many complexities and exceptions in the way that income is taxed. What follows is a broad brush approach to how income is taxed. It gives some important relationships:

Taxable income = (Income − Reliefs − Allowances)
Total income = (Income − Reliefs)
Income tax = Taxable income x the rate(s) of tax

Income is made up of what you earn from your job or self-employment and what you receive as income from other sources, such as investments. But not all the money you receive is income (see p. 6) and some income you receive is tax-free (see p. 309). Some income you receive has had tax deducted (called *net* – see pp. 7 and 62) and some income is paid without tax deducted (called *gross* – see pp. 7 and 312).

Savings income (see p. 62) is a special case. It is normally paid with tax at the savings rate of 20 per cent already deducted. There is no further tax to pay if you are a basic rate taxpayer. You have to pay an extra 20 per cent tax if you are a higher rate taxpayer. Starting rate taxpayers can reclaim part of the tax already deducted. Non-taxpayers can reclaim all the tax or arrange to have the income paid gross.

Income from shares, unit trusts and open-ended investment companies is also a special case. It is paid with tax at 10 per cent already deducted. Again there is no further tax to pay if you are a basic rate taxpayer. But higher rate taxpayers pay 32.5 per cent and non-taxpayers cannot reclaim the tax already deducted.

Reliefs are amounts which you pay out and on which you get tax relief. They reduce your income before your tax bill is worked out. Most give you tax relief at your highest rate of tax, for example pension contributions and donations to charity. But there are exceptions. Up to the tax year ending 5 April 2000, relief on mortgage interest to buy your own home was restricted a certain amount. From 6 April 2000, mortgage interest relief has been abolished for most people though still applies to mortgages linked to some home income plans.

EXAMPLE

Jessica Jones has income from self-employment of £10,000. She pays £1,000 into a personal pension scheme and she can claim a personal allowance for the tax year ending 5 April 2001 of £4,385. Her taxable income is:

	£
Income	10,000.00
Less Reliefs: pension contributions	1,000.00
	9,000.00
Less personal allowance	4,385.00
Taxable income	4,615.00
Tax at 10 per cent on first £1,520	152.00
Tax at 22 per cent on next £3,095	680.90
Total tax bill	832.90

Allowances are amounts to which you are entitled because of your personal circumstances. They reduce your income before your tax bill is worked out. But some allowances get a reduced rate of tax relief. These include married couple's allowance (abolished for people under 65 from 6 April 2000 but still available if you or your husband or wife is aged 65 or more).

Taxable income is the figure on which you work out your tax bill. The amount of your income tax depends on how much taxable income you have and what rate of tax is paid on it (see below).

Total income is a figure that is not important for most taxpayers, but it is for the elderly (those in receipt of age-related allowances). The amount of total income determines whether you can receive these allowances in full or in a reduced amount (see p. 43). Total income can also affect some taxpayers paying life insurance premiums (see p. 68).

Total income is the amount you have after you have deducted some reliefs from income, but before deducting allowances. The reliefs you deduct to arrive at total income include pensions contributions, the gross amount of charitable covenants, charitable donations under Gift Aid and the payroll giving scheme, the gross amount of some maintenance payments (available from 6 April 2000 only if either party is aged 65 or more) and some loan interest (but not on a home income plan mortgage in MIRAS).

The rates of tax
There are different rates of tax:

- starting rate tax (10 per cent for tax years ending on 5 April 2000 and 5 April 2001)
- basic rate tax (23 per cent for tax year ending on 5 April 2000 and 22 per cent for the tax year ending on 5 April 2001)
- higher rate tax (40 per cent for tax years ending 5 April 2000 and 2001)

The levels at which these rates apply can vary from year to year. Here are the levels of income for each of these rates for the tax years ending 5 April 2000 and 5 April 2001:

Tax year ending 5 April 2000

Income band £	Size of band £	Tax rate %	Tax on band £
0 – 1,500	1,500	10	150
1,501 – 28,000	26,500	23	6,095
Over 28,000		40	

Tax year ending 5 April 2001

Income band	Size of band	Tax rate	Tax on band
£	£	%	£
0 – 1,520	1,520	10	152
1,521 – 28,400	26,880	22	5,913.60
Over 28,400		40	

INCOME, RELIEFS, ALLOWANCES AND TAX CREDITS

Income, reliefs and allowances are the three elements in determining your income tax bill – and the three ways in which you can minimise the size of it. Look for opportunities to arrange your income to be tax-free (see p. 309 for a comprehensive list). In the case of a married couple, seek to distribute the income between the two of you to the greatest advantage. And don't forget to claim all your reliefs and allowances, including those from the past that you might have forgotten. You will find tax-saving tips throughout the guide; many of them are gathered together on pp. 32-40.

INCOME

Your income will be made up of money or goods you receive or anything you get in return for a service – but not all payments you receive count as income (see below). The following will all normally be considered as income:

- what you earn from your work, including a job (see p. 195), a partnership (see p. 251) or self-employment (see p. 225). This includes salary, fringe benefits and business profits
- rent from letting out property (see p. 253)
- income from investments, such as interest, dividends and distributions (see pp. 61 and 146)
- pensions (from the state, your previous employer or your own plan)
- social security payments, such as jobseeker's allowance
- until 5 April 2000, maintenance income, if the arrangement was made before 15 March 1988. But, from 6 April 2000, this is no longer taxable
- casual, occasional or miscellaneous income, such as freelance earnings, income received after you close a business, income from guaranteeing loans, dealing in futures, income from underwriting, certain capital payments from selling UK patent rights, accrued income including from gilt strips
- income from a trust.

Payments that are not income
Some payments you receive are not income. For example:

Types of income (for tax year ending 5 April 2001)

Type of income	Tax deducted?	At what rate?	More tax to pay? [1]
Earnings from a job	yes	StR, BR, HR	no
Taxable fringe benefits	yes, from earnings	StR, BR, HR	no
Pension from your former employer	yes	StR, BR, HR	no
Bank, building society [2] interest	yes	SR	yes – HR
British Government stocks [3]	no		yes
Income from annuity (other than pension annuities)	yes [4]	BR	yes – HR
Dividends from shares	yes [5]	10 per cent	yes [6]
Distributions from unit trusts and open-ended investment companies	yes [5]	10 per cent	yes [6]
Income from an executor before a will is sorted out	yes	BR	yes – HR
Income from a trust	yes	generally 34 per cent (see p. 274)	yes – HR
Income from self-employment	no		yes
Income from a partnership	no		yes
Social security benefits	no [7]		yes
Maintenance payments	no		no
Rent from property	no		yes [8]

Key: StR = starting rate; BR = basic rate; HR = higher rate; SR = savings rate

(1) There could, of course, be more tax to pay if insufficient has been collected.
(2) Non-taxpayers can have interest paid without tax deducted – see p. 65.
(3) But you can choose to have interest paid with tax deducted at the savings rate of 20 per cent.
(4) Tax is deducted from the part of the annuity which counts as income, not the part which counts as a return of the capital.
(5) But non-taxpayers cannot claim back the tax deducted.
(6) Higher rate tax payers will pay taxes at the rate of 32.5 per cent (after 10 per cent tax credit, a tax rate of 22.5 per cent, see p. 66)
(7) But if you return to work, tax if due will be deducted from your earnings.
(8) But rent in the Rent a Room scheme is tax-free up to a limit. (For more details see pp. 253-5).

- presents and gifts
- loans
- lottery prizes
- gambling winnings (unless it is your way of making a living)
- what you make from selling an asset (unless this is how you make a living)
- what you receive under a maintenance agreement made on or after 15 March 1988. And, from 6 April 2000, this applies to all income received under a maintenance agreement, no matter when it was made
- money you inherit.

Although these payments are not income, there may be other tax to pay on them – for example, capital gains tax or inheritance tax

Tax-free income
There are many examples of income that are tax-free, including premium bond prizes, interest on National Savings Certificates and income from savings or investments held in an individual savings account (ISA). A comprehensive list is given on p. 309.

How is income paid to you
Income can be paid to you without any tax deducted *(gross)* or with tax deducted *(net)*. The tax can be deducted at the savings rate, the basic rate, the higher rate, and/or some other rate. If it's savings income, tax will be deducted at the savings rate (currently 20 per cent) on most savings and 10 per cent on dividends and distributions from shares and unit trusts. The table on the right lists types of income, whether or not they are paid with tax deducted and if any further tax will be due. There are more details of income in Chapter 13.

If you need to give a figure for gross income when you have received net income, there are ready reckoners which help you to gross it up in Appendix B on p. 312.

RELIEFS

You make certain choices in your life. You might choose to save now to give yourself a pension (over and above the state pension) when you retire. Or you might choose to make gifts to charity. The government decides that it wants to encourage certain of your actions – for example, saving for a pension. So it allows you to deduct some or all of what you pay for these from your income before working out your income tax bill. These items are known as reliefs, outgoings or deductions.

Types of relief (for the tax year ending 5 April 2001)

Type of relief	Amount of relief	How do you get tax relief?
Charity: covenant	StR, BR or HR	StR, BR: make lower payments HR: either PAYE code or tax bill
Charity: Gift Aid[1]	StR, BR or HR	StR, BR: make lower payments HR: either PAYE code or tax bill
Enterprise Investment scheme (up to £150,000)	20%	through your PAYE code or tax bill
Home income plan [2]	23%	make lower payments through MIRAS
Interest on a loan to pay inheritance tax	StR, BR or HR	through your PAYE code or tax bill
Interest on business loans	StR, BR or HR	through your PAYE code or tax bill
Job expenses	StR, BR or HR	through your PAYE code or tax bill
Maintenance payments[3]	10% of £2,000	through your PAYE code or tax bill
Mortgage interest on a home you let	StR, BR or HR	a lower tax bill on rental income
Pension contributions to employers' schemes	StR, BR or HR	through PAYE system
Personal pension payments[4]	Employees BR or HR Self-employed StR, BR or HR	Employees BR: make lower payments HR: through PAYE code or tax bill Self-employed a lower tax bill

Key: StR = starting rate; BR = basic rate; HR = higher rate

(1) You make lower payments by deducting relief at the basic rate. If your top rate of tax is only the starting rate, the Inland Revenue may claw back some of the relief.
(2) Relief not available for loans made on or after 9 March 1999 unless lender has already agreed in writing to advance the loan
(3) From 6 April 2000, available only where one or both parties aged 65 or more. Tax treatment shown is for maintenance paid under the 'new rules'. See p. 180 for details of the 'old rules' and when they apply.
(4) Employees paying into personal pensions get basic rate tax relief by making lower payments. They get the relief even if the amount of tax they pay is less. This treatment will be extended to all stakeholder pension schemes when they are introduced from April 2001.

A further advantage of reliefs is that they may lower the rate at which you pay tax. For example, if you pay pension contributions it might mean you pay tax at the basic rate of 22 per cent rather than the higher rate of 40 per cent. When this happens it means that the cost to you of some of these payments after tax can be low.

How you get tax relief

There are three ways in which you can get tax relief:

- you can make a lower payment by deducting the amount of the tax relief from the payment and keeping it yourself – for example, if you want a charity to receive £50 under the Gift Aid scheme, you hand over just £39
- you can get your tax relief through the PAYE system. It will be included in your Notice of Coding and thus you will pay less tax on your salary each month
- you can get your tax relief by claiming it in your tax return. If you are going to work out your own tax bill you would deduct the amount in your calculation and pay less tax. Or your tax inspector will work out the bill allowing for the deduction.

The table on the right lists types of reliefs and how you get them. There are more details about reliefs in Chapter 14.

ALLOWANCES

Everyone is entitled to an allowance to deduct from their income to ensure that some income is tax-free. This is called the personal allowance. But the amount of the allowance varies with age. There are a few other allowances that you may be able to claim – but these depend on your personal circumstances. There are details of allowances in the table on p. 11 and in Chapter 15.

Details of allowances

Allowance	Age	Tax year ending 5 April	Amount
Personal	up to 65	2000	£4,335
		2001	£4,385
	65-74	2000	£5,720[1]
		2001	£5,790[1]
	75 plus	2000	£5,980[1]
		2001	£6,050[1]
Married couple's [2]	up to 65	2000	10% of £1,970
		2001	no allowance
	65-74	2000	10% of £5,125[1]
		2001	10% of £5,185[1]
	75 plus	2000	10% of £5,195[1]
		2001	15% of £5,255[1]
Blind person's	any	2000	£1,380
		2001	£1,400
Additional personal [3]	any	2000	10% of £1,970
		2001	no allowance
Widow's bereavement [4]	any	2000	10% of £1,970
		2001	10% of £2,000

(1) The amount of these allowances is reduced if total income is above a certain amount. In the tax year ending 5 April 2000 the allowances were reduced if total income was £16,800 and over and in the tax year ending 5 April 2001 the income limit is £17,000. For more details see p. 43.

(2) From April 2000, this allowance is abolished for people under age 65. Where the allowance received by an older person is restricted because of income – see note 1 above – it will not be reduced below £2,000.

(3) This allowance is abolished from 6 April 2000.

(4) This allowance is abolished for deaths occurring after 5 April 2000. Where death occurred during the tax year ending 5 April 2000, the widow also receives the allowance in the tax year ending 5 April 2001.

TAX CREDITS

The government is progressively integrating the state benefits system and the tax system by introducing tax credits. Tax credits work by giving you either cash or tax reductions through the tax system, for example through PAYE or by claiming from your tax office, and reducing the amount you get as your income increases. The following tax credits are in use or on the way:

- **Working Families Tax Credit** This was introduced from October 1999 and replaced a benefit called Family Credit. Working parent(s) on a low income and with at least one child can claim the credit. If their income after deducting tax and National Insurance (and ignoring the amount of credit they receive) exceeds a given threshold (£91.45 a week in the tax year ending 5 April 2001), the credit is reduced by 55p for each £1 income above the threshold
- **Disabled Person's Tax Credit** Introduced in October 1999, this replaced Disability Working Allowance. Again the credit is reduced by 55p for each £1 of income above a set threshold (£71.10 for a single person in the tax year ending 5 April 2001)
- **Children's Tax Credit** This will be introduced from 6 April 2001 and replaces the married couple's tax allowance abolished for people under 65 from 6 April 2000. In the first year, the credit will be 10% of £4,420 given as a reduction in your tax bill. (So the maximum tax saving will be £442.) But you will lose £2 of the credit for every £3 by which your income exceeds the threshold at which higher rate tax starts to be paid
- **Integrated Children's Tax Credit** From 2003, the government plans to combine the child support elements of working families tax credit, income support and jobseeker's allowance with the children's tax credit
- **Employment Tax Credit** From 2003, the government plans to introduce a tax credit for everyone in work and on a low income, regardless of whether they have children
- **Pensioner's Tax Credit** The government is consulting on whether a pensioner's tax credit could be used to boost the income of low-income pensioners.

YOU AND YOUR TAX INSPECTOR

The popular image of the tax inspector is probably close to that of Hector, the character the Inland Revenue uses to publicise deadlines for sending in your tax return. In reality, your tax inspector is nothing like the pin-striped, bowler-hatted Hector. The Inland Revenue is in the middle of a process of streamlining, which is expected to continue until 2002. The interface with the public is being dramatically altered. For most taxpayers the plan is to have one office to send out your tax return, process it when you send it back and issue your PAYE code. A network of high-street Taxpayer Enquiry Centres provides a face-to-face service where taxpayers can talk to tax staff who can call up their records on computer screens and deal with queries.

Along with other government departments, the Inland Revenue is trying to ensure that by 2002, one quarter of dealings with the public can be carried out electronically, through their television, by phone or computer. A major telephone call centre in East Kilbride, Scotland is now being tried out. If successful, it will be rolled out across the country.

You can ask for a free software package to help you complete your tax return if all your income is covered by pages 3 to 8 of the return plus the Employment pages and the Self-Employment pages. The package will not work if you have other income or gains. Telephone 0845 9000 404 or visit www.inlandrevenue. gov.uk/sa.

To encourage you to deal electronically with the Revenue, for one year only, you can get tax discounts if you send in returns by internet and pay your tax electronically (for example, by debit card). The discounts apply

> ## TAX-SAVING IDEA
> Get on-line! Send in your tax return for the year ending 5 April 2000 over the internet and pay any tax due using your debit card (or by asking your bank to arrange an electronic transfer). You will qualify for £10 off your tax bill. You should not deduct the £10 discount when you're working out how much tax is due but you can deduct it from any payment you are making.

to the following returns sent in and tax paid during the year ending 5 April 2001:

- self-assessment tax returns for the tax year ending 5 April 2000 – £10 discount
- VAT returns due from businesses – £50 discount
- End-of-year PAYE returns due from employers – £50 discount plus a further £50 if you're a small employer paying some of your employees Working Families Tax Credit or Disabled Person's Tax Credit.

YOUR OBLIGATIONS

New source of income or capital
Even if you don't receive a tax return, you must notify your tax inspector of any income or capital gains, which have not been previously declared, within six months of the end of the tax year in which you make the income or gain. This applies even if you don't yet know the amount of the income or gain.

There are certain circumstances in which you don't have to notify your tax office. This applies, for example, if all the income comes under the PAYE system or if the income is dividends from shares which is paid with tax deducted at 10 per cent and you pay tax at no more than the basic rate.

Records
You are required to keep records, such as original copies of dividend vouchers, bank statements, certificates of interest received and any cer-

tificates showing foreign tax deductions, which you need to complete your tax return. If you don't have the original certificates, you can complete your tax return using information that can be verified by an external source. You don't have to send in your vouchers and other documents in order to get a tax refund. You must keep the originals in case of Inland Revenue enquiry, but if they are lost you will not be penalised providing you can produce other evidence for the information. You also need to keep a copy of the working papers that you used to work out your calculations.

If you don't run your own business or have letting income, the period to keep records is one year from the date by which you must send back the tax return (31 January). However, this period is extended if there should be an enquiry into your affairs. Records must be kept until the enquiry is complete.

The period to keep records is also extended if you send in your return late or need to correct it after you have sent it in. The documents need to be kept until one year after the end of the quarter in which you amended the return or sent it in late. Quarters end on 31 January, 30 April, 31 July and 31 October.

If you run your own business or receive any income from letting, you need to keep records for five years from the date by which you should send in your tax return (31 January). The records should include what you receive and spend in your business, for example, sales and purchase invoices.

The failure to keep records can result in a swingeing penalty (see p. 20).

THE TAX RETURN

Your tax return asks you for details of your income, deductions and allowances for the tax year just ended, that is the year ending on 5 April 2000. There is one basic tax return of eight pages sent to everyone who should receive a tax return. But there are also a lot of supplementary pages for particular types of income – self-employment, trusts, employment, share schemes, partnerships, land and property, foreign, capital gains and non-residence. You may not receive any of these or, in an extreme case, you might

> ### EXAMPLE
> Ashley Hickie is a self-employed journalist. He also has some savings, such as unit trusts and a building society account. He completes his tax return for the year ended 5 April 2000, including carrying out the calculation of his own tax bill, and returns it by 15 January 2001. Ashley must keep the dividend vouchers and certificate of interest, plus the working papers on this, until 31 January 2002. The records of his business and the working papers relating to it need to be kept much longer. He has to preserve them until 31 January 2006.

receive nine different supplements to the basic return. For more details about these supplements see p. 140.

In the past, it was acceptable to use such phrases as 'as returned' or 'as agreed' for income or the value of benefits. But you are now required to fill in the correct figure – otherwise you will not be able to work out how much income tax or capital gains tax you owe. This means you must get hold of the documents you need, including Forms P60 (your income from your job and the tax you have paid on it), P45 part 1A (your income and tax to date when you leave your job), P11D or P9D (your fringe benefits and expenses for the year), P2 (your notice of coding). Your employer has the responsibility to supply you with these forms (but not P2) by certain dates (see p. 23).

> ### TAX-SAVING IDEA
> If you are an employee paying tax under the PAYE system and you have some other income, for example from investments, on which you will need to pay tax, you should send in your tax return with your tax calculation by 30 September. If you do this, and the amount of tax due is £1,000 or less, you will not have to pay tax on this extra income by 31 January. Instead, it will be included in your PAYE code for the following tax year and you will pay tax on it with your monthly salary, thus spreading out and delaying the payment of your tax bill.

Deadlines for your tax return

There are two important dates to bear in mind. If you want to ask the Inland Revenue to work out your tax bill on your behalf, as your agent, your tax return must be sent in by 30 September. Unless you are using a tax adviser, we recommend that you do this. This is also the date by which you must submit your return even if you do your own tax calculation if you want any previous underpayment (£1,000 or less) to be deducted through the PAYE system, rather than you paying it with the rest of your tax bill.

There is a different date set for returning your tax return if you or your tax adviser choose to calculate what you owe in income tax. This is 31 January.

If you have missed the 30 September deadline and decide that after all you want the Revenue to calculate the tax due, you can still ask for this to happen. But your tax inspector won't guarantee to do this by the 31 January slot, so you may end up paying a penalty for late tax payment.

Where a tax return has been issued after 31 October, you are given three months to complete it and send it back to your tax office. But if the return is issued after 31 July and you want your tax inspector to calculate the tax due, it must be returned within two months.

If you don't send in your tax return

Failing to send back your completed tax return means you can be charged a penalty (see p. 20) and allows the Inland Revenue to issue what's called a determination. Your tax inspector produces an estimate, to the best of his or her belief and using the best information available, of how much tax you should pay. The tax shown on this determination is payable; you cannot appeal against it or postpone it.

The only way you can overturn this estimate is to complete your tax return and tax calculation. You must do this within five years of the date by which you should have sent it in, or, if it is later, within a year of the determination by your tax inspector.

Your tax inspector cannot make a determination if five years have passed since the date by which you should have sent in your tax return. There will also be penalties and interest to pay (see p. 20).

TAX PAYMENTS

After completing your tax return, either you or your adviser or your tax office work out the amount of tax due on all types of income and capital gains. When you return your tax return, at least by the following 31 January, you send in the amount of tax that you have calculated as being due. This is the final bill for income tax for the year.

Interim and final payments

Self-assessment of income tax requires interim payments on account. These will be based on what was due in the previous year, less amounts deducted at source, what is deducted through the PAYE system, tax credits and so on. There is no adjustment for changing levels of income, tax rates or allowances, although you can ask for it to be adjusted.

> **TAX-SAVING IDEA**
> Always check your Statement of Account (see next page) to see if you can claim a reduction in interim payments. But if in doubt, it is better to pay slightly more rather than too little on account – you will be charged interest if you pay too little, whereas tax you have overpaid will earn interest. The rate of interest charged on underpaid tax is roughly twice as much as that added on overpaid tax.

Apart from those paying through the PAYE system, taxpayers will pay income tax due in three instalments. The first interim payment on account (normally half the amount of tax you paid in the previous year less any capital gains tax and tax deducted at source) will be on 31 January during the tax year. The second interim payment on account will be on 31 July following the end of the tax year. The final balancing income tax payment or repayment will be made after completion of the tax return on 31 January following the end of the tax year. Any capital gains tax due will also be paid with this third instalment.

However, there are rules which mean that interim payments will not be required if they are small. Working on the basis of the tax due for the previous tax year, if the total tax payable, net of tax deducted at source (including PAYE), is less than £500 or if tax deducted at source (including PAYE) is more than 80 per cent of the total income tax plus Class 4 National Insurance due, then interim payments won't be required.

The effect of this new system will be that income tax will be paid either monthly through the PAYE system or half-yearly on 31 January and 31 July.

Employees can put off paying a final tax bill of £1,000 or less by asking for it to be included in next year's PAYE code. To achieve this, you have to send in your tax return by 30 September.

Statement of Account

During January 2000, you may have received a Statement of Account giving an estimate of what you should pay on 31 January 2000 and the same figure will be due on 31 July 2000. This estimate is based on the tax you paid for the tax year ending 5 April 1999. For how to check this statement see p. 306. And for how to appeal against it, see p. 307. You will need to use form SA303 to claim to reduce your payments on account.

Interest and surcharges

Interest is payable on tax which is paid late. On the other hand, any tax you have overpaid will also earn interest. The rate of interest due on unpaid tax is based on the average rate of borrowing, whereas that due on overpaid tax is based on average investment returns less tax that would be paid. Any interest charged or received will be shown on your statement of account. Interest is automatically charged on any tax left unpaid by 31 January or 31 July following a statement of account. However, if the statement of account was issued late, although you sent in your tax return on time, the interest will only start 30 days after the date on the statement. Interest is also charged on any tax left unpaid by 31 January following the end of the tax year – that is by 31 January 2001 for the tax year ending 5 April 2000 – unless your tax return was issued late. If the tax is still not paid by 28 February 2001, there is a surcharge of 5 per cent of the unpaid tax. A further 5 per cent surcharge of the amount of tax still unpaid after 31 July 2001 is imposed. Interest will be added to any unpaid surcharge, starting 30 days after the notice of the surcharge.

CHANGES TO YOUR TAX RETURN

Mistakes and corrections

Sometimes you may not know a figure with 100 per cent accuracy by the time it comes to fill in your tax return. What you have to do is to put in your best estimate and work out the tax due on that. When you can supply the final figure, you should do so. If there is more tax to pay, you will have to pay interest (or will receive interest if a refund is due) but no surcharges or penalties unless you have been negligent or fraudulent.

It's also possible that you might make a mistake when you complete the return. You can correct an error at any time within 12 months after the date the return should be sent back – 31 January. If you don't spot a mistake but the Inland Revenue picks up an obvious error, such as an arithmetical mistake or a misunderstanding of principle, your tax office will correct the return within nine months of the date the return was sent in.

Any tax due as a result of the revised self-assessment should be paid either by the normal payment date or 30 days after the making of the self-assessment (but this does not put off the date from which interest is charged).

Enquiries

Your tax inspector has the right to enquire into your tax return – but once only – without giving any reason. A small proportion of all returns is selected at random for enquiry. An enquiry is quite different from your right as a taxpayer or your tax inspector's right to correct or amend your tax return (see above). Once the Inland Revenue has said it is going to enquire into your tax return, you are not able to amend it until after the enquiry is complete.

Your tax inspector must give you written notice of an enquiry. If you sent in your tax return on time, the notice must be made by 31 January the following year. If you sent in your return late, the notice of an enquiry can be issued up to a year after the end of the quarter in which you sent in your return (quarter ends are 31 January, 30 April, 31 July and 31 October). With an amended tax return, the notice can be issued up to a year after the end of the quarter in which you amended it.

Your tax inspector has the right to demand that you produce certain documents. When you receive a notice of an enquiry, you may also receive a notice to produce these within 30 days. You can produce copies, but your tax inspector may insist on seeing the originals. You can appeal within 30 days against this notice to produce documents.

You can also appeal to the general commissioners (see p. 22) if you consider that an enquiry should not have been undertaken or is being continued unnecessarily. The general commissioners can issue a notice to the Inland Revenue requiring it to close the enquiry.

If your tax return or its amendment is the subject of an enquiry your tax inspector will issue you with a formal notice telling you it is completed, how much tax you are considered to owe (if any) and requiring you to amend your self-assessment. You may also be required to amend your self-assessment before the completion of an enquiry if your tax inspector decides that it is too low. You will be given 30 days to amend your self-assessment in line with your tax inspector's conclusions. In certain conditions, you can also use this 30-day period to amend your self-assessment yourself with any changes which you had notified to your tax inspector. If you don't amend your self-assessment, your tax inspector has 30 days in which to do it for you. You can appeal against this Revenue amendment.

What your tax inspector can do if an enquiry has been completed
Although a second enquiry cannot take place, the law allows a discovery assessment if you have been acting fraudulently or negligently. A discovery assessment cannot be made if it is a mistake of arithmetic or principle on your part. Nor can it be made if the correct information was available to the Inland Revenue and it should have been possible to work out the correct tax.

A discovery means that your tax inspector has discovered that some income or gain on which you should have paid tax has not been included in your self-assessment, or the assessment is too low, or the amount of relief given is too much. A discovery assessment would be to collect the tax due. You can appeal against a discovery assessment (see p. 22).

PENALTIES, APPEALS AND COMPLAINTS
Penalties
A whole raft of penalties has been introduced:

- if you don't tell your tax office about a new source of income or capital gain within the required time limit, the maximum penalty imposed can be the amount of tax which would be assessed for that tax year. Interest can be charged on this penalty

- if you don't keep the records required under the self-assessment system, a penalty of up to £3,000 could be imposed. But there are certain exceptions to this, for example, if the documents which you have not kept are dividend vouchers or interest certificates – because there are other ways in which this income can be verified. Interest can be charged on this penalty
- failing to make the annual returns required from employers under the PAYE system and construction industry scheme by 19 May following the year of assessment would bring penalties starting at £100 for each month (or part of a month) by which they are overdue
- you are allowed to claim that you should not make interim payments of your tax bill (see p. 307), either because you will have no tax bill or because it will be covered by payments deducted at source (for example, earnings under the PAYE system or savings income paid with tax deducted). If you make an incorrect statement fraudulently or negligently, the maximum penalty is the amount or additional amount you would have paid on account if you had made a correct statement. Interest can be charged on this penalty
- if you fail to deliver your tax return, you can be fined £100 (or the amount of the tax due if less) and a further penalty of up to £60 a day may be set by the commissioners for each day it is late starting from the day you are notified by the commissioners – but this is likely to happen only if your tax office believes you may owe a substantial amount of tax. If your tax return is still not delivered six months after it was due you can be fined a further £100, and a delay of a year would mean that you could be charged a penalty of the amount of tax that would have been due. You can appeal against these penalties to the commissioners
- if you are in a partnership and you fail to deliver your partnership return, you can be charged the same penalties as above, but not the tax-geared penalty. There is no provision for reducing the £100 penalty
- if you fraudulently or negligently deliver an incorrect return, you can be charged a penalty equal to the amount of tax that would have been due
- if you don't produce the documents your tax inspector asks for during an enquiry, you can be charged a penalty of £50. If you still don't come up with the documents, a daily penalty can be imposed. The amount will be £30, but it could rise to £150 if you are taken to the commissioners.

Penalties which are based upon an amount of tax that is due can be limited by certain factors which your tax inspector could take into account. These include disclosure, cooperation and gravity.

A claim for tax relief, allowance or tax repayment must be made in a tax return, unless it couldn't be included at that time or within the arrangements for correcting a return. If you make a claim independent of a return, you will need documentary proof and you must keep all the records relating to the claim. If you do not keep your records, you may be fined a penalty of up to £3,000, plus interest for each and every claim.

Appeals and complaints

You have the right to appeal against:

- an assessment which is not a self-assessment
- an amendment to your self-assessment by the Inland Revenue after an enquiry into your tax return
- an amendment of a partnership statement where a loss of tax is discovered
- a disallowance, in whole or in part, of a claim or election included in a tax return.

> ### TAX-SAVING IDEA
> You can appeal against the £100 penalty for missing the deadline for sending in your tax return. A reasonable excuse would be, for example, a prolonged postal strike, serious illness, the death of a close relative, or loss of records due to fire, flood or theft. Pressure of work, a failure by your tax adviser or lack of information would not be regarded as a reasonable excuse.

You have to give written notice of appeal within 30 days after the issue of the notice of assessment, amendment or disallowance. But if you want to appeal against an amendment by the Revenue as a result of an enquiry, you cannot appeal until you have received notice that the enquiry is complete.

Even though you are appealing against the tax, it is due unless you also apply to postpone payment of the tax.

If you disagree about the amount of the tax bill, you should first of all exhaust the avenues within the Inland Revenue to try and reach an agreement. It is always worth appealing to your tax inspector – he or she may not have made the original decision. However, if it becomes clear that the two of you are not going to agree, there remains the option of appealing to the commissioners – and if that doesn't work you could appeal to the High Court, then to the Appeal Court and ultimately to the House of Lords.

There are two types of commissioners. The general commissioners are not tax experts, but often local people acting in the same way as magistrates. There will be a clerk with expert knowledge on hand to advise them. The second group are known as special commissioners. These are part of the Civil Service and tax experts in their own right.

If you are dissatisfied with the way the Inland Revenue handles your tax affairs, you should first complain to your tax inspector. If you get no satisfaction, you should direct your complaints to the regional controller responsible for your tax office (ask the tax office for the name and address). If this doesn't work, you should channel your next communication to the independent Revenue Adjudicator. The Adjudicator's remit covers matters such as excessive delay, errors, discourtesy or the way your tax inspector has exercised his or her discretion.

THE PAYE SYSTEM

Your employer is an unpaid tax collector for the Inland Revenue using the PAYE system – Pay As You Earn. Every time employees are paid, tax is deducted from the earnings and sent in a batch to the collector of taxes.

From April 2000, your employer will also be responsible for paying two new tax credits (Working Families and Disabled Person's – see p. 12) along with your pay packet. These tax credits replace two social security benefits, Family Credit and Disability Working Allowance.

Your employer needs various bits of information to operate the PAYE system. The aim is that at the end of the tax year, each employee will have had the correct amount of tax deducted, although this does not always happen. Underpayments of tax might be collected in the following year through the PAYE system or in a tax bill at the end of the year.

The Inland Revenue will tell your employer what your PAYE code is and will also supply tax tables so that your employer can deduct the right amount of tax. If the number in your code is 438, for example, you will be entitled to £4,389 free of tax for the tax year. If you are paid monthly, you will receive one-twelfth of £4,389 (that is £365.75) each month. If you are paid weekly, you will receive £4,389 divided by 52 each week free of tax. This would be £84.40.

The PAYE system is flexible and can be adjusted during the tax year. If your circumstances change, you should tell your tax inspector who should issue a new PAYE code (see Chapter 26). Your monthly after-tax earnings should rise once the new code has been received by your employer.

Your employer must give you certain forms by required dates so that you can use them to fill in your tax return. You should receive your P60 for the tax year ending 5 April 2000 by 31 May 2000. Form P9D or Form P11D should be received by 6 July 2000. Chase your employer if you don't receive them.

DEADLINES

Within 60 days

- Tell your tax office if you disagree with the statement of taxable social security benefits you receive from the benefit office

On or before 31 May 2000

- Form P60 should have been given to all employees by employer

On or before 4 June 2000

- Choose to pay tax in instalments on exercise of option in the tax year ending 5 April 2000 to acquire shares through an approved scheme

On or before 6 July 2000

- Form P9D (or Form P11D) should have been given to employees receiving fringe benefits by employer, plus details of other benefits provided by someone else

On or before 31 July 2000

- Second interim payment of tax due for tax year ending 5 April 2000

On or before 30 September 2000

- Send in tax return if you want Inland Revenue to work out tax due
- Employees who have underpaid tax by £1,000 or less should send in their tax return so that tax will be collected through the PAYE system

On or before 5 October 2000

- Tell your tax inspector about any new source of income or capital gain for year ending 5 April 2000

On or before 30 January 2001

- Claim to reduce payments on account for the tax year ending 5 April 2001 (see p. 307)
- Tell your tax inspector if you have reduced your payments on account by too little
- Send in your tax return, along with calculation of any income and capital gains tax due, plus payment for any unpaid tax for the year ending 5 April 2000
- Make first interim payment on account of tax due for tax year ending 5 April 2001 (statement received from Inland Revenue based on previous year's tax bill or your own self-assessment calculation)
- Choose to carry back personal pension payment made in the tax year ending on 5 April 2000 to the tax year ending on 5 April 1999

On or before 5 April 2001
- Claim for allowances and deductions for tax year ending 5 April 1995

On or before 31 January 2002
- Set losses made in a new business for the tax year ending 5 April 2000 against other income for the previous three tax years
- Set business losses made in the tax year ending 5 April 2000 against other income

On or before 31 January 2006
- Claim for allowances and deductions left out of tax return by mistake for the tax year ending 5 April 1999
- Set business losses made in the tax year ending 5 April 2000 against future profits of the same business

On or before 5 April 2006
- Claim unused relief for retirement annuities and personal pension schemes for tax year ending 5 April 2000.

TAX CHANGES FOR THE TAX YEAR STARTING 6 APRIL 2000

CHAPTER 4

In keeping with previous years, Budget 2000 included measures not just for the immediate tax year but for several years ahead. The Chancellor claimed various 'winners' from the Budget, but only by looking to April 2001. In the tax year starting on April 2000, the main winners were families on very low incomes. Due partly to changes already announced in earlier Budgets, losers included homeowners, married couples, better-off single parents and employees with company cars. The self-employed fared better with generous increases in capital allowances and the capital gains tax treatment of business assets. These measures help to offset the big increase in their National Insurance contributions from April 2000.

The Chancellor used the Budget to take forward his plans to integrate the benefit and tax systems. Working families Tax Credit and Disabled Person's Tax Credit are already up and running. The Children's Tax Credit – which, for now, works in a slightly different way by reducing your tax bill rather than giving you cash – is on the starting blocks and other tax credits are planned for future years.

But the real focus of Budget 2000 was on spending not taxes. The government has a large surplus of funds. Rather than giving money back direct through lower taxes, the government opted for big increases in the amounts it spends on the National Health Service, schools, transport and crime prevention. The tax system came out of the Budget largely unaltered.

Income tax
The starting rate threshold was raised just £20 to £1,520 for the tax year starting 6 April 2000. Other thresholds were increased in line with inflation. As expected, the basic rate of tax was reduced by 1 per cent to 22 per cent. Starting and higher rates were unchanged at 10 per cent and 40 per cent respectively.

Allowances
All allowances were increased in line with inflation, adding for example £50

to the standard personal allowance and £70 to the age-related personal allowances.

As already announced, the married couple's allowance has been abolished for under-65s from 6 April 2000. Associated allowances, such as additional personal allowance, also end. The new children's tax credit does not start until April 2001. So, in the tax year ending 5 April 2001, married couples under 65 and single parents with children lose up to £197 compared with the previous year.

The income limit at which age-related allowances start to be lost was also increased in line with inflation taking it from £16,800 to £17,000.

The component of Working Families Tax Credit for children under 16 increases by an extra £4.35 from June 2000 on top of increases already announced and effective from April 2000.

Tax credits
The Chancellor announced that, from 2003, the child support elements of Working families Tax Credit, Income Support and Jobseeker's Allowance are to be integrated with the Children's Tax Credit. From the same date a new Employment Tax Credit will be introduced for working people on low incomes whether or not they have children. The government is consulting on the introduction of a Pensioners Tax Credit.

Reliefs
As previously announced, tax relief for interest on mortgages is generally abolished from 6 April 2000.

People who have home income plans taken out before 9 March 1999 continue to get interest tax relief on the mortgage element of their plan. The chancellor announced that this relief would now be fixed at 23 per cent (regardless of any changes to the basic rate of tax).

As previously announced, tax relief on payments made to vocational training providers is abolished altogether from April 2000. The scheme is replaced by a system of Individual Learning Accounts.

From 6 April 2000, the Gift Aid scheme is extended to gifts of any size – large or small, regular or one-off. (Previously, gifts had to be at least £250.)

The ceiling (was £1,200 a year) on gifts under the Payroll Giving scheme is abolished from 6 April 2000. For three years from that date, the government will boost your donation by an extra 10 per cent.

Gifts of quoted shares to charities will qualify for income tax relief at your top rate from 6 April 2000.

Savings and investments
As announced in November 1999, the 10 per cent starting rate of tax does after all apply to income from savings. The change is backdated to 6 April 1999.

From 6 April 2000, the yearly maximum you can invest in individual savings accounts (ISAs) had been due to fall from £7,000 to £5,000. The government has relented and the £7,000 limit is retained for the year to 5 April 2001.

The minimum time you must hold shares through Enterprise Investment Schemes or Venture Capital Trusts in order to keep income tax relief on your investment is reduced from five years to three years. The change applies to VCT shares issued on or after 6 April 2000 and EIS shares in companies qualifying on or after that date.

The earnings cap (see p. 69) which limits benefits from and payments into occupational schemes and payments to personal pensions has been raised in line with inflation to £91,800 (from £90,600).

The Finance Act 2000 will include legislation to introduce a new tax system from 2001 for contributions to stakeholder pension schemes (available from 6 April 2001), personal pensions and some types of occupational pension schemes which decide to opt into the new system. Unless you are in an occupational scheme which is not covered by the new sysetm, you will be able to pay up to £3,600 a year into any of the plans and schemes which are covered regardless of your age or earnings. The age- and earnings-related limits which currently apply to personal pensions will apply to extra contributions over and above the £3,600 limit.

Under the new pension contribution system, carry-forward rules (see p. 74) will be abolished. So you have only until 5 April 2001 to use up any unused contribution relief from previous years. After 5 April 2001, the unused relief will be lost for good.

Inheritance tax
The threshold at which tax starts to be paid was increased in line with inflation to £234,000 for the tax year beginning 6 April 2000 (up £3,000 from £231,000).

Capital gains tax

The amount of net capital gains which an individual can make each year without paying capital gains tax is increased by £100 to £7,200 for the tax year starting 6 April 2000. Most trusts will be exempt on the first £3,600 of gains.

The starting rate of tax newly applies to capital gains from 6 April 2000. This means gains may be taxed at 10 per cent, 20 per cent or 40 per cent depending on the size of the gain and your taxable income.

Taper relief for business assets has been made more generous. For disposals from 6 April 2000, maximum relief of 75 per cent is now available when you have held the asset just four or more years. If you are a higher-rate taxpayer, this reduced the effective tax rate to just 10 per cent.

The extra year credited for taper relief where you were holding the asset on 17 March 1998 is abolished for business assets disposed of from 6 April 2000 onwards.

From 6 April 2000, all holdings of unquoted shares will count as business assets for the purpose of taper relief whether or not you are employed by the company. All quoted shares will qualify if you are an employee (full-time or part-time); otherwise quoted shares qualify where they give you at least 5 per cent of the voting rights. These changes enable many more share holdings to qualify as business assets.

Stamp duty

The rate of duty on the transfers of property (excluding shares) on or after 28 March 2000 is increased by 0.5 per cent where the price is more than £250,000. This brings the rate to 3% on property costing more than £250,000 but less than £500,000 and 4 per cent on property costing more than £500,000. The old rates will apply to transfers made after 28 March if the contract was made on or before 21 March.

Other rates are unchanged.

Businesses

From 1 April 2000, a new 10 per cent starting rate of corporation tax is introduced for companies with taxable profits of £10,000 or less. The 20 per cent small companies rate and 30 per cent main rate are unchanged.

Business assets will attract more generous capital gains tax treatment from 6 April 2000 – see *Capital gains tax* above.

Changes to the EIS and VCT schemes aim to attract more people to invest in small high-risk companies – *Savings and investments* above. From 1 April 2000, a new Corporate Venturing Scheme will give tax benefits to companies investing in small higher risk trading companies.

The existing temporary 40 per cent first-year capital allowance on machinery and plant is made permanent.

A new 100 per cent first-year allowance for spending on information and communication technology equipment is introduced for spending during a three-year period from 1 April 2000. This means you can set off the whole cost of items such as computers and internet-enabled mobile phones in the year you purchase them.

The payroll threshold below which employees can make PAYE payments quarterly rather than monthly is increased from £1,000 to £1,500 a month for periods beginning after 5 April 2000.

The threshold for VAT registration has been lifted from £51,000 to £52,000 from 1 April 2000.

In the year ending 5 April 2001, you can qualify for tax discounts if you send in self assessment, VAT and/or PAYE returns, and make payment, electronically – see p. 13.

Employees

There are no changes to the taxable value of a company car for the year starting 6 April 2000, but the system changes completely from 6 April 2002. The tax charge will then be based on a percentage of the purchase price of the car determined by the car's carbon dioxide emissions. The taxable value will range from 15 per cent of purchase price for the most efficient cars to 35 per cent for the least efficient. Business mileage and age-related discounts will be abolished from that date.

For the tax year starting 6 April 2000, fuel scale charges increase by 40 per cent (see p. 95). The fuel scale charge is the amount on which you pay tax if your employer provides you with free fuel for your private use of a company car.

Employers (but not employees) must pay National Insurance contributions on the value of most fringe benefits they provide. The chancellor announced that workplace nurseries, the provision of places at commercial nurseries, hiring the services of a childminder and so on would be exempt. He hopes this will encourage employers to provide childcare facilities for employees.

From 6 April 2000, you can join a new type of employee share scheme if your employer runs one. Under the scheme, your employer can give you up to £3,000 of free shares which may be linked to reaching work targets. You can buy up to a further £1,500 of 'partnership shares' out of your pre-tax pay and your employer may award up to two 'matching shares' for every partnership share you buy. Provided you keep the shares in the plan for at least five years, there's no income tax or National Insurance on them. In addition, there is no tax on capital gains made while the shares are in the plan.

Savings-related share option schemes and company share option schemes are unchanged. But approved profit sharing schemes are to end – no further awards can be made after 5 April 2002.

Employers can offer share options worth up to £100,000 to up to 15 key employees as an incentive to take up jobs with that employer. The options will be free of income tax.

National Insurance
From 6 April 2000, employees pay no National Insurance contributions (NICs) on the first £76 a week of earnings. Above that level, employees who are not contracted out pay NICs at a rate of 10 per cent on weekly earnings between £76 and £535. From 6 April 2001, the threshold at which NICs start to be paid will be aligned with the income tax personal allowance (£84 a week in the tax year starting 6 April 2000).

Employers pay no NICs for employees earning up to £84 a week. Above that level, the contribution is 12.2 per cent of earnings, which includes the taxable value of company cars, free fuel and most other taxable benefits. Employees do not pay contributions on benefits.

The self-employed pay flat rate Class 2 contributions of £2 a week from 6 April 2000. Class 4 contributions are due at a rate of 7 per cent (increased from 6 per cent) on profits between £4,385 and £27,820.

Taxpayers who get a tax return
In the year ending 5 April 2001, if you send in your tax return, and pay any tax, electronically, you can qualify for a £10 tax discount – see p. 13.

SEVENTY-FIVE WAYS
TO SAVE TAX

CHAPTER 5

Here are 75 tips to cut your tax bill. None of them requires you to turn your life upside down in search of tax savings.

All taxpayers

- Make sure you keep all your records, including the originals of certificates and your working papers. You can be fined for not keeping your records (p. 14).

- Keep careful records – apart from the legal requirement, it could help you pay less tax. Note down all the expenses you could claim: if you are an employee (see p. 211); if you are self-employed (see p. 230); if you let out property (see p. 256).

- Don't be late sending in your tax return. The 2000 tax return must be sent back by 30 September if you want the Inland Revenue to work out your bill (p. 16) and by 31 January 2001 if you want to avoid an automatic £100 penalty (see p. 20).

- If you send in your tax return over the internet and pay any tax due electronically, £10 will be knocked off the bill (p. 13).

- Always check your tax forms. As soon as you receive a Tax Calculation or PAYE Coding Notice make sure your tax inspector has got the sums right (see Chapter 25).

- If you are asked to make payments on account, check that you're not paying more than you need to. The figures will be based on last year's tax bill. If you expect your income to be lower this year or your allowances and reliefs to be higher, you can make reduced payments (see p. 307).

- Investigate the past. It may not be too late to claim an allowance or deduction you have forgotten about. Some of the more important deadlines for claims are given on pp. 24-5.

- If you want to give money to charity, think about payroll-giving schemes and Gift Aid – you'll get tax relief on the gifts, large or small, regular or one-off. There are more details on pp. 183-5 and p. 199.

- Look closely at any gifts you make to charity by covenant or through Gift Aid. If you are a non-taxpayer, you will not be able to keep the tax relief you deduct at the basic rate from the gifts (p. 184). If your husband or wife pays tax, it may be better if he or she makes the gifts. The same will be true if he or she pays tax at the higher rate and you don't.

- Think about giving quoted shares to charity. You will get income tax relief at your highest rate of tax (see p. 28).

Married

- If you are married, consider reorganising your investments so your investment income is paid to the partner who pays least tax on it.

- Married couples where one partner has a low income and can't use up all their allowances can transfer the blind person's allowance to their partner (see p. 194). This is also possible for the married couple's allowance (abolished for the under-65s from 6 April 2000 – see p. 42).

- If you are single and there is a child under 18 living with you at the start of the tax year, you may have been able to claim the additional personal allowance of £1,970 until 6 April 2000. You may also have been entitled to claim this allowance if you were married but separated, or married to someone who was totally unable to look after himself or herself (see p. 191).

Employees

- If you pay tax under the PAYE system and have some other income, for example from investments, on which you will need to pay tax, make sure you send your tax return back by 30 September – even if you are working out your own tax bill. If the amount of tax due is £1,000 or less, the tax on this extra income will be deducted from your earnings under PAYE in the tax year which begins on 6 April 2001 – not as a lump sum by 31 January.

- There is a long list of fringe benefits which are tax-free whatever your level of earnings – try to take advantage of them in your negotiations with your boss. These perks are still free of tax: entertainment by your suppliers or customers at cultural or sporting events (within certain rules); air miles (which enable you to make cheap flights); and non-cash gifts costing up to £100 from a third party (see p. 83).

- Fringe benefits which are not tax-free can still be a tax-efficient way of being paid. The taxable value put on them may be much lower than the value to you. There is a rundown of how they are taxed in Chapter 9 (p. 83).

- If you have a company car, keep an eye on your business mileage as the end of the tax year approaches or if you are about to change your car. If your business mileage is approaching a rate of 2,500 or 18,000 miles a year, try to use the car for work enough to qualify for the reduction in the tax bill if you travel more than either of these amounts on business (see p. 92). Keep good records of your business mileage so you can substantiate your claims.

- Be aware that if you want a large, luxurious company car, you will be taxed fairly heavily for the privilege (see p. 92). Do your sums carefully before accepting a company car if your taxable income is just below the limit for paying higher rate tax (£28,400 in the tax year beginning 6 April 2000). If you have the option, consider a cheap, lightly taxed company car and take the rest of the car allowance in cash to invest in a tax-free investment, such as additional contributions to your pension plan.

- Choosing a new company car? From April 2002, the tax will be linked to its carbon dioxide emissions (see p. 94). Pick a low-polluting car to keep the tax bill down.

- Use your bicycle at work? Your employer can pay you a tax-free cycling allowance or even provide a bicycle for commuting to work without a tax bill. If your employer doesn't pay a mileage allowance, you can claim bicycle mileage as an allowable expense (see p. 85).

- Working parents should try to persuade their employers to provide childcare facilities, as this fringe benefit is tax-free. Your private childcare arrangements are not eligible for tax relief (see p. 84).

- If you often work away from home or your normal workplace, you may be able to claim the costs of travel (see p. 211). Start keeping a note now of your costs of normal commuting.

- If you can arrange your work so you count as self-employed rather than an employee, you will be able to claim a wider range of expenses (see p. 234). But remember there may be disadvantages in not having the protection of employment law. For more about the distinction between employees and the self-employed, see pp. 195 and 225.

- Persuade your employer to set up a new-style all-employee share scheme. Your employer can give you up to £6,000 of shares tax-free so long as you keep them in the scheme for five years (p. 31).

- If you are an employee, see if you can negotiate the introduction of share option schemes (p. 215).

- If you borrow to buy shares in a company where you work, you may be able to get tax relief on the loan (see p. 179). The company must be largely owned by its employees or you must have a large stake in it.

- If you become unemployed and are not claiming social security benefits, ask your tax inspector for a rebate of tax paid when you were working.

Self-employed

- If you leave a job in the middle of a tax year to become self-employed, ask your tax inspector for a rebate. It will help your finances, although not cut your actual tax bill.

- If you are self-employed or in partnership and your turnover is less than £15,000 a year, take advantage of the ability to send in three-line accounts (see p. 231). This won't save you any tax, but it may cut your book-keeping and accountancy fees.

- You can still claim as an expense for your business something you use partly for business and partly in your private life, for example, using your home for work, sharing the car (p. 234).

- You can get a 100 per cent capital allowance in the year that you buy information technology and communications equipment. This concession, for three years from 1 April 2000, covers things like computers, software and internet-enabled mobile telephones (p. 30).

- When you first start your business, claim capital allowances on any equipment you already own but take into the business, for example, a car, desk and so on (see p. 243).

- You do not have to claim all the capital allowances you are entitled to. It may save you more tax to claim less and carry forward a higher value to the next year when your profits may be higher or your personal allowances lower (p. 242).

- If you are married and run your own business, consider employing your spouse if he or she does not work. It could save money if your spouse's tax rate (including National Insurance contributions – see p. 248) would be lower than yours.

- If you make a tax loss in your business, there are several ways this can be used to reduce tax on other income (see p. 246).

Investments

- The government offers lots of tax incentives to persuade you to save for a pension. Take advantage of them. Chapter 8 (p. 68) tells you how to take them up.

- If you're approaching retirement, consider making extra contributions towards a pension. If you work for an employer, you can get tax relief on additional voluntary contributions (AVCs) to your employer's scheme (p. 70). With contributions to a personal pension scheme, you can get tax relief on a higher proportion of your earnings as you get older (p. 73).

- Take advantage of the rules that allow you to backdate contributions to personal pensions (see p. 74). You may be able to get a higher rate of tax relief – for example, if you paid tax at the higher rate in a previous tax year.

- If you haven't made the maximum contributions to personal pensions in the last six tax years, you can claim the unused relief this year. The carry-forward rules are being abolished from 6 April 2001, however – so this is your last chance to take advantage of unused relief (see p. 76).

- If you pay tax at the top rate of 40 per cent, tax-free investments can be attractive. Even if you could get a higher rate of return on a taxable investment, the after-tax return could be considerably lower.

- Non-taxpayers investing in banks, building societies and other investments where tax is deducted from the income should claim it back from the Inland Revenue. With interest from banks and building societies, you can arrange for it to be paid without deduction of tax if you are a non-taxpayer (see p. 65).

- If you want to give some capital to your children, any income it produces over £100 a year will be counted as yours (see p. 275). Choose investments that produce a tax-free income or gain (see pp. 309 and 100).

- If you are elderly, watch out for the income trap – the level of income where the higher tax allowances paid to people aged 65 or over are withdrawn. The withdrawal is phased, but it means you are effectively taxed at a higher-than-normal rate on each extra £1 of income (see p. 43). Consider tax-free investments if this is the case.

- If you have invested in shares, investment trusts or unit trusts through a personal equity plan before PEPs were replaced by Individual Savings Accounts on 6 April 1999, try not to sell it. There's no tax to pay on the income or gains and you can keep PEPs going even if you have an ISA.

- If you have a tax exempt special savings account (TESSA) opened before the closing date for new accounts of 5 April 1999, you can get tax-free interest on up to £9,000 of savings until the end of the five-year term. You can go on adding to it up to the maximum each year – see p. 80.

- Saving through an individual savings account (ISA) means no tax to pay on income or gains on the investments (see p. 76). You won't lose the tax relief if you withdraw your money, so you can use an ISA even for temporary savings and boost the returns.

- If you receive shares through an employee profit-sharing scheme or a savings-related share option scheme you can transfer them into an ISA – the value of the shares will count towards the annual investment limit for the ISA (see p. 77). This will mean no income tax on the dividends and no capital gains tax when you eventually sell the shares.

- Investors should consider having some investments which give a capital gain rather than income. There is a tax-free allowance of net capital gains (£7,200 in the tax year beginning 6 April 2000) which you can make each tax year (see p. 67).

- If you took out a life insurance policy before midnight on 13 March 1984, the chances are that you get tax relief on the premiums (currently at 12.5 per cent). However, altering the policy (for example, increasing the benefits unless this is done automatically under the policy) could mean losing the tax relief (see p. 67). Consider carefully before altering – perhaps you can achieve your objective in another way.

- If you get income from trusts, it comes with a tax credit – you can reclaim some or all of this if it is more than you should have paid (see p. 275). Unless you pay tax at the higher rates, you are almost certainly entitled to a tax rebate on income from discretionary trusts.

- People investing in growing businesses can claim tax relief on up to £150,000 in a tax year through the Enterprise Investment Scheme – and the minimum period for an investment has fallen from five to three years (p. 80). There is also tax relief for investing in venture capital trusts (see p. 82).

- If you get income from investments abroad on which you have paid foreign tax, tax credit relief can reduce the amount of UK tax you pay (see p. 266).

Homeowners

- If you are away from your home for quite long periods keep an eye on the capital gains tax position – don't lose private residence relief which means you pay no capital gains tax on your only or main home (see p. 58).

- Do you have more than one home? You may have to pay capital gains tax when you sell your second home (p. 56). But you can choose which of your homes counts as your main one, make sure you nominate the home that is likely to incur the biggest capital gains tax bill.

- Do you want an income of over £80 a week tax-free? If you let out a room in your home under the rent a room scheme, you can take £4,250 of gross rent a year tax-free. This relief can reduce your tax bill even if the income is higher (see p. 253).

- If you let out your home, don't forget to claim the interest you pay on the mortgage as an expense against letting income. You get the tax relief at your highest rate of tax (see p. 55).

- If you let out your second home, try to make sure you meet the conditions for the rent to be taxed as income from furnished holiday lettings (p. 255). You can claim a wider variety of deductions against tax, and you may be able to avoid capital gains tax when you sell the home.

- You can claim a tax allowance for the wear and tear incurred in letting out furnished property (see p. 264).

- If you have made a loss letting out property, you may be able to use this to reduce other parts of your tax bill (see p. 265).

- If you've let out part or all of your home, lettings relief could mean no capital gains tax to pay when you dispose of it (see p. 60).

Capital gains tax

- Try to use the tax-free allowance for capital gains tax every year – you can't carry over unused allowances to other years. Think about selling some shares showing a profit and buying them back a month later to make a gain that uses up the allowance (see p. 112).

- Husband and wife are each entitled to the tax-free allowance of net capital gains – £7,200 for the tax year beginning 6 April 2000 (see p. 122). Consider reorganising your possessions so each of you can use up the limit before either starts paying capital gains tax.

- If you are going to dispose of assets, split the disposals over several years. You can then claim the tax-free allowance for capital gains to reduce the bill each year.

- If you are facing a capital gains tax bill on the disposal of one large asset, you could sell assets that are showing losses to set against the gain. If you don't really want to get rid of these other assets, you can buy them back some time later (see p. 117).

- Selling shares in the company you work for? From 5 April 2000, you can claim taper relief at the rate for business assets, so you pay capital gains tax on only one-quarter of the chargeable gain after four years (see p. 114).

- If you own valuables such as antiques, a second home or collectables, keep careful records of what they cost you to buy and maintain. You could face a capital gains tax bill when you dispose of them – allowable expenses can reduce the tax bill (p. 106).

- If you are thinking of making a gift to charity of an asset which is showing a loss, think again. It might be better to sell the asset and give the money to the charity (see p. 100).

- Do not forget to claim losses if you dispose of something like shares or valuables at a loss. Losses can be set off against taxable gains, and carried over to later years. But you must claim them within time limits (see pp. 111-3). Keep careful records so you don't forget them later!

- If you face a big capital gains tax bill, think about investing the gain in growing companies. Reinvestment relief can defer the bill (see p. 123).

Inheritance tax

- Draw up a will. There are simple steps you can take to minimise the tax payable on your estate when you die and to reduce the complications for those you leave behind (see p. 131). Making a will helps you to start thinking about inheritance tax.

- Make as full use as possible of the gifts you can make which do not fall into the inheritance tax net. Gifts on marriage and those made out of normal income are tax-free (p. 130).

- Share your wealth with your husband or wife so you can each make tax-free gifts. There is no capital gains tax to pay on gifts between a married couple (p. 132).

- Use life insurance to blunt the impact of inheritance tax. Policies written in trust go straight to the beneficiary and don't form part of your estate (see p. 133). If you pay the premiums out of your normal income, they are tax-free gifts (see p. 130).

- If you own a small business or farm, take professional tax advice. There are extensive tax reliefs which can mean you pay little or no capital gains tax (p. 124) or inheritance tax (p. 134), but they are complicated and need careful planning.

- There are steps you can take to reduce an inheritance tax bill after a death (see p. 138). In particular, you can rearrange inheritances in ways that reduce the amount of tax.

MARRIAGE AND DIVORCE

Married couples are treated as two independent taxpayers by the Inland Revenue. They are taxed on their own income and gains and have their own allowances. Each is responsible for filling in their own tax return and paying their own tax bills. There is no longer a tax allowance for married couples unless they were 65 or over on 5 April 2000.

However, there are some aspects of the tax system which recognise that husband and wife are more than just two individuals living together. One is that they can transfer some allowances between them in certain circumstances. Gifts between husband and wife don't normally fall into the net for capital gains tax or inheritance tax. And by sharing their wealth, a couple can each use their tax-free allowances to reduce the amounts paid in tax.

This chapter explains the opportunities to save tax in marriage. It sets out the rules for what happens when marriages come to an end, and the taxation of maintenance payments. And it gives some brief guidance on what happens if you are widowed. For how marriage affected mortgage interest tax relief, see p. 53; information about capital gains tax is on p. 102, and on inheritance tax on p. 132.

MARRIAGE

Personal allowances

A husband and wife are each entitled to a personal tax allowance in the same way as single people – £4,385 for the tax year beginning 6 April 2000. This personal allowance is deducted from income in arriving at

> ## TAX-SAVING IDEA
>
> If one of you pays tax at a higher rate than the other, you should consider giving investments which produce a taxable income to the spouse who would pay least tax on the income.
>
> Gifts between married couples must be genuine – you can't hand them over with strings attached. If you are reluctant to give away the investments completely, consider putting them into joint names with your spouse so the income is shared equally (see p. 45).

the taxable income on which the individual's tax bill is calculated (see p. 4).

Married people aged 65 or over during the tax year can claim the higher amounts of personal allowance for older people in the same way as single people. The rates are £5,790 for the tax year beginning 6 April 2000, rising to £6,050 for those aged 75 and over. The additional amount is gradually reduced if 'total income' is above a certain level – £17,000 for the tax year beginning 6 April 2000. The personal allowance is reduced by £1 for every £2 over the limit until it reaches the amount for under-65s. Total income is broadly all your income less deductions such as pension contributions (see p. 4).

(see p. 4).

EXAMPLE

Janet Lardon is a high flier on a salary of £60,000 a year and interest from savings accounts of £5,000 a year before tax. She pays tax at the higher rate of 40 per cent on her earnings – and that will be the rate for any savings interest.

She decides to share the savings accounts with her husband Ted, who pays tax at the basic rate only. She puts them in their joint names, so £2,500 of the interest is taxed as his. He has to pay tax on interest at 20 per cent (see p. 62), so they save higher rate tax of 20 per cent of £2,500, that is £500 a year.

Married couple's allowance

Until 6 April 2000 married couples could claim an extra tax allowance that could be allocated to either partner or split between them. But from that date the married couple's allowance ended except where one of the couple was born on or before 5 April 1935. A new children's tax credit worth up to £8.50 a week will be introduced from 6 April 2001 for all families supporting children – whether the couple is married or not (see p. 12).

For the tax year ending 5 April 2000, the married couple's allowance for people under the age of 65 was £1,970. Unlike the personal allowance, the married couple's allowance reduced their tax bill by a fixed amount – it was not used to reduce their income for tax purposes. Tax relief was given at 10 per cent against this amount, giving a maximum tax-saving of £197 for the tax year (£3.79 a week). This went automatically to the husband unless before the start of the tax year both husband and wife had asked for it to be given to the wife, or either had asked for it to be split equally between them.

For those aged 65 or over

Married people who were 65 or over at any time during the tax year ending 5 April 2000 received higher rates of married couple's allowance for that tax year, as with personal allowances. They are also entitled to keep claiming a married couple's allowance after it has ended for everyone else on 6 April 2000 – or to claim it if they marry on or after that date. But people who reach 65 on or after 6 April 2000 will not be able to claim married couple's allowance.

The figures for this tax year and the last tax year are given in the table below. The table also gives the maximum tax-savings with the relief given at 10 per cent.

Age of older partner during tax year	Tax year ending 5 April 2000		Tax year beginning 6 April 2000	
	maximum allowance £	maximum tax-saving £	maximum allowance £	maximum tax-saving £
Under 65	1,970	197.00		
65-74	5,125	512.50	5,185	518.50
75 and over	5,195	519.50	5,255	525.50

The married couple's allowance for over-65s will normally be given to the husband. £1,000 or £2,000 of the allowance can be switched to the wife for the tax year beginning 6 April 2000, but the rest always goes to the husband.

This allowance is gradually reduced if the husband's 'total income' is above a certain level – even if the couple are getting the allowance because of the wife's age. However, it never falls below a minimum amount – £2,000 for the tax year beginning 6 April 2000.

TAX-SAVING IDEA

If one of you is 65 or over and the husband's 'total income' is £17,000 or more in the tax year which began on 6 April 2000, see if you would save tax by giving investments that produce a taxable income to the wife. Even if the husband is under 65, his total income could be reducing the amount of married couple's allowance you get.

If the husband's total income in the tax year beginning 6 April 2000 is £17,000 or more, his personal allowance is first reduced by £1 for each extra £2 over the limit until he is getting the same allowance as the under-65s. So if he is 65-74, his personal allowance falls to the £4,385 for under-65s when his 'total income' reaches £19,810. If he is 75 or over, the personal allowance falls to the under-65s level when his 'total income' reaches £20,330. If his income is higher, the married couple's allowance is similarly reduced until it falls to the minimum amount, which would be when his total income reached £26,180 (£26,840 if he is 75 or over, or £26,320 if he isn't but his wife is).

If the husband is under 65, he won't get the higher personal allowance, so if his total income is over £17,000 it will immediately start to reduce the married couple's allowance. He will end up with the minimum allowance if total income is £23,370 (£23,510 if his wife is 75 or over).

The total income limit for the tax year ending on 5 April 2000 was £16,800.

Transfer of allowances because of low income

If either husband or wife has a tax bill which is too low to use up all their married couple's allowance, they can ask to have the unused part deducted from the tax bill of their spouse. You can do this after the end of the tax year in which you got the allowance – see p. 194 for how to claim this. The same is true if you get blind person's allowance and can't fully use it because your income is too low. It can be transferred to your partner even if not blind.

> ## EXAMPLE
> Jasper Duffy, 68, has a total income of £20,750 – of which £9,300 a year is from savings and investments. Because his total income is over the £17,000 limit, it reduces the amount of personal allowance he gets to the amount for under-65s. But it is also high enough to reduce the married couple's allowance the Duffys get by £1 for each £2 over £17,000.
>
> He decides to share his savings and investments equally with his wife Ellen, whose total income is well below the £17,000 limit. He puts them all into their joint names, which means only half the income they produce is his. This reduces his total income by half of £9,300 = £4,650 to £16,100.
>
> The Duffys will thus get the full amount of married couple's allowance for people aged 65 and over. And Jasper will get the full higher personal allowance for those aged 65 and over.

You have up to five years and ten months after the end of the tax year to transfer the unused allowances. So for the tax year ending 5 April 2000, you can make a claim any time up to 31 January 2006. But if you know in advance that your income will not be big enough to benefit from these allowances, you can ask your tax inspector to transfer the part you estimate will be unused to your spouse's PAYE code.

Allowances in the year of marriage
In the tax year of your marriage, you get one-twelfth of the married couple's

allowance for each month or part-month you are married during the tax year. The proportion depends on the date of the wedding – the table below shows the amount someone under 65 got in the tax year ending 5 April 2000. If you had a child living with you when you married, you could carry on claiming the full additional personal allowance for single parents (which was the same as the married couple's allowance) instead of a fraction of the married couple's allowance.

| | Tax year ending 5 April 2000 | |
Date of marriage before	maximum allowance £	maximum tax-saving £
6 May	1,970	197.00
6 June	1,806	180.60
6 July	1,642	164.20
6 August	1,478	147.80
6 September	1,313	131.30
6 October	1,149	114.90
6 November	985	98.50
6 December	821	82.10
6 January	657	65.70
6 February	493	49.30
6 March	328	32.80
6 April	164	16.40

Jointly owned assets

If you have investments which are jointly owned, your tax inspector will assume the income from them is split equally between you. If the investments are not owned in equal proportions, you can have the income divided between you to reflect your actual shares of it. You do this by both signing a declaration of beneficial interests on Form 17 (available from tax offices) and sending it to your tax inspector.

The new split of joint income applies from when the declaration is signed – it can't be backdated. If you acquire new assets on which the 50:50 split is not to apply, you must make a further declaration. Note the split for income will also be used to allocate any gain on selling an asset between you when you dispose of it (see p. 102).

SEPARATION AND DIVORCE

You should tell your tax inspector when you separate – even if you have yet to make a deed of separation or seek a court order. The Inland Revenue will treat you as no longer living with your husband or wife if you have parted in circumstances that make it look as if the separation is permanent.

You should tell the Inland Revenue even if you weren't paying tax before – contact your local tax office (under Inland Revenue in the telephone book). You will be asked to fill in a form about the separation and provide documentation about it. You must also tell your tax inspector if you get back together again or remarry.

Tax allowances

Each of you retains your personal allowances. And each of you will retain any married couple's allowance you were getting before the separation – but only for the rest of the tax year. This means that if the separation happens on or after 6 April 2000, only couples where one of the partners was 65 or over before that date retains any married couple's allowance. Other couples have no such allowance since it ended on 6 April 2000.

Until 6 April 2000, if either of you had a child under 18 at the start of the tax year who was living with you, you could claim additional personal allowance – worth the same as married couple's allowance (see p. 42).

Where a couple separated on or before 5 April 1990, the husband could continue to receive married couple's allowance so long as he wholly maintained his wife by making voluntary payments. This could carry on until the couple divorced but has ended for under-65s since 6 April 2000 with the ending of the married couple's allowance for this age group.

> ## Example
>
> Joe and Jenny Barrett separated on 15 April 1999. They have three children under 18, one of whom now lives with Joe while the other two live with Jenny. Before separation they split the £1,970 married couple's allowance between them.
>
> For the tax year which ended on 5 April 2000, each got the personal allowance of £4,335, an additional personal allowance for having a child living with them of £1,970 and half the married couple's allowance – £985. That made total allowances of £7,290 each. Of this total tax relief was at 10 per cent only on the £2,955 of additional personal and married couple's allowances.
>
> In the tax year which began on 6 April 2000, each gets the personal allowance only. Neither is any longer entitled to the married couple's allowance which ended from that date for under-65s – as did additional personal allowance.

Maintenance payments

Maintenance can take several forms, including direct payments of cash or the provision of support such as a home to live in. Where this is provided voluntarily – that is, payment cannot be enforced – the person paying it gets no tax relief and the person getting it does not have to pay tax on what they receive. Thus the person receiving the maintenance can have other income up to the amount of the personal allowance (£4,385 for the tax year beginning 6 April 2000) before paying income tax.

This is now also true of maintenance payments made under enforceable agreements, such as a deed of separation, court order or assessment by the Child Support Agency. The rules have changed from 6 April 2000 onwards and the only people for whom this is different are couples where one or both was born on or before 5 April 1935. Because there is still a married couple's allowance for these couples, there is tax relief for the person making the payments equivalent to the amount of the allowance.

So for the tax year beginning 6 April 2000, a person born on or before 5 April 1935 gets tax relief of 10 per cent of the payments made up to the level of the married couple's allowance of £5,185 (more if either is over 75). The tax relief is available only on regular payments made direct to someone you were married to (so not to children). It ends if the ex-spouse remarries. The maximum is the same however many former spouses you are paying, but the tax relief is in addition to any other tax allowances such as any married couple's allowance you get in the year of separation.

You get the tax relief on these maintenance payments through your PAYE code (see p. 301) or through an adjustment to your tax bill. You do not deduct any tax from the maintenance payments you make.

Before 6 April 2000

The amount of tax relief the giver got on maintenance payments before 6 April 2000 – and how the recipient was taxed on them – depended on when the arrangements were made. There's an explanation on p. 180 where details are given of what to enter in the 2000 tax return.

The change in the taxation of maintenance payments means lots of people who previously got tax relief on the payments they made will no longer do so. The maximum for most was 10 per cent of the old married couple's allowance of £1,970 or £197. Some people making payments under arrangements made before 1988 were getting higher amounts of tax relief, however, and the recipients had to pay corresponding amounts of tax on part of the payments.

Example

Damian Boland makes enforceable maintenance payments of £2,100 a year to his ex-wife Debbie under an agreement originally drawn up in 1986 to support her and their child. But he has been steadily raising the amount over the years – he paid £1,300 in the tax year ending 5 April 1989. So the amount he gets tax relief on under the old rules is pegged at £1,300. He gets tax relief of 10 per cent of £1,300 – £130 a year.

Under the new rules, Damian would have got tax relief on maintenance payments for the tax year ending 5 April 2000 up to the level of the married couple's allowance – £1,970. He would be better off switching, when he would get tax relief of 10 per cent on £1,970 = £197.00.

Switching from the old rules to the new

Everyone has had to switch to the new rules from 6 April 2000. But it could pay you to switch for the previous year if you would get more tax relief on the maintenance payments you made.

This could happen if you made maintenance payments of less than £1,970 in the tax year ending 5 April 1989 and you are now paying more than this. Under the old rules, you are restricted to tax relief on what you paid then; under the new rules, you would get tax relief on the equivalent of the married couple's allowance – £1,970 for the tax year ending 5 April 2000.

But if you switch to the new rules, you would lose any tax relief on payments you made to your children under a court order.

You can switch from the old rules for taxing maintenance payments to the new rules, simply by filling in Inland Revenue Form 142. To have the payments for the tax year ending 5 April 2000 taxed under the new rules, you must tell your tax inspector on or before 5 April 2001.

What happens to your home?

Once you are separated, you are likely to need two homes. You could each get tax relief on interest you pay on loans to buy your only or main home until 6 April 2000 when mortgage interest tax relief was abolished (see p. 50).

Capital gains tax and inheritance tax on separation

You can carry on making gifts to your ex-husband or ex-wife in the year of separation without falling into the net for capital gains tax. After this, gifts may lead to a capital gains tax bill in the same way as for any other gifts (see p. 99).

However, if one of you moves out of the family home and gives or sells it to the other within three years of the separation, there will be no capital gains tax to pay. Even after that, there may be no capital gains tax if your ex-spouse is still living there and you have not claimed any other property as your only or main home.

If you bought a home for your ex-spouse on or before 5 April 1988, there will be no capital gains tax to pay when you dispose of it, as long as the ex-spouse has lived in it rent-free ever since.

Gifts between a separated husband and wife are free of inheritance tax (see p. 130). Once you are divorced, gifts may fall into the inheritance tax net unless they are for the maintenance of the ex-spouse or any children.

WIDOWED

When your husband or wife dies, you keep any married couple's allowance you were getting for the rest of the tax year in which the death happens. In the tax year ending 5 April 2000, you could also get additional personal allowance if you had living with you a child or children under 18 at the start of the tax year.

Widows could also get widow's bereavement allowance of £1,970 for the tax year beginning 6 April 1999. The amount of tax relief was restricted in the same way as for married couple's allowance – the rate was 10 per cent. This allowance could also be claimed in the tax year after the one in which you were widowed.

From 6 April 2000, the married couple's allowance has ended for under-65s, as has the additional personal allowance and widow's bereavement allowance for everyone. So there is no longer an extra allowance for women widowed on or after 6 April 2000. Women who were widowed in the tax year ending 5 April 2000 will still be entitled to the second year widow's allowance of £2,000 for the tax year beginning 6 April 2000.

HOME AND TAX

Buying a home is probably the biggest purchase you will make. Your mortgage payments are almost certainly the largest outgoing in your household budget. And your home is also likely to be your most valuable asset.

For decades, people buying a home were entitled to help with their mortgage costs in the form of tax relief on the interest. The amount of tax relief was gradually scaled down and was ended altogether from 6 April 2000. This chapter explains the rules for the last year of mortgage interest tax relief – and what will happen to home income plans which take advantage of the tax relief to top up the income of older people. It also explains how to make sure you don't pay a hefty capital gains tax bill if you sell your home for a lot more than you paid for it.

MORTGAGE INTEREST TAX RELIEF

You could get tax relief until 6 April 2000 on interest you paid on loans of £30,000 or less to buy your only or main home. Your only or main home is normally the one you live in for most of the time, although you could get tax relief on loans for homes you were not living in (see p. 54).

The rate of tax relief had fallen to 10 per cent. Although this tax relief is no longer available, the rules are set out below in case it affects your tax bill for the tax year ending 5 April 2000.

How you got the tax relief
In most cases, you got the tax relief in the form of lower monthly payments to the lender. For example, if £100 interest was due on your mortgage, you paid £100 minus tax relief of 10 per cent: £100 – £10 = £90. You got the tax relief even if you didn't pay tax, or you paid less than the tax relief you got.

This system was known as mortgage interest relief at source (MIRAS) and was operated by most lenders such as building societies, banks and insurance companies. They reclaimed the tax relief direct from the Inland Revenue.

MIRAS did not include loans which were only partly for buying a home. If this applied to your loan – or your lender was not in MIRAS – you had to claim the tax relief direct from the Inland Revenue (see p. 178). In this case, you got tax relief only if you have enough income to pay tax.

Which loans qualified for relief?
The relief was available on loans to buy a house or flat, leasehold or freehold, in the UK or the Republic of Ireland. You could also claim it for a houseboat designed to be used as a home. And loans for a caravan (or mobile home) used as your only or main home were also eligible.

You could get tax relief on the interest paid on most sorts of loans used to buy your only or main home, including personal loans from banks and other lenders. The loan didn't have to be a mortgage secured on your home to qualify. But you didn't get tax relief on interest paid on a bank overdraft or credit card debts – even if these were incurred on your home. And there was no tax relief on interest for loans which had to be repaid within a year of being taken out, unless the lender was a bank, stockbroker or discount house.

You could still get the tax relief if part of the loan was used to pay the costs of buying the home such as stamp duty, valuers' fees, legal bills and insurance premiums (for example, for a mortgage indemnity policy). And if the loan had been increased because you fell behind on the payments or to cover insurance premiums, the amount of loan on which you could get mortgage interest tax relief was increased by up to £1,000 (or 12 months' payments arrears, if greater).

If you remortgaged your home to change lenders or borrow more, you got mortgage interest tax relief on the new loan provided you got it on the old loan it replaced.

Bigger mortgages
If your loan to buy your only or main home was more than £30,000, you got the tax relief on only a proportion of the interest. For example, if your loan was £40,000, the proportion of interest on which you got tax relief was:

$$\frac{£30,000}{£40,000} = \frac{3}{4}$$

If your loan was in MIRAS, it automatically gave you the right amount of tax relief.

If you were buying your home with two or more loans which added up to over £30,000, you got the tax relief on the earliest loans first, up to the

£30,000 limit. For example, if you had a loan of £25,000 topped up with another £10,000 loan, you got tax relief on all the interest on the first loan. That would have left unused mortgage interest tax relief of £30,000 – £25,000 = £5,000. So you got tax relief on the following share of the interest on the second loan:

$$\frac{£5,000}{£10,000} = \frac{1}{2}$$

Your loan could have crept up above £30,000 if you had missed some interest payments (or didn't increase your payments when the mortgage rate went up). You got tax relief on all the interest you paid as long as no more than £1,000 of interest had been added to the loan.

Bridging loans
If you took out a bridging loan to buy a new home before you sold your old one, you got tax relief on the interest for up to £30,000 of the bridging loan, as well as on £30,000 of loans on your old home. This second lot of tax relief was available for up to 12 months (longer if you could persuade your tax inspector there was good reason for the delay in selling your old home).

It didn't matter which of the homes you lived in during the transitional period. But you had to pay back the second lot of relief if you did not move into the new home at the end of the bridging period.

Home income schemes
People aged 65 or over can still get tax relief on the interest paid on a mortgage loan taken out as part of a home income scheme before 9 March 1999. Under such a scheme, an insurance company lent up to £30,000 against the security of the home. The loan was used to buy an annuity which pays a regular income that leaves the homeowner with money to spend after making the mortgage payments.

Provided 90 per cent or more of the loan was used to buy the annuity, tax relief is given on the interest payments at a rate of 23 per cent. Provided you took out the scheme before 9 March 1999, you go on getting tax relief even though mortgage interest tax relief ended on 6 April 2000 – even if you move house or take out a new mortgage.

Rolling the mortgage over to a new home
Normally, when buying a new home you pay off the old loan and take out a new one. However, if you carried a loan over from one home to another, you could go on getting tax relief on the interest until it ended on 6 April 2000.

This concession was introduced in 1993 to help people who wanted to move but could not repay their mortgages because their homes were worth less than the loan outstanding (this is known as negative equity). Provided the lender agreed, they could sell the home and carry the loan over to the new one.

Married couples
A married couple got tax relief on interest they paid for loans of £30,000 or less in total. If the loan was in one of their names only, that person got all the tax relief. With a mortgage in their joint names, the mortgage interest tax relief was divided 50:50 between them. But you could allocate the tax relief between husband and wife in any way you chose, simply by signing a form.

For loans covered by MIRAS it made no practical difference how the relief was allocated. However, if the loan was outside MIRAS and one partner paid little or no tax, it paid to allocate all the interest to the other partner to get the tax relief in full.

To change the way relief was allocated, both husband and wife had to sign Form 15. You had up to a year after the end of the tax year to make the choice. So for the tax year ending 5 April 2000, you have until 5 April 2001 to send in Form 15. The allocation could be varied from year to year, simply by filling in a new Form 15. To revert to a 50:50 split, you should withdraw the allocation on Form 15-1.

Newlyweds
If a newly married couple each owned homes before marriage and moved into one of them after the wedding, they could go on getting tax relief on the interest on the other for up to a year. If they had decided to buy a new matrimonial home, they could go on getting tax relief on the mortgage interest for the two other homes for up to a year after the wedding – effectively getting three lots of tax relief.

Sharers
If two or more single people bought a home together, or a married couple bought with another couple or single person, the tax relief was restricted to interest on £30,000 of loans per home – irrespective of the number of people sharing it.

For example, two single people got half the tax relief on the interest paid for £30,000 or less of loans (that is on £15,000 of loans each). Where a married couple shared with a single person, the couple got tax relief on interest they pay on two-thirds of the £30,000 limit (£20,000) with one-third (£10,000) for the single person. If a sharer had a loan smaller than his or her entitlement, the unused part could be transferred to the other sharers.

Sharers who took out loans before 1 August 1988 to buy a home in which they still live were each entitled to tax relief on £30,000 of mortgage interest. So two single people who had shared a home since before that date got tax relief on the interest paid on up to £60,000 of such loans. These rules applied until the loans were paid off, replaced with a new loan or switched to a new home. If two such sharers married, the maximum amount of loans on which they got tax relief immediately fell from £60,000 to £30,000.

Home-improvement loans
If you took out a loan before 6 April 1988 to improve your only or main home, the interest paid on it could be added to the interest paid on loans to buy it when calculating your mortgage interest tax relief. You could go on getting the tax relief for such home improvement loans until 6 April 2000 when mortgage interest tax relief ended. If you paid off the loan and replaced it with a new one – at a lower rate of interest, say – you didn't get tax relief on the interest on the new loan.

A home for an ex-spouse or dependent relative
You could get tax relief on a loan taken out on or before 5 April 1988 to buy or improve a home for a separated or former spouse or dependent relative. You could go on getting the tax relief on such loans until 6 April 2000 as long as the ex-spouse or dependent relative continued to live in the home as their only or main residence. If you paid off such a loan and replaced it with a new loan – at a lower rate of interest, say – you didn't get tax relief on the interest on the new loan.

Dependent relatives are:

- your mother or mother-in-law if widowed, separated or divorced
- any relative of yours or your spouse who is unable to look after themselves because of permanent illness, disablement or old age (over 64 at the start of the tax year).

The tax relief was given only if the dependent relative lives in the home rent-free.

Absence from home
Mortgage interest tax relief was meant for your only or main home. But you could be away from the home for up to a year without losing tax relief on the mortgage interest payments. And if you moved out but had not yet sold the home, you could go on getting the tax relief for up to a year (longer if

you could persuade your tax inspector that selling the home was proving difficult).

You may also have been able to go on getting tax relief if work took you away from home. If you worked for an employer who required you to live away from home, you could go on getting mortgage interest tax relief for up to four years provided you were expected to return within that period. If you were still away after four years, the tax relief ended. But if you moved back in for at least three months, further such absence of up to four years was allowed.

Servants of the Crown who moved abroad because of their jobs could be away indefinitely without losing the tax relief. So could those who had to live in job-related accommodation, provided they intended to live in the house they owned eventually. Job-related accommodation is living accommodation provided for one of the following reasons:

- it is necessary to live in it to do the job properly – for example, a residential housekeeper
- it is customary to live in it for that sort of work and living there helps do the job better – a hotel manager
- it is essential for security reasons.

There was a similar exemption for the self-employed who had to live in work-related accommodation (for example, over the shop or at the club). They could go on getting mortgage interest tax relief on their own homes provided they intended to live in them eventually.

Working from home
If you used part of your home for business, you could still get mortgage interest tax relief through MIRAS – provided the business use was incidental. For example, if you occasionally worked from home or used part of it on occasions as an office or place to store work tools.

If you used your home for more substantial work or business purposes, the loan may have had to leave MIRAS. In this case you should still have got mortgage interest tax relief on it (and perhaps also been able to set off some of the interest against business income – see p. 239).

If you let your home
If you let out no more than one-third of your home, you could go on getting mortgage interest tax relief through MIRAS. But if you let out more than one-third, you no longer got mortgage interest tax relief through MIRAS – although you could claim it directly from the Inland Revenue if you were still entitled to it.

Whether or not you were in MIRAS, you might have been better off not claiming mortgage interest tax relief but deducting the interest from rental income when working out the profit or loss of your letting business (see pp. 257, 262). There were several possible advantages:

- all the interest qualified for tax relief – mortgage interest tax relief covered interest on £30,000 of loans only
- the tax relief was at your highest rate of tax – not just the 10 per cent that was given for mortgage interest tax relief
- if the interest was more than your property income in one tax year, you could carry forward the loss to set against property income in the future.

If your loan was not in MIRAS, you could choose each year whether to claim mortgage interest tax relief or set the interest against letting income. If your loan was in MIRAS, you had to opt out of it if you wanted the interest to be set against letting income. You had to write and tell your tax inspector within 22 months of the end of the tax year in which you first wanted this to happen. So if you want the interest paid in the tax year ending 5 April 2000 to be set against letting income for that year, tell the tax inspector by 5 February 2002. Once you had opted out of MIRAS, you could not return to it unless the letting business ended.

CAPITAL GAINS TAX ON HOMES

If you sell most types of investments (including property) for more than you paid for them, there may be capital gains tax to pay (see Chapter 10). But if you sell your only or main home, there is normally no capital gains tax to pay unless the garden is excessively large (see opposite) or you are making a business out of buying and selling homes. This exemption from capital gains tax is known as private residence relief.

However, if you own more than one home, only one of them qualifies for private residence relief. And you might lose the relief if you use the home for business, leave it for prolonged periods or let it out. If you do have to pay capital gains tax on selling a home, it can mean a hefty tax bill – the gain, adjusted for inflation, can be taxed at up to 40 per cent.

Which homes?
Private residence relief is given for your only or main home, whether it is a house or flat, freehold or leasehold, and wherever in the world it is situated. You must occupy the home exclusively as your residence if it is to be free of capital gains tax. If part of the home is used for work or business, you may have to pay tax on part of the gain (see p. 58). And letting out some or all of your home can also mean a capital gains tax bill (see p. 60).

If you live in a caravan or houseboat, there's normally no capital gains tax to pay on it, even if it is not your only or main home. Caravans and boats count as wasting assets with a useful life of 50 years or less – and are thus outside the net for capital gains tax (see p. 100). But if you own the land on which a caravan stands, you might have to pay capital gains tax if you sell it, unless the caravan was your only or main home.

A home which an ex-spouse or dependent relative lives in rent-free is also free of capital gains tax provided it fell into this category on or before 5 April 1988 (see p. 54 for who qualifies). This exemption lasts only as long as the ex-spouse or dependent relative continues to live in the home.

Gardens
Private residence relief applies to both your home and garden. But there are rules to stop people taking advantage of it to avoid capital gains tax on dealing in land.

If the area of your home and garden exceeds half a hectare, there may be tax to pay on the gain you make on the excess. The gain on any excess will be free of tax only if you can convince your tax inspector that a garden of that size is appropriate for the home (for example, it is a Capability Brown garden designed for the house).

If the area of the home and garden is less than half a hectare, you can sell part of the garden without having to pay capital gains tax. But if you divide the garden to build a second home which you sell off, there could be tax to pay on the gain. And if you sell the home and keep some of the land, there may be capital gains tax to pay when you eventually sell the land.

If you own more than one home
If you own more than one home, you can choose which of your homes is your main one and thus free of capital gains tax. It doesn't have to be the one you live in most of the time, or the one on which you got mortgage interest tax relief.

So you should think about which home is likely to make the largest gain and nominate it for private residence relief. You must make your choice and tell your tax inspector in writing within two years of buying the second home. Newlyweds who have kept the two homes they owned while single should tell their tax inspector which is to get private residence relief within two years of the marriage.

You can alter your choice at any time, but you cannot backdate the change by more than two years. Again, write and tell your tax inspector that you wish to change your choice and when you want the change to run from.

If you don't nominate one of your homes for private residence relief, your tax inspector will decide – probably on the basis of which home you spend the most time at. You can appeal against this decision in the normal way (see p. 22), but you will have to produce proof that the other home really is your main one.

Working from home
If any part of your home is used exclusively for work, there may be a capital gains tax bill when you sell the home. This applies to work for your own business (if you are self-employed) and work for an employer.

So if you use one or more rooms entirely for work (as an office or workshop, for example), there will be tax to pay on a proportion of the gain when you come to sell the home. You will have to agree the proportion with the tax inspector, who may calculate it by reference to the number of rooms you use or their floor area. If you claim a proportion of the rent and council tax as business expenses (see p. 236) or as expenses of employment (see p. 214), the same proportion of the gain is likely to be taxable. But in modest cases you may be able to persuade your tax inspector to allow you the expenses without a capital gains tax bill.

For details of how the taxable gain will be worked out – and ways to reduce the tax bill – see Chapter 10.

Away from home
If you don't live in your home for all the time you own it, you might lose some of the private residence relief – even though it is the only home you own or you have nominated it as your main home. Normally you will have to pay capital gains tax on the following proportion of the taxable gain:

$$\frac{\text{Number of complete months of absence}}{\text{Number of complete months of ownership}}$$

Only months of ownership or absence since 31 March 1982 count in working out the proportion – gains before that date are outside the scope of the tax (see p. 109).

In practice, you can be away from the home for considerable spells of absence without losing any private residence relief. You can retain it during absence for the following periods:
- the first year of ownership while you are building, rebuilding or modernising the home, or because you can't sell your old home. This can

be extended for another year if you can convince the tax inspector it is necessary. To retain the exemption, you must move in within the one-year (or two-year) period

- the last three years of ownership – even if you have already moved out
- any other absences totalling up to three years, provided you live in the home both before the first absence and after the last.

You may also be able to retain private residence relief if work takes you or your spouse away from home. If you work for an employer who requires you to live away from home in the UK, you can go on getting private residence relief for up to four years of absence, provided you return to the home afterwards (unless you are prevented by the job). If your employer requires you to work abroad, you can get private residence relief indefinitely.

Provided you intend to live in your home in the future, private residence relief continues if you or your spouse are required to live in job-related accommodation (see p. 55). Self-employed people who have to live in work-related accommodation (for example, over the shop or at the club) can go on getting private residence relief on their own homes as long as they intend to live in them eventually.

EXAMPLE

Linda March bought a house on 24 June 1989. On 6 July 1992 her employer sent her on an overseas posting lasting until 10 November 1994. On Linda's return to the UK, her employer sent her to work away from home until 15 August 1998. She lived in the home until 22 October 1998, when she bought a new home, eventually selling her old home on 27 February 2000.

During the ten years and nine months Linda owned the home, she was absent for three periods totalling seven years and three months. But she will get private residence relief for the entire time she owned the house:

- the two years and four months from July 1992 to November 1994 count for private residence relief because they are a period of employment spent entirely abroad
- the three years and nine months from November 1994 to August 1998 are less than the four years of employment elsewhere in the UK possible without losing private residence relief
- the year and four months from October 1998 to February 2000 are part of the last three years of ownership.

You can add together some or all of these reasons to continue getting private residence relief for longer periods of absence – as the example shows.

Capital gains tax on lettings

There is no capital gains tax to pay if you take in a lodger who is treated as a member of the family – sharing your living rooms and eating with you. But in other circumstances, there may be capital gains tax to pay when you sell a home that has been let out wholly or in part.

If you let out the whole house for a period, the gain attributable to that period is taxable.

If you let part of your home, you may have to pay capital gains tax on the part that is not occupied by you. If you let two of your six rooms, for example, one-third of the gain on selling the home is taxable (less if you haven't let the two rooms for all the time that you've owned the home).

However, there may still be no capital gains tax to pay if you can claim lettings relief, for homes which have been wholly or partly eligible for private residence relief. Lettings relief reduces the taxable gain by £40,000, or the amount of private residence relief if this is lower – the example shows how it works.

Property dealings

If you regularly buy and sell houses for profit, there might be a capital gains tax bill when you sell one – even if you have been living in it as your only or main home. This is meant to catch people who are making a business out of doing up unmodernised homes for sale.

If your property dealings are on a substantial scale, you could find yourself classified as a dealer in land. You would then have to pay income tax on the profits like any other self-employed person (see p. 225).

SAVING AND INVESTING

The ordinary saver faces a wider choice of investments than ever before. Banks, building societies and National Savings are vying to look after your spare cash. Many more people have become shareholders through employee share-ownership schemes, privatisations and the conversion of building societies into companies. And millions are saving for their retirement through personal pensions.

To encourage savings, the government has introduced a series of tax incentives for investors, including a lower tax rate on savings income for basic-rate taxpayers and tax relief on pension contributions. There are also special tax rules to tempt savers into long-term life insurance policies, the Enterprise Investment Scheme (EIS), venture capital trusts (VCTs) and individual savings accounts (ISAs). And if you still own personal equity plans (PEPs), tax-exempt special savings accounts (TESSAs) and Business Expansion Scheme (BES) investments, you can continue to enjoy the tax benefits – even though they are no longer available for new investors.

This chapter guides you through the various types of savings and investments and how they are taxed. It tells you how to cash in on the tax breaks offered by the government. It explains the rules for the new individual savings accounts. And it sets out the position of PEPs and TESSAs taken out before ISAs were introduced.

INCOME TAX ON INVESTMENTS

Income from some investments is tax-free (that is, there is no income tax to pay). For a list of these, see p. 309.

All other investment income is taxable. With more and more investments, tax is deducted from the income before it is paid to you. There is no further tax to pay on such income unless you pay tax at the higher rate. If you should have paid less tax than was deducted, you will normally be able to get a refund.

Interest paid after deduction of tax
Interest on most kinds of savings is now normally paid after tax has been deducted from it. This applies to building society accounts, bank accounts, local authority loans and bonds and National Savings First Option Bonds.

On these types of interest, tax is deducted at 20 per cent from the gross income before handing it over to you. There is no further tax bill if you pay tax at the basic rate on your income – which is the case for the vast majority of taxpayers. If you pay tax at the higher rate, there will be extra tax to pay on this income (see opposite). If your income is too low to pay tax or you pay tax on the rest of your income at the lower rate of

EXAMPLE
Sonny Dasgupta pays tax at 40 per cent on his income. National Savings certificates offer him an average return of 3.5 per cent a year tax-free over five years. He could get 6.5 per cent a year over the same period in a bank high interest account.

Sonny invests in the National Savings certificates, since that will give him 4.5 per cent a year whatever his tax rate. The interest rate he would get on the bank account after paying tax at 40 per cent would be 60 per cent of 6.5 per cent, that is 3.9 per cent a year.

GROSSING-UP
If you receive investment income after some tax has been deducted from it, what you receive is known as the net income. But you may need to work out how much the income was before tax was deducted from it (the gross income).

You can find the gross income by grossing-up the net income (that is the income after deduction of tax) using the ready reckoners in Appendix B (p. 312), or by using the following formula:

$$\text{Amount paid to you} \times \left(\frac{100}{100 - \text{rate of tax}} \right)$$

For example, if you receive £50 of income after tax has been deducted at 20 per cent, the grossed-up amount of the income is:

$$£50 \times \left(\frac{100}{100 - 20} \right)$$
$$= £50 \times \frac{100}{80}$$
$$= £62.50$$

10 per cent only, you should be able to reclaim some or all of the tax which has been deducted (see overleaf).

The savings income is treated as your top slice of your income. This means it does not reduce the amount of earnings or other income that can be taxed at the lower rate – the £1,520 taxable at 10 per cent in the tax year beginning 6 April 2000.

Higher rate tax on income paid after deduction of tax

If you get interest after tax has been deducted and pay tax at the higher rate of 40 per cent, there will be a further tax bill to pay – as the example below shows. The higher rate tax will be collected by the Inland Revenue in one of two ways:

- by increasing the amount of tax you pay on your earnings through PAYE (see p. 304)
- through the payments you have to make in January and July under the self-assessment system (see p. 17).

EXAMPLE

Niamh Fagan gets £80 interest on her building society account in the tax year beginning 6 April 2000. Tax has already been deducted from the interest at 20 per cent before it is credited to her account, so this £80 is the net (that is, after deduction of tax) amount.

To work out the gross (before deduction of tax) amount of interest, Niamh must add the tax back to the net amount. The grossed-up amount of interest is:

$$£80 \times \left(\frac{100}{100 - 20} \right)$$
$$= £80 \times \frac{100}{80}$$
$$= £100$$

In other words, Niamh has paid £100 – £80 = £20 in tax and this covers her basic rate tax on the interest.

If Niamh should pay tax at 40 per cent on this interest, her overall tax liability is 40 per cent of £100 = £40. Since she has already paid £20 in tax, she has to pay only £40 – £20 = £20 in higher rate tax. This leaves her with £80 – £20 = £60 of interest after higher rate tax has been paid.

Too much tax deducted?

If too much tax has been deducted from your interest, the excess can be claimed back. This would happen if the rest of your income is below the level at which you pay tax or you pay tax at the lower rate of 10 per cent only on the rest of your income – as the next example shows.

Example

Niall O'Halloran has earnings of £4,000 in the tax year beginning 6 April 2000 and received interest from his savings of £400. Tax has been deducted from this interest at 20 per cent but Niall reckons he should be paying tax on it at the lower rate of 10 per cent only. He checks to see if he is due a rebate.

First he works out the gross amount of interest he received – the amount before deduction of tax at 20 per cent:

$$£400 \times \left(\frac{100}{100 - 20} \right)$$
$$= £400 \times \frac{100}{80}$$
$$= £500$$

This means he has been paid a gross amount of £500 from which £100 of tax has been deducted.

He adds the £500 to the £4,000 of earnings to find his total income of £4,500. Like all taxpayers, he is entitled to a personal allowance of £4,385 for the tax year, so his taxable income is £4,500 – £4,385 = £115.

Lower rate tax of 10 per cent is due on the first £1,520 of taxable income, so that is the rate he should have paid on the £115 of gross interest. 10 per cent of £115 is £11.50, so he is due a rebate of £100 – £11.50 = £88.50 on the interest.

To claim back tax, ask your tax inspector for Tax Claim Form R40. Fill this in and send it back with the certificates showing the amount of tax deducted (the bank or building society can supply these). You can send in the completed form before the end of the tax year to get the repayment as soon as possible so long as the amount of tax involved is more than £50 and you've had all the savings income for the tax year paid to you after tax has been deducted (including share dividends – see opposite).

When the 10 per cent lower rate of tax was introduced from 6 April 1999, it applied only to non-savings income. This meant that there was no rebate for lower-rate taxpayers who had had tax deducted from their savings income at 20 per cent. But in November 1999, the chancellor decided to extend the 10 per cent lower rate to all income and backdate the change to 6 April 1999. If you had already sent in your Tax Claim Form or want advice on whether you can claim a rebate, call the special Inland Revenue helpline on 0845 307 5555 (calls charged at local rates).

Not a taxpayer?
If your income is too low to pay tax, you can arrange with the bank or building society to be paid interest without deduction of tax. Fill in Form R85 which is available from banks, building societies and post offices, as well as from tax offices. A copy is in Inland Revenue leaflet *IR110 A guide for people with savings*, which also contains useful hints on checking whether you will pay tax or not. A new Inland Revenue website will help you do the sums – it's at www.inlandrevenue.gov.uk/taxback.

Arranging for interest to be paid without deduction of tax not only saves you claiming back the tax which has been deducted, you also get the money much earlier. However, interest on joint accounts can be paid without deduction of tax to just one of the two account-holders only if the bank or building society can arrange it. There are hefty penalties for making a false declaration.

Gilt-edged stock
Interest paid on government stock (gilts) you buy through the National Savings Stock Register is paid gross – without deduction of tax. With gilts you buy directly, interest used to be paid net, after deduction of tax. But with gilts bought on or after 6 April 1998, interest is paid gross unless you ask the Bank of England to pay it net. Interest on gilts you owned before 6 April 1998 will continue to be paid net unless you ask the Bank of England to pay it gross.

Shares and unit trusts
Dividends from UK companies and distributions from authorised unit trusts are paid with a tax credit – the amount is given on the tax voucher which comes with the dividend or distribution. There is no further tax bill if you pay tax at the lower or basic rate only on your income – which is the case for the vast majority of taxpayers.

For dividends and distributions paid on or after 6 April 1999, the tax credit is 10 per cent of the gross amount. So if you receive a dividend of £80, the grossed-up amount of this dividend is:

$$£80 \times \left(\frac{100}{100 - 20} \right)$$
$$= £80 \times \frac{100}{90}$$
$$= £88.89$$

The tax credit was £88.89 − £80 = £8.89.

The tax on the grossed up amount of dividends and distributions is 10 per cent for lower rate and basic rate taxpayers. Since this is the same amount as the tax credit, they need pay nothing extra. Note that the 10 per cent tax credit does not eat up any of your lower rate band: you can still have up to £1,520 of other income taxed at the 10 per cent lower rate in the tax year beginning 6 April 2000.

EXAMPLE

Maggie East has income of £13,100, made up of £8,900 in pensions, £2,500 in dividends (grossed-up at 10 per cent to include the tax credit) and £1,700 in interest (grossed-up with the 20 per cent tax deducted before it is paid). She has a personal allowance of £5,790 and wonders how the tax bill is allocated between these different types of income.

Her taxable income is £13,100 – £5,790 = £7,310. So she will pay tax at no more than the basic rate.

Of the taxable income of £7,310, £2,500 is dividends where the tax is covered by the 10 per cent tax credit. The basic rate tax on the £1,700 of interest is covered by the 20 per cent deducted before it is paid. So £2,500 + £1,700 = £4,200 is already taxed, leaving £7,310 – £4,200 = £3,110 to be reckoned with.

Now of that £3,110, £1,520 is taxed at the lower rate of 10 per cent – remember that the tax credit and tax deducted from the interest do not reduce the £1,520 taxable at the lower rate. This leaves £3,110 – £1,520 = £1,590 taxable at the basic rate of 22 per cent for the tax year beginning 6 April 2000.

So tax on the pensions is:

10 per cent of £1,520	£152.00
22 per cent of £1,590	£349.80
Total tax	£501.80

If you pay tax at the higher rate, there is extra tax to pay. Higher rate taxpayers pay tax on the grossed-up amount of dividends and distributions at 32.5 per cent. So on a net dividend of £80, your total tax bill is 32.5 per cent of the grossed-up amount of £88.89 = £28.89. Since you have a tax credit of £8.89, the higher rate tax due is £28.89 – £8.89 = £20. That leaves you with £80 – £20 = £60 after paying the higher rate tax.

The effect of this arrangement is that there is no difference for a higher rate taxpayer between dividends and distributions which come with a 10 per cent tax credit and interest paid after deduction of tax at 20 per cent. If the net income received is £80, a higher rate taxpayer ends up with £60 whether it is a dividend or interest.

The tax credit cannot be claimed back if the income is not taxable in your hands. So if your income is too low to pay tax you cannot claim it back, and you would be better off investing in shares through an individual savings account (ISA) which can reclaim the tax credit (see p. 77).

This also means that if most or all of your income is dividends and distributions, you might not get the full value of your tax allowance. There is no refund of the tax credit even if some of your dividend income could be set against the allowance.

INVESTING FOR CAPITAL GAINS

One way of reducing your income tax bill is to invest for capital gains rather than income. Capital gains tax is paid on increases in the value of investments – for example if the value of shares rises. The chargeable gain is added to your income and taxed at the same rate as interest or dividends.

But there's no tax to pay if your total net capital gains in the tax year beginning 6 April 2000 are below £7,200. A husband and wife can each make total net capital gains of this amount before paying capital gains tax. And you can make paper gains of more than the £7,200 limit, because of the deductions you can make in calculating your total net capital gains. These include expenses incurred in acquiring, owning or disposing of the investment and losses on other investments. There's indexation allowance to take account of gains due to inflation between 1982 and 1998. And taper relief reduces the tax bill to take account of how long you have owned the investment since 6 April 1998.

For more about capital gains tax and how to minimise it, see Chapter 10, p. 99.

LIFE INSURANCE POLICIES

Life insurance can be used as a form of investment, since some types pay out a tax-free lump sum when the policy matures. There are various conditions to be met if the proceeds of a life insurance policy which pays out in your lifetime are to be tax-free – in particular, that the policy involves paying regular premiums for at least ten years. With most endowment, unit-linked and whole life policies, these conditions are normally met so you don't have to pay tax on the proceeds. There may be some tax to pay if you cash in a savings-type life insurance policy after less than ten years or three-quarters of the term, if this is shorter (see p. 164).

Some insurance companies make a deduction from the proceeds of unit-linked policies to cover their capital gains tax. This deduction is your share of the company's tax bill, not a tax charge on you personally – so you cannot claim it back if you don't pay capital gains tax.

Tax relief on life insurance premiums

With certain types of life insurance policies taken out before 14 March 1984, you were able to get tax relief on the premiums (within limits). Provided you haven't substantially changed the policy, you can go on getting the tax relief which is now $12^1/_2$ per cent of the premiums. In most cases you get it by paying reduced premiums to the insurance company – you pay $87^1/_2$ per cent of the gross premium and the insurance company reclaims the $12^1/_2$ per cent tax relief from the Inland Revenue.

You can get tax relief on no more than £1,500 of gross premiums (£1,312.50 of net premiums) in any tax year – or one-sixth of your total income if this is greater. If you pay more than the limit, the taxman will reclaim the excess tax relief you have been given by paying reduced premiums. If you change the policy, you may lose the tax relief. For example, you will lose the tax relief if you extend the term of the policy, increase the cover or convert it to a different type of policy. But you won't lose the tax relief if the value of the policy increases automatically as part of the policy (for example, if it increases by 5 per cent every year). Check with the insurance company.

PENSIONS

The government offers handsome tax incentives to encourage you to provide for your retirement by saving with an employer's pension scheme or through your own personal pension. These mean that saving for the future through a pension often provides a better return than any other type of investment:

- there is tax relief on your contributions to the scheme (within limits)
- any employer's contributions made for you are not taxable as your income or as a fringe benefit
- the fund the money goes into pays no further income tax or any capital gains tax

> **TAX-SAVING IDEA**
> Everyone should try to make sure that they are saving for retirement through a pension – and the earlier you start, the better the pension you should get at the end. Don't delay. You can get tax relief at your highest rate of tax. This means a contribution of £1,000 costs you just £600 if you are a higher rate taxpayer, and just £780 if you are a basic rate taxpayer for the year beginning 6 April 2000. The fund into which you pay your contributions pays no income or capital gains tax.

- you can trade in some pension to get a tax-free lump sum when you retire.

Personal pensions will become part of the new stakeholder pension to be introduced on 6 April 2001. This will allow even people not at work to save for their retirement (see brief details on p. 76).

Employers' pension schemes

The tax incentives for saving through an employer's pension scheme are available only if it is approved by the Inland Revenue. Approved schemes must offer benefits within set limits:

- the maximum pension is two-thirds of your final salary
- the maximum tax-free lump sum is $1^1/_2$ times your final salary
- the maximum lump sum payment which can be made on death in service (the life insurance cover) is four times your final salary.

There are also limits on the benefits that can be paid out to widows and widowers. For example, the maximum widow's or widower's pension is two-thirds the pension the deceased would have got.

There is a further restriction on the pension benefits from an approved scheme set up on or after 14 March 1989, or if you joined an older scheme on or after 1 June 1989. The amount of final salary which can be taken into account is limited by the pension scheme earnings cap which is £91,800 for the tax year beginning 6 April 2000 (£90,600 for the tax year ending 5 April 2000). If the cap applies to you, the maximum you can draw in the tax year which began on 6 April 2000 are:

- a maximum pension of £61,200 a year (two-thirds of £91,800)
- a maximum lump sum of £137,700 ($1^1/_2$ times £91,800)
- a maximum payment for death in service of £367,200 (four times £91,800).

> ## EXAMPLES
>
> Marion Mould is an employee. Her monthly contributions of £50 to an employer's pension scheme are deducted from her salary before tax is worked out under the PAYE scheme.
>
> Margaret May is an employee. She doesn't contribute to her employer's pension scheme, but saves in a personal pension scheme instead. She saves £50 a month, but hands over only £39 to the pension provider, because she has deducted £11 (basic rate tax at 22 per cent for the year beginning 6 April 2000). The pension provider claims back the £11 from the Inland Revenue.
>
> Marcia Mumps is self-employed, saving £50 a month in a personal pension scheme. She hands over £50 each month to the pension provider. She claims her basic rate tax relief in her tax return, deducting it from her income before working out how much tax she should pay on 31 January.

Other benefits such as widow's and widower's pensions are also subject to the pension scheme earnings cap.

Contributions to an employer's scheme
The amount you are required to contribute to an employer's pension scheme is decided by your employer, but cannot exceed 15 per cent of your earnings (this can include the value of fringe benefits). Provided the pension scheme is approved by the Inland Revenue, you get tax relief at your highest rate of tax on these contributions. Your contributions will be deducted from your income before working out how much tax has to be paid under PAYE (although your National Insurance contributions are worked out on your full pay, that is, before deduction of pension contributions).

However, if the scheme was set up on or after 14 March 1989, or you joined it on or after 1 June 1989, contributions are restricted to 15 per cent of earnings up to the pension scheme earnings cap mentioned above. For the tax year beginning 6 April 2000, that means you can get tax relief on maximum contributions of 15 per cent of £91,800, that is £13,770.

If you leave an approved pension scheme within two years of joining, your pension contributions can be repaid only after tax has been deducted at a flat rate of 20 per cent, to recover the tax relief you have had.

Additional voluntary contributions
Very few people qualify for the maximum permitted amount of an employer's pension – if only because job changes usually mean losing some pension entitlement. If you are in this position and want to save for your retirement, you should consider additional voluntary contributions (AVCs). These enjoy the same tax benefits as an approved pension scheme, so should grow faster than if you invested the money yourself.

You can choose between two different ways of investing your AVCs:
- through your employer's pension scheme (in-scheme AVCs), which should be considered first
- by making your own arrangements with an insurance company, bank, building society or unit trust manager (free-standing AVCs).

You get full tax relief on AVCs, provided the total amount you contribute in pension contributions does not exceed the 15 per cent limit. So if your employer's pension scheme contributions are 6 per cent, you can pay up to 15 – 6 = 9 per cent in AVCs.

AVCs can be used to increase the pension you will get, the widow's or widower's pension and your life cover. But you can increase the tax-free lump sum only if the AVCs began on or before 7 April 1987. You cannot use AVCs to buy pension benefits greater than the maximum limits set by the Inland Revenue for approved schemes. If you inadvertently contribute so much that the benefits would exceed the limits, some of the AVCs will be paid back when you retire, with a deduction to cover the tax relief you have had on the contributions.

Personal pensions

If you save through a personal pension plan, you can build up a fund with an insurance company, bank, building society or other pension provider that provides you with an income for retirement. Your employer can also contribute to your personal pension plan, as will the government if you contract out of the state earnings-related pension scheme (SERPS) into an appropriate personal pension plan. You can begin to draw this pension any time after the age of 50 (younger for certain professions such as sports-playing).

The amount of pension you draw depends on the size of the fund – which in turn depends on the amount contributed and the investment performance of the fund. However, there are limits on the size of the tax-free lump sum you can take: the maximum is a quarter of the fund accumulated from your contributions and your employer's, with a cash limit of £150,000 if you took out the personal pension on or before 26 July 1989.

Personal pension plans taken out before 1 July 1988 are known as retirement annuity contracts and are subject to slightly different rules. The maximum tax-free lump sum is three times the pension the remainder of the fund will buy – which is usually more than you can take with a new-style personal

---

E X A M P L E

Brenda Robertson earns £28,000 a year from a job and does not belong to her employer's pension scheme. She is 44 and is therefore entitled to tax relief at her top rate of tax on personal pension contributions of up to 20 per cent of her net relevant earnings.

To work out her net relevant earnings, Brenda adds the £28,000 salary to the £1,890 value of her fringe benefits and deducts the £180 of allowable expenses she can claim. Thus her net relevant earnings are £28,000 + £1,890 – £180 = £29,710.

So Brenda can get tax relief on personal pension contributions of 20 per cent of £29,710 = £5,942. If her top rate of tax is 22 per cent in the tax year which began on 6 April 2000 her tax bill will be reduced by 22 per cent of £5,942 = £1,307. The £5,942 of contributions will cost Brenda only £4,635 after allowing for the tax relief.

pension. On the down side, your employer can't get tax relief on contributions to a retirement annuity contract, and you can't start drawing the pension until you are 60. If you have a retirement annuity contract, you can convert it into a personal pension plan at any time simply by telling the insurance company.

How much tax relief?

The amount of contributions you can get tax relief on depends on three factors:

- your net relevant earnings (see below)
- your age
- whether you are saving in a personal pension plan or a retirement annuity contract.

Net relevant earnings for employees are earnings from non-pensionable jobs, including the taxable value of fringe benefits but after deduction of allowable expenses. For self-employed people, it is taxable profits after deducting certain payments made to your business after deduction of tax (for example, patent royalties or covenant payments). In the case of a partnership, it is your share of the partnership profits. With furnished holiday lettings, net relevant earnings are your profits from the lettings.

The amount of your net relevant earnings on which you can get tax relief depends on your age at the start of the tax year and the type of personal pension:

TAX-SAVING IDEA

If you are saving through a retirement annuity contract and your earnings are below the pension scheme earnings cap, consider taking out a personal pension plan as well. You can contribute a higher percentage of your net relevant earnings with a personal pension, allowing you to save more.

EXAMPLE

Shelagh Fitzherbert is contributing to both a retirement annuity contract and a personal pension plan – this gives her more flexibility about when she starts drawing benefits and spreads the risk in case either turns out to be a poor investment. Her earnings for the tax year beginning 6 April 2000 are £40,000 and she is 52.

This means she can invest 20 per cent of £40,000 = £8,000 in her retirement annuity contract, or 30 per cent of £40,000 = £12,000 in her personal pension plan. Tax relief is always given for the retirement annuity first, and she chooses to put £8,000 into it. That leaves her with £12,000 – £8,000 = £4,000 that she can invest in her personal pension plan.

Age at 6 April	Personal pension %	Retirement annuity %
35 or less	$17^{1}/_{2}$	$17^{1}/_{2}$
36-45	20	$17^{1}/_{2}$
46-50	25	$17^{1}/_{2}$
51-55	30	20
56-60	35	$22^{1}/_{2}$
61-74	40	$27^{1}/_{2}$

Any contributions made by your employer to your personal pension plan count towards the limits above. And the maximum net relevant earnings that can be used to calculate the amount you can get tax relief on with a personal pension plan is the pension scheme earnings cap which applies to employers' pensions (see p. 69). For the tax year beginning 6 April 2000, the pension scheme earnings cap is £91,800 – so the maximum for someone aged 35 or less is $17^{1}/_{2}$ per cent of £91,800 – that is, £16,065.

As noted above, your employer can't get tax relief on contributions to a retirement annuity contract. But there is no earnings cap with a retirement annuity, so highly paid people can save more. If you are saving with both, the tax relief goes first to the retirement annuity contributions, and the amount reduces the maximum you can put into a personal pension plan.

Life insurance cover
If you die before drawing a personal pension or retirement annuity, the

contributions are normally paid into your estate – usually with interest. But many personal pension providers also offer some sort of optional life insurance cover, and you can get tax relief on the premiums for this up to a maximum of 5 per cent of your net relevant earnings. Whatever is spent on this life insurance cover is deducted from the maximum amount you can contribute to your personal pension.

Backdating contributions and unused tax relief

You can claim extra tax relief on payments to personal pension plans or retirement annuity contracts until 5 April 2001 by backdating contributions to a previous tax year or claiming unused tax relief for up to six previous tax years. The rules are known as 'carry-back', 'bring back' and 'carry-forward' – and they allow you to make maximum use of the tax relief even if you do not have enough cash to save in a particular year.

You can choose to carry back payments made in one tax year to the previous tax year. For example, you could carry back payments made in the tax year beginning 6 April 2000 to the tax year ending 5 April 2000. And if you had no net relevant earnings in the year ending 5 April 2000, you could carry the payments back to the year ending 5 April 1999 – but no further. You might choose to carry back payments if your rate of tax in the previous year was higher than your current rate of tax, thus saving money – see the example below.

> **TAX-SAVING IDEA**
> If you haven't made the maximum contributions for the last six years, you have until 5 April 2001 to claim the unused relief. After that date you won't be able to use unused relief from earlier years.

> ### EXAMPLE
> Alan Perry is 37 and has a retirement annuity contract into which he pays £5,000 a year – normally well within his limits for tax relief. But the year beginning 6 April 2000 is a bad one and he earns only £20,000 – so his maximum contribution is $17^1/_2$ per cent of that, or £3,500. He gets tax relief for that year at 22 per cent, his top rate of tax – 22 per cent of £3,500 saves him £770.
>
> But the previous year he had earnings of £45,000, and could have made contributions to his retirement annuity of $17^1/_2$ per cent of that figure, or £7,875. Since he had paid in his usual £5,000, he had £7,875 – £5,000 = £2,875 of unused allowance.
>
> He can backdate £1,500 of the contribution made in the tax year beginning 6 April 2000 to the previous year. But he decides to backdate £2,875, since he paid tax at 40 per cent in that tax year and will get more tax relief.

James Loch's net relevant earnings for the last six complete tax years are set out below. He has his 36th birthday in February 2000, which means the maximum personal pension contributions on which he can get tax relief rises from $17^{1}/_{2}$ per cent of net relevant earnings to 20 per cent from 6 April 1999.

Tax year ending 5 April	Net relevant earnings £	Maximum premiums £	Premiums paid £	Unused relief £
1995	20,000	3,500	2,000	1,500
1996	15,000	2,625	2,000	625
1997	20,000	3,500	2,000	1,500
1998	22,000	3,850	2,000	1,850
1999	24,000	4,200	2,000	2,200
2000	22,000	4,400	2,000	2,400

James contributed £2,000 a year to his personal pension, which means that by the end of the tax year ending 5 April 2000, he had unused relief for the previous six years of £10,075. He could make a lump sum payment of £10,075 in the tax year beginning 6 April 2000 in addition to whatever contribution he could make based on his earnings for that year. The tax relief is at his highest rate of tax in the year he makes the payments – the one beginning 6 April 2000.

Alternatively, you can carry forward unused tax relief from the previous six tax years. You can do this only if you have already made your maximum contribution for the current year, and the tax relief will be at the tax rates for the year in which you use it up. Unused relief from the earliest years is used first, as the example above shows.

For what happens from 6 April 2001 onwards, see overleaf.

How do you get the tax relief?
If you are self-employed, you get tax relief on contributions to either a personal pension plan or a retirement annuity contract by claiming it in your tax return. This means you make the payments gross to the pension provider – that is, without deducting any tax relief.

If you are an employee, you will get tax relief on contributions to a personal pension plan by paying them net of basic rate tax. So if the basic rate of tax is 22 per cent and you contribute £1,000 to a personal pension plan, you would hand over £780 (that is, £1,000 less 22 per cent of £1,000). If you are a higher rate taxpayer, you will have to claim the extra tax relief on your tax return – see p. 172.

With a retirement annuity contract, you make your payments without deducting any tax relief. You must claim the tax relief in your tax return (see p. 172). Your PAYE code may be adjusted to give you the tax relief through lower tax deductions from your earnings (see p. 301).

Stakeholder pensions

From 6 April 2001, the government is introducing stakeholder pensions, aimed at people who currently do not save for their retirement. They will work in much the same way as personal pensions: contributions go into a fund which is used to provide an income when you retire, with the option to take one-quarter of the accumulated fund as a tax-free lump sum. Personal pensions can continue in their present form, but the tax rules will change to the same basis as for stakeholder pensions.

The main points about the new tax rules are:

- You can contribute up to £3,600 a year irrespective of your earnings and even if you are not in paid work (so people raising children, students and carers can take out a stakeholder pension)
- You can contribute more than £3,600 if your earnings are high enough – the limits will be as for personal pensions. You can go on making these higher contributions for up to five years even if your earnings fall or cease altogether
- You will get tax relief on contributions, paying them net of basic rate tax even if you are self-employed. You will have to claim higher rate tax relief
- Up to 10 per cent of the contributions can be used for life insurance cover
- You will not be able to carry forward unused tax relief from earlier years – 'use it or lose it'. But you can carry back a contribution to the previous tax year provided it is made before 31 January.

One other new feature of stakeholder pensions is that shares from an approved employee share scheme can be put into the pension, up to the maximum contribution you are entitled to make. Once in the scheme, there is no income tax on the dividends and no capital gains tax if the shares are sold.

INDIVIDUAL SAVINGS ACCOUNTS

The individual savings account (ISA) was introduced from 6 April 1999 for anyone aged 18 or over. It allows you to save in three ways without paying tax on the income and capital gains:

- cash savings accounts with banks, building societies or National Savings
- stockmarket investments such as shares, unit trusts and gilt-edged stock

- specially designed life insurance policies.

The accounts are provided by ISA managers – banks, building societies, supermarkets, insurance companies, investment managers and other financial institutions. You can save up to £7,000 in ISAs in the tax year beginning 6 April 2000 (the maximum is due to fall to £5,000 from 6 April 2001). A husband and wife can each save through ISAs, so a married couple can save £14,000 in the tax year beginning 6 April 2000 and £10,000 a year thereafter.

Any interest, dividends or distributions paid out are free of income tax – you don't need to declare them on your tax return. You can take your money out at any time and there will be no capital gains tax to pay when you cash in part or all of an ISA.

There's an added benefit for people whose income is too low to pay tax. ISA managers can claim back the 10 per cent tax credit that comes with dividends and distributions paid until 5 April 2004 and add them to your account. Non-taxpayers cannot claim back the tax credit if they own the shares or unit trusts outside an ISA (see p. 67).

Note that you have to be resident in the UK (unless you are a Crown servant working abroad) to put money into an ISA, but if you go abroad after starting one, you don't have to cash it in – it still goes on getting tax relief.

Investing in ISAs
You can put all your investment for the year in a single ISA which can combine cash savings accounts, stockmarket investments and life insurance – this is known as a maxi-ISA. Or you can have up to three mini-ISAs, one for each of the three types of savings. You can't change your mind about which option to go for after you have started your ISA savings for the tax year.

The most you can invest in a cash savings account in the tax year beginning 6 April 2000 is £3,000 – the same as the previous year (this limit is due to fall to £1,000 from 6 April 2001). The maximum for life insurance policies is £1,000 a year. So this means if you have three mini-ISAs, the most you can have in the stockmarket investment one is £3,000. With a single maxi-ISA, you can save more than £3,000 in stockmarket investments if you invest less than the maximum in the cash savings part and life insurance – up to the maximum of £7,000 a year (£5,000 from the tax year beginning 6 April 2001).

If you receive shares under employee share-ownership schemes – such as savings-related share option schemes (see p. 218) and employee profit-sharing schemes (see p. 217) – you can transfer them into an ISA up to the maximum you are allowed to invest. So for the tax year beginning 6 April 2000, you can transfer £7,000 of such shares into an ISA provided you made no other ISA investments in the tax year. There will be no capital gains tax to pay on the transfer, no income tax on the dividends and no capital gains tax on the profits on selling the shares – provided the transfer takes place within 90 days of the shares being issued.

You can save more than the normal maximum amount in ISAs if you have a tax-exempt special savings account (TESSA) taken out on or before 5 April 1999 which reaches the end of its five-year term. The capital – what you invested – can be invested in the cash savings account part of an ISA, up to the maximum TESSA investment of £9,000. The money must be transferred within six months of the end of the TESSA, and if it is more than the maximum you can invest in cash in a maxi- or mini-ISA, you can put it in a special TESSA-only ISA.

If by mistake you realise you have taken out too many ISAs, tell the manager of the last one you bought. The tax due on any income or gains on it will have to be paid by the manager and you will be sent details for entering on your tax return.

Choosing an ISA

Managers have different rules for their ISAs on matters such as the minimum amount you need to invest, the types of savings available, the notice required for withdrawals and charges. The government has set voluntary standards for ISA managers on Charges, Access and Terms (CAT standards). To meet the CAT standards, ISAs must be simple, clear and fair – meeting the following conditions:

- cash ISAs must have no regular or one-off charges, allow withdrawals within seven working days and pay interest no lower than 2 per cent below base rate
- stockmarket investment ISAs cannot charge more than 1 per cent of net asset value a year and must allow you to save as little as £50 a month or £500 in a single lump sum
- life insurance ISAs cannot demand minimum premiums of more than £25 a month and must offer reasonable surrender values if cashed in early.

You can only have one maxi-ISA each year, but you can change managers from year to year. If you decide to go for two or three mini-ISAs, they can be with different managers. And you can switch investments within each of the three categories – you can move stockmarket investments from one share to another, for example.

If your ISA manager does not offer the investment you want to switch to, you can change manager. In the year the ISA was taken out, however, you can do this only by closing the old ISA and switching everything in it to a new one. Once the tax year in which you took out the ISA has ended, you can switch part of it to another manager – you don't have to close the old one. Note that there may be charges for switching.

> **TAX-SAVING TIP**
> Invest as much as you can each year in an ISA – up to £7,000 in the tax year beginning 6 April 2000. This maximises the amount you are saving free of income tax and capital gains tax – and you can get your money back if you need it.

PERSONAL EQUITY PLANS (PEPs)

A personal equity plan (PEP) is a way of investing in various stock-market investments such as shares and unit trusts without paying income tax or capital gains tax on the proceeds. PEPs came to an end on 5 April 1999, so you can no longer invest in them. But you can continue to own PEPs taken out on or before that date and get the tax benefits.

> **TAX-SAVING TIP**
> Keep your old PEPs going if you can afford to – together with saving through ISAs, you can build up a sizeable chunk of savings with no tax to pay on income or gains.

There is one circumstance under which tax might be due on PEP proceeds: if some of your money is held as cash on deposit and earns interest which is paid out to you. If more than £180 of interest is paid out to you in a year, the plan manager must deduct tax at 20 per cent and hand this over to the Inland Revenue. The net interest is treated in the same way as any other interest you receive after deduction of tax – higher-rate taxpayers face an additional tax bill (see p. 63).

TAX EXEMPT SPECIAL SAVINGS ACCOUNTS (TESSAs)

A tax exempt special savings account (TESSA) allows you to save with a bank or building society without paying income tax on the interest, provided you save for five years. The last date for starting a TESSA was 5 April 1999, but if you started one on or before that date it can continue until its five-year term is up.

The maximum you can save is £9,000 over five years which you can build up by regular savings (up to £150 a month), by lump sum deposits or a combination of both. No more than £3,000 can be invested in the first year of your first TESSA, and the maximum in each of the remaining years is £1,800. But if you opened a second TESSA within six months of the first one completing its five years, you could put in all the capital saved in the first one – though not the interest. A husband and wife can each invest up to £9,000 in a TESSA – a total of £18,000.

If you need income from your TESSA, you can draw out up to 80 per cent of the interest. But you must leave at least 20 per cent – the equivalent of the tax which would have been deducted from the interest with a normal savings account. If you draw out more than this – or withdraw any of the capital – the TESSA comes to an end and tax will be deducted from all the interest added to your TESSA at the 20 per cent rate for savings income. If you are a higher-rate taxpayer, there could be extra tax to pay (see p. 63). If your income for the tax year is too low to pay tax, you might be able to claim back some or all of the tax deducted (see p. 64).

If a TESSA reaches the end of its five-year term, some or all of the capital – what you invested – can be invested in the cash savings account part of an ISA. This could be up to the maximum you can invest in a TESSA of £9,000, and doesn't count against the maximum you are allowed to invest in ISAs for the tax year. The money must be transferred within six months of the end of the TESSA, and if it is more than the maximum you can invest in cash in a maxi- or mini-ISA, you can put it in a special TESSA-only ISA – see p. 78. If you want to invest the accumulated interest on your TESSA, this counts as part of the annual amount limit of £5,000 for the tax year beginning 6 April 2000.

INVESTING IN GROWING BUSINESSES

Enterprise Investment Scheme (EIS)
If you invest £500 or more in new shares issued by certain unquoted trading companies, you can get tax relief on the investment – provided you hold the shares for a minimum period. For investments on or before 5 April 2000, the

minimum period was five years, but this has fallen from 6 April 2000 to three years from the issue of the shares (or when the company starts trading if this is later). Investments in EIS approved investment funds which invest in such companies also qualify – even if less than £500.

If you dispose of the investments after the minimum period, there will be no capital gains tax to pay when you sell your investment. To further encourage you to invest in growing companies, a series of investments in EIS shares will be treated as a single investment when working out taper relief for capital gains tax – see p. 113. This means that 'serial investors' can reduce the capital gains tax bill on EIS shares held for less than the minimum period.

You get income tax relief at 20 per cent on up to £150,000 of such investments in any tax year. But if you make the investment on or after 6 April and on or before 5 October of the same tax year, half the investment up to a maximum of £25,000 can be set off against your income for the previous tax year. With a married couple, husband and wife can each invest up to these limits.

Making EIS investments can also allow you to put off paying capital gains tax on disposing of other assets if you are able to claim reinvestment relief (see p. 123). To get the relief, you must reinvest the proceeds within a period starting one year before and ending three years after making them.

The companies you can invest in must be unquoted; this includes those with shares traded on the Alternative Investment Market (AIM). They have to be trading companies, which excludes those engaged in banking, insurance, share-dealing, dealing in land or property, leasing and legal or accountancy services. The company must be trading in the UK, but it does not have to be registered or resident in the UK. Investments in schemes where a substantial part of the return is guaranteed or backed by property made on or after 2 July 1997 are also excluded because they do not carry the degree of risk envisaged when the EIS was introduced.

You won't get tax relief on investments if you are connected with the companies – broadly this means being an employee or director or owning over 30 per cent of the shares. In deciding how much of a company you own, you must include the holdings of connected persons – your spouse and you and your spouse's children, parents and grandparents (but not brothers or sisters) – and associates such as business partners. Once you have made your EIS investment, however, you can take part in the active management of the company as a paid director (or 'business angel') provided you had not been connected with the company before you made the EIS investment.

You can't claim the tax relief until the company has carried out its qualifying trade for at least four months, and you lose it if it ceases to do so within three years. If you sell the shares within the minimum period, you lose tax relief on the amount you sell them for (that is, if you sell them for more than they cost you, you have to pay back all the relief). If you sell the shares after the minimum period and the company still qualifies under the scheme there will be no capital gains tax to pay on any gain you make. If you make a loss, this can be set off against other income or capital gains – reducing your overall tax bill for the year.

Business Expansion Scheme

The Business Expansion Scheme (BES), which used to offer tax relief on a wider range of investments than the Enterprise Investment Scheme, came to an end on 31 December 1993. But although no new investments have been possible under the BES since, there is still no capital gains tax to pay when you sell BES investments which you made after 18 March 1986.

Venture capital trusts

If you buy new ordinary shares in a venture capital trust (VCT) which invests in or lends money to certain unquoted trading companies, you can get tax relief on an investment of up to £100,000 in any tax year. A venture capital trust is similar to an investment trust and must be quoted on the Stock Exchange. Unquoted trading companies are defined in broadly the same way as for the Enterprise Investment Scheme.

You get income tax relief at 20 per cent on your investment, provided you hold the shares for the same minimum period as EIS investments. Any dividends paid out by the venture capital trust and gains you make when you sell the shares are tax-free. In addition, you can claim reinvestment relief on VCT investments – which puts off the capital gains tax bill on other assets (see p. 123).

FRINGE BENEFITS

Many employers give their employees non-cash fringe benefits as part of their pay package. Typical examples are employer's contributions to a pension scheme, company cars, luncheon vouchers or interest-free loans to buy your season ticket for the railway.

Many fringe-benefits are tax-free, and even those which are not can remain good value for employees because the taxable value put on them may be less than it would cost you to pay for the benefit yourself.

TAX-FREE FOR ALL

There are many fringe benefits which are tax-free for all employees regardless of what you are paid – see the list below. There are also a number of other benefits which are tax-free for some employees, but not all. There are more details of these on p. 90.

Your employer's own products or services provided to you at less than the price to the general public are tax-free as long as providing them does not cost your employer anything; for example, goods sold to you at the wholesale price, cheap conveyancing for solicitors which does not require the firm to take on extra staff, or free bus travel for bus company employees which does not displace fare-paying customers.

The following are also tax-free:

- free or subsidised meals at work, provided they are available to all employees and are not provided in a public restaurant
- changing room and shower facilities at work, provided they are available to all employees
- luncheon vouchers (or equivalent) up to a maximum of 15p a day

> **TAX-SAVING IDEA**
> There is a long list of fringe benefits which are tax-free whatever your level of earnings – try to take advantage of them in your negotiations with your boss.

- your employer's contributions to a pension, life insurance or sick pay insurance policy for you (but premiums to a private medical insurance policy for you do count as a taxable fringe benefit)
- loans on preferential terms where the total loan outstanding is not more than £5,000

- routine medical check-ups or medical screening for you or your family
- the costs of medical treatment while you are working abroad (or insurance to cover it)
- nurseries and playschemes run by your employer (if the childcare is not on your employer's premises, then the employer must participate in financing and arranging the care)
- living accommodation provided it is either necessary for you to do your job, or beneficial and customary for someone in your line of work (for example, a caretaker). This benefit is not tax-free if you are a director, unless you have no material interest in the company, and you are either a full-time working director, or a director of a non-profit-making company or charity
- living accommodation provided as part of special security arrangements, and other security precautions, if there is a threat to your security because of your job
- if you live in accommodation which is tax-free for one of the two reasons above, any council tax paid by your employer is also a tax-free benefit
- the provision of a car-parking or bicycle-parking space at or near your work
- travelling expenses paid for your spouse if he or she has to accompany you on a business trip abroad because your health does not allow you to travel abroad alone
- reasonable extra travel or overnight subsistence expenses paid to you because of disruption to public transport by industrial action
- the cost of transport home if you are occasionally required to work late after public transport has shut down or cannot reasonably be used
- financial help with the cost of travelling between home and work if you are severely and permanently disabled and cannot use public transport
- some retraining and counselling costs paid for by your employer when you leave your job, providing you have worked for your employer for at least two years
- the cost of fees and books for further education or training courses paid for by your employer if the course is either necessary or directly beneficial for your work, or if you are under 21 when starting a general educational course. If you have to be away from your normal workplace

for not more than 12 months, and will return to it after training, some travel and subsistence costs may be tax-free

- truly personal gifts from your employer of an appropriate size and nature (excluding cash), including gifts on marriage, and long-service awards of things or shares in the company. However, long-service awards are tax-free only if they are to mark service of 20 years or more, they do not cost more than £20 for each year of service, and you have received no similar award in the previous ten years

- suggestion scheme awards (see Incentive awards on p. 199)
- entertainment for you or your family provided by someone other than your employer purely as a gesture of goodwill – but not if there are any strings attached, or if it counts as payment for your services
- small non-cash gifts from someone other than your employer. To qualify, the total cost of all gifts you received from the same donor must not be more than £150 in any tax year, and they must not be provided on any sort of condition, for example, that you will provide some particular service
- annual parties or similar functions, such as a Christmas dinner or summer party, which are open to staff generally and cost no more than £75 a head per year to provide
- sports facilities generally available to all staff and their families (and not available to the general public)
- incidental overnight expenses paid or reimbursed by your employer if you are away overnight on business, such as newspapers and phone calls home. The maximum payment is £5 a night (£10 outside the UK); if more is paid, the whole of the payment becomes taxable, not just the excess
- relocation expenses if you move house for your job, such as the costs of buying and selling homes, some travel and subsistence expenses, and bridging loan expenses. There is a maximum of £8,000 per move; you will be taxed on anything over this figure
- private use of a mobile phone provided by employer
- work buses which can transport 17 or more employees, general subsidies to public bus services used by employees (as long as employees pay the same fare as the general public), bicycles and cycling safety equipment for employees to get between home and work
- the loan of a computer from your employer will be tax-free.

TAXABLE FOR ALL

There are four types of benefits which are always taxable. These are:

- assets transferred to you or payments made for you
- vouchers and any goods or services paid for by credit card
- living accommodation provided by your employer (apart from the few exceptions listed on p. 84)
- mileage allowances if you use your own car for work.

Assets transferred to you or payments made for you

Your employer may give you as a present, or allow you to buy it cheap, an item such as a television set, furniture, groceries or your employer's own product. These payments in kind may be taxed in a number of ways depending on how much you earn and whether you have the alternative of cash instead.

If you earn less than £8,500 (see p. 90)
The taxable value is the second-hand value of the payment in kind (whether or not you actually sell it). Since many assets have a much lower second-hand value than the cost of buying them new this can be advantageous to you.

If you earn at the rate of £8,500 or more (see p. 90)
The tax rules are tougher for those who earn at a rate of £8,500 or more, or directors. They pay tax on the larger of:

- the second-hand value, or
- the cost to the employer of providing the asset, including ancillary costs such as installation or servicing. Remember, though, that if it is the employer's own product, you pay only the extra cost to the employer. So if it does not cost the employer anything (after taking into account anything you have paid for it) it should be tax-free, unless it has a second-hand value.

If you are being given something you have already had the use of (apart from a car, telephone or mobile phone), the taxable value is the larger of the following, less any amount you have paid:

> **T**AX-SAVING IDEA
> Fringe benefits which are not tax-free can still be a tax-efficient way of being paid. The taxable value put on them may be much lower than the value to you.

- the market value when you are given it, or
- the market value of the asset when it was first loaned out (either to you or to anyone else), less the total amount on which tax has already been charged. This is because assets which have been on loan will already have had some tax paid on them.

If you are given a car, telephone or mobile phone, for example on leaving a job, you are taxed on its second-hand value when you are given it, less anything you pay for it. If you buy your company car for a low price, you may have to pay tax on the difference between the price you paid and what your tax office reckons it would fetch on the open market.

Cash or perks?

You may be given the alternative of either a particular payment in kind, such as free board and lodging, or cash. If you have a perk you can convert into money either immediately or at short notice, you have to pay tax on the value of the cash alternative, even if you opt for the perk. However, note that there is a concession for some workers, including farm workers, and for cash alternatives to cars (see p. 94).

Payments made for you

However much you earn, you pay tax on the full amount of any bill paid directly by your employer on your behalf, such as:

- your phone bill
- your personal credit card bill
- your council tax (unless it is tax-free because you live in tax-free accommodation, see p. 84)
- rent paid direct to your landlord
- a tax bill.

Note, though, that this normally applies only to payments settled directly by your employer, for example to the telephone company, the credit card company or your landlord. If you were given cash to settle the bill yourself, it should already have been added to your other pay on your payslip and taxed through PAYE.

Vouchers and credit cards

You may be given a voucher for a particular service (for example, a season ticket), a credit token or a company credit or charge card. If so, you are taxed on their cash equivalent unless they appear in the list of tax-free fringe benefits on p. 83 (for example, luncheon vouchers, gift vouchers which count as a small gift). Cash vouchers worth a specified amount of cash will usually be taxed under PAYE.

For vouchers and cards which do count as a taxable fringe benefit, broadly speaking you pay tax on the expense incurred by the person who provided them, less any amount that you have paid yourself. You will not have to pay tax on any annual card fee or interest paid by your employer.

Company credit cards and charge cards are often provided as a convenient way of paying business expenses. But you will have to pay tax on anything which is not an allowable business expense.

Living accommodation

In some cases living accommodation may count as a tax-free fringe benefit – see the list on p. 83. But if it does not, it counts as a taxable perk however much you earn. It includes houses, flats, houseboats and holiday homes but not board and lodging or hotel-type accommodation where typically you get food and other services.

The taxable value of the accommodation is based on the higher of:

• the rateable value of the property, or
• if the property is let, the rent paid for it.

From the taxable value, you can deduct anything you pay for the accommodation, and also, if part of the property is used exclusively for your work, a proportion for that.

Rateable values are still used, although rates are no longer payable. However, for properties in Scotland, where rateable values were revalued more recently than elsewhere, only a percentage of the rateable value is used (found by multiplying the rateable value by 100 and dividing by 270). If there is no rateable value your employer will have to agree a value with your tax office.

If the tax is based on the rateable value, there may be an extra charge if the property cost more than £75,000, including the cost of any improvements made before the current tax year, but deducting anything you paid towards the cost. Broadly, you pay interest at the Inland Revenue's official rate at the start of the tax year (6.25 per cent at 6 April 1999) on the excess over £75,000, reduced in line with the number of days you do not have the property if it is provided for only part of the year. You can deduct any rent you pay not already deducted when working out the basic taxable value, and an amount for business use.

Mileage allowances

If you use your own car for work most employers pay you a mileage allowance which can be quite generous. Any profit you make on your mileage allowance will be taxable.

There are three different methods of working out your profit. You can choose which suits you best. Inland Revenue leaflet *IR125 Using your car for work* is helpful. Note that:

- business mileage excludes travel between home and work – see p. 211 for how 'grey areas' are treated
- motoring expenses are fuel, insurance, servicing, repairs, road tax and tax relief on loan interest to buy the car (or capital allowances if you buy it outright).

Method 1: Exact

You keep records of your business mileage, your overall mileage and your overall motoring expenses. At the end of the tax year, you divide your business mileage by your overall mileage to find what percentage of your mileage is down to your work. Then multiply your overall expenses by the same percentage to find out how much of these you can claim as business expenses. If your mileage allowances come to more than this, the excess is your profit (unless your employer has a dispensation, see p. 202).

Method 2: Quick

You need only keep records of your business mileage. The Inland Revenue has a scale of pence per mile (the Fixed Profit Car Scheme scales) which it estimates to be the average cost of running a car of various engine sizes, including fuel, insurance, depreciation, servicing and road tax. You pay tax only on any mileage allowance you receive above this scale. At the end of the tax year you multiply your business mileage by the appropriate pence per mile. If your mileage allowances come to more than this, the excess is your profit.

Scale charges under the Fixed Profit Car Scheme

	Tax-free rate per mile	
	on the first 4,000 miles in the tax year	*on each mile over 4,000 miles in the tax year*
	2000-01	2000-01
Size of car engine		
up to 1,000 cc	28p	17p
1,001-1,500 cc	35p	20p
1,501-2,000 cc	45p	25p
over 2,000 cc	63p	36p
Rates for 1999-2000 are the same		

Method 3: Fixed Profit Car Scheme

Your employer has agreed with your tax office that method 2 should apply when working out employees' profit. If so, the figures will not appear on your P11D, but your employer should give you the taxable figure, or the information you need to work it out. If your employer's mileage allowances are not worked out using the same engine sizes as those shown in the table, the scale charges are matched as closely as possible. If the same allowance is paid whatever the size of car, the average of the two middle bands is used.

> **TAX-SAVING IDEA**
> Check out which method of calculation (see p. 89) will give you the lowest profit on your mileage allowance.

Which method?

You do not have to stick with the Fixed Profit Car Scheme, even if your employer operates it, but using the scheme's scales is much simpler than keeping full records. Keep records for a few months to see how similar your actual cost per mile is to the Fixed Profit Car Scheme scale. Then:

- if your car happens to be more expensive to run than average, choose the exact method (but you must keep records of all your expenses)
- if its running costs are average, or cheaper than average, choose the Fixed Profit Car Scheme if your employer runs one, or the Quick method
- if you find that your mileage allowance comes to less than the amount of your actual business expenses, you will be able to claim a loss.

TAXABLE FOR SOME, TAX-FREE FOR OTHERS

The following benefits are tax-free if you earn at a rate of less than £8,500 and are not a director:

- a company car or van
- private medical or dental insurance
- services without a second-hand value, such as hairdressing at work
- loans of things or money.

However, these benefits are taxable for employees who earn at the rate of £8,500 or more. You cannot get around this by asking to be paid under £8,500 and getting substantial perks instead. To work out whether you earn at a rate of £8,500 a year, you need to take into account two rules:

Rule 1

Your earnings for this purpose are any kind of pay you receive for the job – that is, including your expenses and the taxable value of any perks worked out as if you earned £8,500 or more. However, you can exclude any tax-free profit-related pay, your contributions to an employer's pension scheme, and payroll giving donations.

Rule 2

The earnings are worked out assuming you work full-time for a whole year. So if you leave a job half-way through the year, having earned £5,000, you will still count as earning more than £8,500 – because in the second part of the year you would have earned another £5,000, that is, £10,000 in total.

If you are a director you are automatically counted as earning £8,500 or more unless all of the following three conditions apply:

- you are either a full-time working director or a director of a charity or non-profit-making concern
- you do not own or control more than 5 per cent of the share capital
- you earn under £8,500.

Your employer should take account of your rate of earnings when filling in your taxable benefits and their cash equivalent: you can tell what category you fall into depending on whether you get a form P11D (which is the form for people who earn at a rate of £8,500 or more) or P9D (the alternative form if you earn under £8,500).

Company cars

The rules for taxing company cars have become less favourable over the years and many employers now give their staff the choice of whether to take a car or cash. If you only need a car for work occasionally, note that a 'pool car' is tax-free. To qualify it must not normally be kept overnight near your home, it must be used by more than one employee, and any private use must be a consequence of business use. But before you can work out which option is better for you, you need to be able to work out the taxable value of a company car and any free fuel you get.

E X A M P L E

Sanjay O'Rourke got a new company car in March 1997 with a price of £15,000. The basic taxable value for each tax year was 35 per cent of this, £5,250. But he does at least 2,500 miles on business in it each year, so the tax charge for the year ending 5 April 2001 is lower, 25 per cent, that is £3,750 and this is added to his pay for tax purposes, when working out his PAYE code.

However, in March 2001 the car had its fourth birthday. This means that he can claim a one-quarter deduction for the whole of the tax year ending 5 April 2001. The deduction is one-quarter of £3,750, that is £937.50, so the car's taxable value for the tax year ending 5 April 2001 was £2,812.50. Had the car been registered just a month later, after 5 April 1997, he would have had to wait until the tax year ending 5 April 2002 for the further reduction.

To complicate matters further, the system for taxing company cars is changing from 1 April 2002.

Company cars: the current system

The baseline for a car's taxable value is 35 per cent of its price. So a £15,000 new car has a basic taxable value of £5,250. The price is defined as the list price of the car at registration (not the dealer's price), including delivery charges, VAT and car tax (but not road tax). Any contribution you make towards the cost of the car is deducted from its price, up to a limit of £5,000, and the maximum price for tax purposes is capped at £80,000. For cars without a list price, your employer will have to reach agreement with the Revenue, usually on the basis of published car price guides. The market value is used for classic cars worth at least £15,000 and aged 15 years or more at the end of the tax year.

You cannot create an artificially low price by getting a basic model and adding accessories. The price includes any accessories fitted before the car was made available to you, and any accessories or set of accessories worth more than £100 which are fitted after that. Accessories needed because you are disabled are excluded.

From 6 April 1999, the tax charge varies depending on the number of business miles you drive in the car each tax year. If you drive in the year:

- less than 2,500 miles, the tax charge is 35 per cent of the price.
- between 2,500 and 17,999 miles, the tax charge is 25 per cent of the price.
- 18,000 or more miles, the tax charge is 15 per cent of the price.

You are also taxed on free fuel you get (see p. 95), although other running costs borne by your employer, such tax, servicing and insurance, are tax-free. You can reduce the basic taxable value if:

- the car is more than four years old at the end of the tax year in question – deduct one-quarter of the taxable value you ended up with after any

business mileage adjustment
- you have to pay towards your private use of the car – deduct the amount you pay. Note that you cannot deduct a contribution you make voluntarily, in order to get a better car, say.

Changing, getting or losing a company car

At some point your company car is almost certain to be unavailable for part of a tax year, because you changed it, or you started or stopped getting one. The tax system recognises this by reducing the taxable value of the car in line with the number of days in the tax year for which the car was unavailable. The same applies if you didn't have the car (or a replacement) for at least 30 days at a stretch during the tax year. The number of miles you need to do to qualify for the business mileage reductions is also reduced proportionately.

However, you may want to work out your own figures during the tax year to decide whether a company car will be beneficial for you. If so, beware of confusion if you have to adjust the figures to account for time when the car was unavailable. The method shown in the example below is the simplest but the Revenue tends to talk in terms of days unavailable, and then deducts a figure for those days from the full-year figure. So in the example, Sanjay's tax office would probably work out the days for which the first car was unavailable (254) and then deduct $254/_{365}$ths from the full-year figures.

Two company cars?

If your employer provides you and your household with two company cars, from 6 April 1999 that the second car will be taxed on 35 per cent of the price of the car (25 per cent if business mileage in the second car is also 18,000 miles or more in the year).

E X A M P L E

Sanjay changes his company car on 1 August 2000. He has had his old company car for only 117 days in the tax year, so the taxable value is $117/_{365}$ of the full year's value. But first he needs to check that he is still entitled to the business mileage deduction he usually gets. He multiplies the normal business mileage limit that applies (2,500 miles) by $117/_{365}$ to get 801 but his actual mileage is comfortably above this. The taxable value for a full tax year would be £2,333; the taxable value for the 117 days is £2,333 x $117/_{365}$ = £747.

Sanjay has to do a similar calculation for his brand new company car, using its price, but this time he cannot claim the reduction for a car aged four years or more. This time he adjusts all the figures by the number of days he had the new car: 365 – 117 = 248.

Giving up cars for cash

If you do decide that you would rather have cash than a company car, you will of course be taxed on the cash. Employees have to pay National Insurance contributions on extra cash but not on company cars. However, there is no employees' National Insurance to pay on earnings over £27,820 (in the tax year ending 5 April 2001) so if you are over this limit there would be no extra National Insurance to pay anyway.

Company cars: the system from 6 April 2002

From 6 April 2002, the tax charge for a company car will be a percentage of the purchase price based on the car's carbon dioxide (CO_2) emissions. The charge will range from 15% of the car's price for the least polluting cars to 35% for the most polluting.

Although diesel cars produce less CO_2 than petrol versions, there will be an extra 3% charge for diesel cars, subject to the maximum 35%. This is because diesel engines generally produce higher levels of other pollutants.

Under the new system, business mileage discounts and age-related discounts will be abolished.

There may be discounts for environmentally friendly cars, such as very low emission diesel cars, electric cars and so on.

Working out the charge

As under the current system for taxing company cars, the starting point is the purchase price (see p. 92) and the official CO_2 emissions figure for the particular type of car.

For all cars first registered from November 2000, a CO_2 figure for tax purposes will be recorded on the registration document. The Society of Motor Manufacturers and Traders will provide an emissions enquiry service for cars registered from January 1998 onwards. Where no emissions figure is available, the taxable value will be based on engine size, as follows:

Engine capacity cc	Taxable value as % of purchase price	
	Post January 1998 cars with no emissions data	Pre-January 1998 cars (for which reliable emissions data is not available)
0-1,400	15%	15%
1,401-2,000	25%	22%
2,001 or more	35%	32%

Where the CO2 emissions are below a given threshold, the taxable value of the car will normally be 15 per cent of the car's price. The threshold will be reduced each year to encourage the development and use of more efficient cars. Thresholds will be 165g/km in the tax year starting 6 April 2002, 155g/km in the year starting 6 April 2003 and 145g/km for the year starting 6 April 2004. In general, the proportion of purchase price on which tax is charged increases by 1 per cent for each 5g/km increase in emissions.

Fuel for company cars

If you get a company car, you may get free fuel for private use as well. This is taxed according to a fixed scale of charges added to your taxable income. The only reduction you get is if you have the car for only part of the year, in which case the scale charge is worked out in line with the number of days, in the same way as for cars. The only way in which you can avoid the scale charge is by being required by your employer to reimburse all the cost of fuel used for private purposes, and actually doing so. However, fuel provided for the travel between home and work for disabled employees is tax-free.

Car fuel scale charges

	Engine size, cc		
	0-1,400	1,401-2,000	2,001+
Petrol			
1999-2000	£1,210	£1,540	£2,270[1]
2000-01	£1,700	£2,170	£3,200[1]
Diesel			
1999-2000	£1,540	£1,540	£2,270
2000-01	£2,170	£2,170	£3,200

[1]These figures also apply for cars without a cylinder capacity

Car fuel scale charges rose by 41 per cent for the tax year starting 6 April 2000 and are set to rise by 20 per cent a year or more each year until the tax year ending 5 April 2003. This is to discourage employers from offering, and employees from accepting, free fuel.

Vans

A van provided by your employer for your private use is lightly taxed, compared with a company car. The basic taxable value of a van is £500, and there is no tax charge for free fuel. You may also qualify for the following reductions:

- the taxable value is reduced to £350 if the van is aged four years or more at the end of the tax year
- if the van is shared with other employees and is not exclusively yours for any period of more than 30 days at a stretch, the taxable value is split between all the employees concerned
- the taxable value is reduced in line with the number of days within the tax year for which it is unavailable (as for company cars, see above)
- any amount you have to pay for the use of the van is deducted from the taxable value.

Cheap or free loans

The basic rule is that if your employer provides a cheap or interest-free loan, you have to pay tax on the difference between the interest you pay and the interest worked out at an official rate – 6.25 per cent for 1999/2000 and 2000/2001. You do not need to worry about any of this, however, if:

- your employer lends money as part of its normal business, comparable loans were available to members of the general public (a substantial proportion actually being sold to them), and the loan was made to you on the same terms as those comparable loans. Such loans are tax-free from 6 April 1994, even if they were first taken out before then
- the total loans you have outstanding are no more than £5,000 throughout the tax year. If you have several loans, one of which qualifies for tax relief, then the qualifying loan is ignored when deciding whether the other loans fall within the limit.

To work out the tax on a loan, you take the average amount owing during the year (the whole amount, not just the amount above £5,000), adjusted if the loan was only outstanding for part of the year. You then multiply the average loan by the average official rate of interest for the period in the year during which the loan was outstanding (your tax office should be able to tell you this). Lastly, you deduct the interest you were actually liable to pay during the tax year, to find the amount on which you will be taxed.

If you think that you will lose out under this averaging method, you can choose to calculate the figures using the daily amounts of the loan and official rates of interest. However, you have to use the same method for all your taxable loans, and the calculations can get quite complex. If you want to make this choice, you have to tell your tax office within roughly 21 months of the end of the tax year in question.

Note that under either method, if the loan qualifies for tax relief, you get tax relief on both the interest you actually paid and the difference between that and the official rate of interest. Effectively, the tax relief is worked out

Example

Lene Mikkelsen has a £10,000 loan from her employer to help buy her flat, at a special low interest rate of 5 per cent (compared with the official interest rate of 6.25 per cent). She paid off £1,000 of the loan halfway through the year. The taxable value of the perk is £118.75 for 1999/2000, worked out as follows:

Amount outstanding:	
At start of tax year	£10,000
At end of tax year	£9,000
Average:	£19,000 ÷ 2 = £9,500.
Interest payable at official rate	£9,500 x 6.25% = £593.75
Actual interest payable	£475.00
Difference (taxable value)	£118.75

As the loan qualifies for tax relief, Lene can claim tax relief on both the actual interest payable (£475) and the difference between that and the interest payable at the official rate (£118.75), a total of £593.75. As the loan is to buy a home, the tax relief for the year ending 5 April 2000 is 10 per cent of the total – a £59 saving.

But she will be charged tax on the benefit £118.75 at her top rate.

assuming you paid the official rate of interest.

Private medical or dental insurance
If your employer pays premiums for a private medical expenses policy for you (for example, through a group scheme for all employees), the amount is a taxable benefit. The same applies to dental insurance schemes. You pay tax on the cost to your employer, less any amount you pay for the benefit.

Other benefits
There is a variety of other perks taxable only if you earn at the rate of £8,500 a year or more. These include:

- relocation expenses which would normally be tax-free but which are above the £8,000 tax-free limit for each move
- childcare provided by your employer – workplace nurseries and playschemes – should be tax-free, but if your employer just pays for you to arrange your own childcare, this will count as a taxable benefit
- services supplied, such as free hairdressing, holidays, gardening or a free chauffeur – but remember that you pay tax only on the extra cost to your

employer, so services that your employer provides as part of their normal business may be tax-free
- share schemes or share options which are not tax-free. See Chapter 17 for more on these
- subscriptions and fees paid for by your employer for you to join professional bodies, societies, leisure or sports clubs etc. Note that if you pay for these yourself, you may be able to claim them against your tax if they are necessary for your work (see p. 213)
- any income tax paid for you by your employer, other than through PAYE – but only if you are a director. This may sometimes apply if PAYE was not deducted from your pay at the proper time, and the tax was later paid for you
- the value of anything provided for your use, except for cars, vans, mobile phones and living accommodation (for example, a television, furniture, a yacht or aircraft). The value is 20 per cent of the market value when it was first provided (to you or to anyone else), plus any expense of providing it met by your employer. If you are later given whatever it is, you will be taxed as explained on p. 87
- help with educating your children (unless this is nothing to do with your job, for example it is pure coincidence that your child gets one of the generally available scholarships your employer's firm provides).

MINIMISING CAPITAL GAINS TAX

If you own items which increase in value, you may find yourself paying capital gains tax. For example, shares, unit trusts, land, property and antiques can increase in price, giving you a capital gain. If you sell them – or even give them away – you may be faced with a tax bill at up to 40 per cent of the chargeable gain

The average taxpayer is unlikely to pay capital gains tax, however. There is a long list of assets on which gains are tax-free, including your only or main home, private cars and other personal belongings (see p.100). If you do part with an asset which falls into the capital gains tax net, you can deduct from the gain any money you've spent acquiring and owning it. You can also deduct any losses you've made on other assets.

Then there is indexation allowance to reduce the part of the gain caused by inflation between 1982 and 1998 and taper relief reduces it to take account of how long it has been owned since 6 April 1998. There are special reliefs which can reduce or eliminate the gain made on selling business assets, farms or growing businesses. And if there is still any chargeable gain left after all these deductions, there is an annual tax-free allowance that can swallow up another £7,100 of chargeable gains in the tax year ending 5 April 2000, £7,200 for the tax year beginning 6 April 2000.

This chapter explains how capital gains tax works and the details of the various reliefs and allowances. It tells you how to keep your capital gains tax to a minimum. And it sets out the complicated rules for calculating the tax when you buy and sell shares. But it begins with a guide to when you might face this tax.

When do you have to pay capital gains tax?
You may have to pay this tax whenever you dispose of an asset. What is meant by dispose is not defined by law. But if you sell an asset, swap one asset for another or give something away, this will normally count as a disposal. So will the loss or destruction of an asset (although not if you replace or restore it by claiming on an insurance policy, or by using some types of

compensation from an overseas government).

There are some occasions when there is no capital gains tax to pay, regardless of what is being disposed of or how much it is worth:

- assets passed on when someone dies
- gifts to a husband or wife, unless separated (p. 48)
- gifts to charity.

Although there are no taxable gains in these circumstances, there are also no losses if the asset is worth less than when you acquired it.

<table>
<tr>
<td>

TAX-SAVING IDEA
If you are thinking of making a gift to charity of an asset which is showing a loss, think again. You won't be able to claim the loss to reduce other taxable gains (though with gifts of quoted shares, you may be able to claim income tax relief – see p. 28).

Ideally, find something which is showing a taxable gain to give – there will be no tax to pay on the disposal. Alternatively, sell the asset which is showing a loss and give the proceeds to the charity. That would create an allowable loss which could reduce your tax bill on other disposals.

</td>
<td>

EXAMPLE
Leonie Dale wants to give a house she used to let out to students to a charity for the homeless. It has become badly run-down and would produce a capital loss of £40,000 if sold on the open market.

However, she also owns shares which are showing a chargeable gain of much more than £40,000. She decides to sell the house to produce an allowable loss and at the same time sells some shares to produce a similar gain – saving around £10,000 in capital gains tax. She gives the proceeds of the house sale to the charity together with a donation of £5,000 towards the expense of buying another house for their purposes.

</td>
</tr>
</table>

Tax-free gains
There is no capital gains tax to pay on any gain you make on the following assets:

- your home (though not a second home in most cases – see p. 56)
- private cars
- personal belongings – known as chattels – sold for less than £6,000 (see p. 111)
- wasting assets with a useful life of 50 years or less (for example, a boat or caravan), so long as you could not have claimed a capital allowance on it
- British money, including sovereigns dated after 1837
- foreign currency for your personal spending abroad (including what you

spend on maintaining a home abroad), but not foreign currency accounts
- gains on insurance policies, unless you bought them and were not the original holder (though you may have to pay part of the insurance company's capital gains tax bill – see p. 67)
- betting, pools or lottery winnings
- National Savings investments such as National Savings Certificates and Capital Bonds
- Individual savings accounts (ISAs) – see p. 76
- Personal equity plans (PEPs) – see p. 79
- Business Expansion Scheme (BES) shares bought after 18 March 1986, provided you have owned them for at least five years and they carried on their qualifying activity for at least three years (see p. 82)
- Enterprise Investment Scheme (EIS) shares, provided you have owned them for a minimum period and they carried on their qualifying activity for at least three years – see p. 80
- shares in venture capital trusts (VCTs) – see p. 82
- terminal bonuses on Save-As-You-Earn (SAYE) contracts
- British Government stock and any options to buy and sell such stock
- certain corporate bonds such as company loan stock and debentures issued after 13 March 1984 and options to buy and sell such bonds
- interests in trusts or settlements, unless you bought them
- decorations for bravery, unless you bought them
- certain gifts for the public benefit (p. 130)
- damages or compensation for a personal injury or wrong to yourself or in your personal capacity (for example, libel)
- compensation for being given bad investment advice that left you worse off after being persuaded to buy a personal pension between 29 April 1988 and 30 June 1994.

Disposals of land to housing associations may also be free of capital gains tax.

If an asset is one where there is no capital gains tax to pay on disposal, any loss you make on it cannot normally be used to reduce your overall tax bill. But if you dispose of a chattel worth £6,000 or less at a loss, you may be able to use this to reduce your tax bill (see p. 111).

Who has to pay?
Capital gains tax applies to you as an individual in your private life or in your business whether self-employed or in partnership. Trustees may also have to pay capital gains tax on the assets that are held in trust (see overleaf).

Any capital gains tax for the tax year ending 5 April 2000 will have to be paid by 31 January 2001, along with the final payment for any income tax still unpaid from the same tax year. Capital gains tax for the tax year beginning 6 April 2000 will have to be paid by 31 January 2002.

Married couples

A husband and wife are treated as two single people for capital gains tax purposes, and each is responsible for paying their own capital gains tax bills. With assets jointly owned by husband and wife – second homes, shares, valuables and so on – the gain or loss should be split 50:50 between you unless you have told your tax inspector that they are not owned equally.

If assets are held in your joint names unequally, you need to complete a declaration of beneficial interests using Form 17. If the asset produces income, you may already have filled in Form 17 to allocate the income other than 50:50 (see p. 45). There is no need to fill in another for capital gains tax purposes.

Trusts

Where assets are held in trust, the trustees are liable for capital gains tax on disposals of the assets in the trust, in much the same way as individuals. The rate of capital gains tax paid by trustees is 34 per cent.

Trusts are entitled to a tax-free capital gains tax allowance in the same way as individual taxpayers. For most trusts, the allowance is half the figure that applies to individuals. So for the tax year ending 5 April 2000, the first £3,550 of net chargeable gains is free of tax for a trust; for the tax year beginning 6 April 2000, the tax-free allowance for trusts is £3,600. Trusts for certain disabled people get the same tax-exemption as individuals: £7,100 for the tax year ending 5 April 2000; £7,200 for the tax year beginning 6 April 2000.

HOW TO WORK OUT THE GAIN OR LOSS

The gain or loss on an asset disposed of in the tax year ending 5 April 2000 is worked out broadly as follows (and see the example on pp. 104-5):

Step 1: Find the final value of the asset – what you get for selling it or its market value if given away.

Step 2: Find its initial value – normally what you paid for it or its market value (see p. 104). There are special rules for valuing the initial value of assets owned on or before 31 March 1982 (p. 109) and for shares and unit trusts (p. 115).

Step 3: Deduct the initial value from the final value to find the gross capital gain or gross capital loss.

Step 4: If you incurred any allowable expenses in acquiring, owning or disposing of the asset (p. 106), these can be deducted from the gross capital gain or loss to give the net capital gain or net allowable loss.

Step 5: If you have made a net capital gain on an asset owned on or before 5 April 1998, you can reduce this by claiming indexation allowance which reflects the impact of inflation before that date on the figures (p. 108).

Step 6: You may be able to claim special reliefs to reduce a gain further or increase a net allowable loss – for example, when disposing of your only or main home (p. 56) or retiring from your business (p. 124).

Step 7: Subtract your total allowable losses for the year from the total of your chargeable gains to find your net chargeable gain or your net allowable loss. If the losses exceed the gains, there is no capital gains tax to pay and your net allowable loss can be carried forward to set against gains in future years (p. 111).

Step 8: If you have made a net chargeable gain, you can deduct any losses carried over from previous years (p. 112). If the result is equal to or less than the the tax-free capital gains tax allowance for the tax year (£7,100 for the tax year ending 5 April 2000), there is no capital gains tax to pay.

Step 9: If the result of deducting losses from previous years from your net chargeable gain is more than the tax-free allowance, you must next work out if you are entitled to taper relief on any of the gains you have made in this tax year. If you have owned an asset for more than a year after 5 April 1998, taper relief reduces the net capital gain on it according to the number of whole years it was owned after that date (p. 113). Assets owned before 17 March 1998 and sold on or after 6 April 1998 qualify for one bonus year of taper relief (but not business assets disposed of on or after 6 April 2000).

Step 10: Now deduct your losses for the tax year and previous tax years from the net capital gains made on each asset, starting with those that do not qualify for taper relief, going on to those with the lowest rate of taper relief, then to those with the next lowest rate and so on.

Step 11: When all the losses are used up, you can reduce each of the remaining chargeable gains by the appropriate rate of taper relief

Example

Ben Barber bought a painting for £2,000 in April 1985, paying a buyer's fee to the auction house of £200. In the same week, he spent £500 having the painting cleaned. The painting was sold in May 1999 for £20,000, with a seller's fee of £3,000 for the auction house. Ben calculates the tax due as follows:

Step 1: The final value of the painting is what he sold it for – £20,000.

Step 2: The initial value is what he paid for it – £2,000.

Step 3: He deducts the initial value from the final value to find the gross capital gain of £18,000.

Step 4: He incurred allowable expenses of £3,700: the £200 fee paid when buying the painting, the £500 spent on cleaning it and the £3,000 fee paid when selling it. He deducts this from the £18,000 gross capital gain to get the net capital gain of £14,300.

Step 5: He can claim indexation allowance for the £2,000 cost of buying the painting, the £200 buyer's fee and the £500 cleaning charge. The allowance is £1,933 (for how he calculated this, see p. 108). Ben subtracts this indexation allowance from the net capital gain of £14,300 to get a chargeable gain of £12,367.

Step 6: Ben can claim none of the special reliefs against capital gains tax.

Step 7: This is his only chargeable gain for the tax year and he has no allowable losses from the same tax year to deduct from it.

Step 12: Add the net tapered gains together to get the total net tapered gain for the tax year. Deduct the tax-free capital gains tax allowance for the tax year from the total – this was £7,100 for the tax year ending 5 April 2000.

Step 13: Add the result to your taxable income for the year. If the total is less than £28,000 for the tax year ending 5 April 1999, the rate of tax on the capital gain is 20 per cent. If the total is more than £28,000 tax on the amount over the limit is charged at 40 per cent.

Initial and final value

In most cases, the value of an asset when you acquire or sell it is what it cost you to acquire it or what you get on selling it. If you acquired something by inheritance, its initial value is its probate value.

Step 8: Ben has £3,500 of allowable losses from previous tax years to set off against this chargeable gain. Deducting this from his £12,367 net chargeable gain gives £8,867 – well above the £7,100 capital gains tax-free allowance for the tax year, so he will pay capital gains tax.

Step 9: He will be entitled to taper relief on the chargeable gain made on the painting. He has owned it for one full year after 5 April 1998 and he gets a bonus year for having owned it before 17 March 1998. But because it is not a business asset, there is is no taper relief for two years of ownership (see table on p. 114) and, he must pay capital gains tax on 100 per cent of the gain.

Step 10: Ben deducts the £3,500 loss from previous tax years from his net chargeable gains of £12,367 to get £8,867.

Step 11: There is no deduction to be made for taper allowance, so Ben's net tapered gains come to £8,867.

Step 12: The tax-free allowance for the tax year ending 5 April 2000 is £7,100. He subtracts this from the total chargeable gain to get £1,767.

Step 13: The £1,767 is added to Ben's taxable income for the tax year ending 5 April 1999 and income tax is charged on it. His income is already high enough for him to be paying tax at the higher rate of 40 per cent, so that is the rate he pays on the gain.

So Ben must pay 40 per cent of £1,767 – a capital gains tax bill of £706.80.

With a gift, the value is its market value: what anyone selling it at the time of the gift would get for it on the open market. However, in certain circumstances, the initial value of a gift may be what the giver acquired it for if you agreed at the time of the gift to take over the giver's capital gain (see overleaf).

The market value is also the final value if you dispose of an asset to a connected person, however much you sell it for. For capital gains tax, a connected person includes your husband or wife, your business partner and their spouse, a relative of yours or these others (brother, sister, parents, child, grandchild) and the spouse of one of these relatives.

There are special rules for valuing assets owned before April 1982 (see p. 109).

Gifts

With some things you are given, you may have agreed to take over the giver's capital gains tax bill by agreeing to a claim for hold-over relief (see p. 123). Since 14 March 1989, this can be done for only a limited range of gifts, but before that date it could be done with almost anything.

When you come to dispose of an asset on which hold-over relief has been claimed when you got it, its initial value is what the giver acquired it for, not its market value when you were given it.

> ### EXAMPLE
> In December 1988 Suzy Richmond gave an antique diamond ring valued at £8,500 to her daughter Emma. Suzy had bought the ring herself four years previously at a cost of £4,000. They claimed hold-over relief.
>
> In December 1999 Emma sold the ring for £12,000. Because hold-over relief had been claimed on the gift, her net gain was not £12,000 – £8,500 = £3,500. Instead, Suzy's original purchase price of £4,000 is taken as the initial value. And Emma can claim as an allowable expense the £200 bill for restoring the ring paid by Suzy in June 1986.
>
> So Emma's net gain (ignoring indexation allowance) was £12,000 – £4,000 – £200 = £7,800.

Allowable expenses

Deducting the initial value of an asset from its final value gives you the gross capital gain or gross capital loss. However, you can then deduct certain allowable expenses in computing the gain on an asset for capital gains tax. These include:

- acquisition costs, such as payments to a professional adviser (for example, surveyor, accountant, solicitor), conveyancing costs and stamp duty, and advertising to find a seller
- what you spend improving the asset (though not your own time)
- what you spend establishing or defending your rights or title to the asset
- disposal costs, similar to acquisition costs, but including the cost of valuing it for capital gains tax.

Deducting these expenses gives you the net capital gain or net allowable loss. If the asset was a gift to you and the giver got hold-over relief (see above), you can also claim any allowable expenses incurred while the giver owned it.

EXAMPLE

When Melanie Hill sold her holiday cottage in September 1999 for £108,000, she feared an enormous capital gains tax bill – she had bought it in August 1988 for £52,000. But she soon realised there were a lot of expenses she could claim to reduce the capital gain:

- acquisition costs of £1,735 – the £790 legal bill incurred in buying it, the £520 stamp duty and the £425 surveyor's fee for inspecting and valuing it
- improvement costs of £18,750 – the cost of installing modern plumbing and central heating, rewiring and building an extension which were all paid for in May 1989
- disposal costs of £3,575 – legal bills for the sale of £1,725 and £1,850 commission paid to the estate agent.

The net capital gain is worked out as follows:

Final value		£108,000
minus allowable expenses:		
original cost	£52,000	
acquisition costs	£1,735	
improvement costs	£18,750	
disposal costs	£3,575	
Total allowable expenses		£76,060
Net capital gain		**£31,940**

However, Melanie won't pay capital gains tax even on this net capital gain of £31,940 – she can claim indexation allowance (see overleaf) and taper relief (p. 113).

Part disposals

If you dispose of part of an asset, you will need to allocate expenses between the part you are getting rid of and the part you have kept.

Any expense connected only with the part being disposed of can be fully deducted from the proceeds in working out the gain. Anything connected only with the part you are keeping cannot be deducted. But some of the expenditure will be impossible to allocate in this way, and will thus have to be divided between the two parts, in proportion to their value. The proportion of such a cost that you can deduct from the gain is as follows:

$$\frac{\text{Disposal proceeds}}{\text{Disposal proceeds} + \text{Value of the part retained}}$$

There are special rules for allocating costs to shares and unit trusts where holdings are divided or added to (see p. 115).

EXAMPLE

Martin Thompson buys a house which he converts into a pair of flats. He spends £5,000 converting one into a weekend retreat for himself and £3,000 on doing up the other one to sell off.

Each of the flats is given identical valuations at the time of the sale. So any money spent on the whole house can be divided equally between the two flats. He can therefore claim the following expenses to reduce the gain on flat he sells off:

- the £3,000 spent improving the flat he sells off
- the expenses of selling the flat
- half the expenses of buying the house including the purchase price.

Indexation allowance

If you end up with a net capital gain after deducting allowable expenses from the gross capital gain, you can claim indexation allowance to remove some or all of the gain created by inflation if you owned it between 1 April 1982 and 31 March 1998. If there is a net capital loss, you can't claim indexation allowance, however – indexation allowance cannot be used to create or increase a loss.

To calculate indexation allowance for assets held on 5 April 1998, the initial value and each allowable expense is multiplied by the indexation factor for the month in which the money was spent. The factors are in the table opposite – for example, if the money was spent in June 1994, the factor is 0.124.

EXAMPLE

Ben Barber works out the indexation allowance he can claim on the painting he disposed of in May 1999 (see p. 104). He can claim the allowance for the original cost of £2,000, the buyer's fee of £200 and the cleaning costs of £500 – all of this £2,700 was spent in April 1985 when the indexation factor was 0.716.

The indexation allowance is as follows:

$$£2,700 \times 0.716$$
$$= £1,933$$

Ben's chargeable gain on the painting is therefore £14,300 – £1,933 = £12,367

Indexation factors

Year	Jan	Feb	Mar	Apr	May	Jun	Jul	Aug	Sep	Oct	Nov	Dec
1982			1.047	1.006	0.992	0.987	0.986	0.985	0.987	0.977	0.967	0.971
1983	0.968	0.960	0.956	0.929	0.921	0.917	0.906	0.898	0.889	0.883	0.876	0.871
1984	0.872	0.865	0.859	0.834	0.828	0.823	0.825	0.808	0.804	0.793	0.788	0.789
1985	0.783	0.769	0.752	0.716	0.708	0.704	0.707	0.703	0.704	0.701	0.695	0.693
1986	0.689	0.683	0.681	0.665	0.662	0.663	0.667	0.662	0.654	0.652	0.638	0.632
1987	0.626	0.620	0.616	0.597	0.596	0.596	0.597	0.593	0.588	0.580	0.573	0.574
1988	0.574	0.568	0.562	0.537	0.531	0.525	0.524	0.507	0.500	0.485	0.478	0.474
1989	0.465	0.454	0.448	0.423	0.414	0.409	0.408	0.404	0.395	0.384	0.372	0.369
1990	0.361	0.353	0.339	0.300	0.288	0.283	0.282	0.269	0.258	0.248	0.251	0.252
1991	0.249	0.242	0.237	0.222	0.218	0.213	0.215	0.213	0.208	0.204	0.199	0.198
1992	0.199	0.193	0.189	0.171	0.167	0.167	0.171	0.171	0.166	0.162	0.164	0.168
1993	0.179	0.171	0.167	0.156	0.152	0.153	0.156	0.151	0.146	0.147	0.148	0.146
1994	0.151	0.144	0.141	0.128	0.124	0.124	0.129	0.124	0.121	0.120	0.119	0.114
1995	0.114	0.107	0.102	0.091	0.087	0.085	0.091	0.085	0.080	0.085	0.085	0.079
1996	0.083	0.078	0.073	0.066	0.063	0.063	0.067	0.062	0.057	0.057	0.057	0.053
1997	0.053	0.049	0.046	0.040	0.036	0.032	0.032	0.026	0.021	0.019	0.019	0.016
1998	0.019	0.014	0.011									

Assets owned on or before 31 March 1982

If you owned an asset on or before 31 March 1982, only the gain since that date is liable to capital gains tax. Any gain made before 1 April 1982 is effectively tax-free. With such assets, the initial value is normally its market value on 31 March 1982. You cannot deduct expenses incurred on or before that date. Indexation allowance runs from March 1982.

In some circumstances, using the 31 March 1982 value could artificially inflate your gain or loss. Suppose, for example, you bought something in 1978 which fell in value before 31 March 1982 and has risen in value since. Basing the gain on the 31 March 1982 value would make the gain larger than the amount you've actually made since that date. Similarly, if you dispose of something which rose in value while you owned it before 31 March 1982 and fell in value afterwards, this could produce a bigger loss than you actually made.

Thus when calculating the gain or loss on assets owned before 1 April 1982, you need to work out the sums using two different methods:

- the rebased chargeable gain – using the value on 31 March 1982 and ignoring costs incurred on or before that date

- the actual gain – using the original cost you paid for it and allowing for allowable expenses incurred on or before 31 March 1982 (with indexation allowance on them running from that date).

The two answers are then compared in what the Inland Revenue calls the kink test:

- if both methods produce a gain, the smaller gain is used to calculate your tax bill
- if both methods produce a loss, the smaller loss is allowable
- if one produces a gain and the other a loss, the disposal is assumed to produce no gain or loss.

To avoid all this palaver, you can make a rebasing election, which means all your gains and losses on assets owned on or before 31 March 1982 will be based on their market value on that date. This will avoid having to keep complicated records (although it could mean paying more tax if you have assets which fell in value before 31 March 1982 and have risen in value since).

If you want to make a rebasing election, tell your tax inspector in writing within two years of the first disposal of such an asset on or after 6 April 1988. This is likely to be the first disposal to which the rebasing rules apply. The election is irrevocable – so make sure it will pay for you. For more details, see Help Sheet *IR280 Rebasing – assets held at 31 March 1982*.

E X A M P L E

Jim Brooke carries out the kink test on the home he rents out which he sold for £120,000 in December 1999.

He had bought it in June 1979 when he had paid £20,000 for it, with acquisition costs and other allowable expenses before 1 April 1982 of £2,000. Its value at 31 March 1982 was £16,300.

The net capital gain using the 31 March 1982 value as the initial value would be £120,000 – £16,300 = £103,700. The net capital gain based on what he paid for it in June 1979 and expenses before 1 April 1982 would be £120,000 – £20,000 – £2,000 = £98,000.

Both methods produce a gain, so the capital gains tax bill will be based on what Jim paid for it in June 1979 since that produces the smaller gain. If Jim had already opted for all his pre-1 April 1982 assets to be treated as if they were acquired on that date, his tax bill would be based on the larger figure produced by using the market value on 31 March 1982.

Special rules for personal belongings – chattels

If personal belongings, known as chattels by the Inland Revenue, are sold for less than £6,000, the gain is tax-free. Chattels are defined as tangible, movable property and include furniture, silver, paintings and so on. A set (for example, a silver tea-set) counts as one chattel for this exemption.

If a chattel is sold for more than the tax-free limit, the taxable gain is restricted to $5/3$ of the amount of the disposal over the limit. So the maximum gain on a chattel sold for £7,200 would be $5/3$ of £7,200 – £6,000 = $5/3$ of £1,200 = £2,000.

> ## EXAMPLE
> William Baxter bought a piece of furniture for £4,000 and sold it for £7,500 in the tax year ending 5 April 2000. This produces a gain of £7,500 – £4,000 = £3,500. The sale price is over the £6,000 chattels limit so the gain is not tax-free. But for capital gains tax purposes, the gain cannot be more than $5/3$ of £7,500 – £6,000. This is $5/3$ of £1,500 = £2,500, thus reducing William's taxable gain by £1,000.

In most cases, disposing of an asset that would produce a tax-free gain means that you cannot claim any allowable loss made on such an asset. With a chattel, you can claim a loss even if it is sold for less than £6,000 – but the loss is calculated as if it had fetched £6,000.

> ## EXAMPLE
> William Baxter sold another piece of furniture for £4,500 which he had bought for £9,500. His gross loss is calculated as if he had sold it for £6,000: it is therefore £9,500 – £6,000 = £3,500 – rather than the £5,000 loss William actually made.

For more about chattels, ask for Help Sheet *IR295 Chattels and capital gains tax*.

Capital losses

If the initial cost of an asset and its expenses add up to more than its final value, you have made a net capital loss on that asset. Net capital losses are deducted from your chargeable gains to find the total chargeable gain on which your capital gains tax bill is based. If your net capital losses are bigger than your total chargeable gains, the difference – your net allowable loss – can be carried over to reduce your chargeable gains in later tax years.

Note that a loss made when you dispose of an asset to a connected person (p. 105) can be set off only against a gain made to a connected person. This is called a 'clogged loss' and applies even if the loss was made when you disposed of the asset for a genuine commercial value.

The tax-free allowance
The first slice of total chargeable gain in any tax year is free of capital gains tax. For the tax year ending 5 April 2000, the tax-free allowance is £7,100; for the tax year beginning 6 April 2000, the allowance is £7,200.

If you don't use all your tax-free allowance in one year, you can't carry the unused part over to another year. So try not to reduce your total chargeable gain below the level of the tax-free allowance by claiming too much by way of losses. You have to deduct losses from gains made in the same tax year, even if this reduces your net chargeable gain below the tax-free level.

Example
Gus Henry made chargeable gains of £7,500 in the tax year ending 5 April 2000 and allowable losses of £3,250 in the same year. All the losses have to be set off against the gains for this tax year, even though this brings the net chargeable gain below the tax-free allowance of £7,100 for the tax year.

So his net chargeable gain is £7,500 – £3,250 = £4,250 – on which no tax is payable.

Losses from previous years
If your net chargeable gain for the tax year is bigger than the tax-free allowance, you can use any losses from previous tax years to reduce your tax bill. If you have enough such losses, you can reduce your total chargeable gain to the level of the tax-free allowance and pay no capital gains tax at all. Note that – unlike with losses from the same tax year – you don't have to deduct more than is necessary to get down to the tax-free amount.

If your losses from previous tax years are not sufficient to reduce your total chargeable gain below the level of the tax-free allowance, then they can be used to reduce your capital gains tax bill. The carried-forward losses are subtracted from the chargeable gains on individual assets in a way that ensures the biggest possible reduction in your tax bill by maximising the amount of taper relief you can claim – see opposite.

Losses can never be carried back to an earlier tax year, except in the year when you die. Your executors will be able to carry back these losses to set against gains you made in the three previous tax years – starting with the gains in the most recent year. There is further information in Help Sheet *IR282 Death, personal representatives and legatees*.

Example

Elizabeth Ong has a total chargeable gain for the tax year ending 5 April 2000 of £8,000. The tax-free amount for that tax year is £7,100, which would mean paying capital gains tax on £8,000 – £7,100 = £900. But she has losses of £3,500 carried over from previous years and she can use £900 of this amount to reduce her total chargeable gain to nil – with no capital gains tax to pay.

This still leaves her with £3,500 – £900 = £2,600 of unused losses to be carried forward to the tax year beginning 6 April 2000 and beyond.

Claiming losses

You have to claim losses within five years and ten months of the end of the tax year in which they were made. So losses made in the tax year ending 5 April 2000 must be claimed by 31 January 2006.

You can claim the losses by giving details on the Capital gains pages of the tax return – enter the net loss on each asset on pages CG1 or CG2 of the Capital gains supplementary pages (pp. 282, 285). If you haven't been sent these pages, write and tell your tax inspector about your losses.

Taper relief

Taper relief is a rough and ready way of reducing chargeable gains on assets owned for more than a few years, to allow for the effects of inflation. It reduces the amount of the gain according to the number of complete years the asset has been owned after 5 April 1998. The reduction is bigger for business assets, which from 6 April 2000 includes shares owned by employees in trading companies.

For a non-business asset owned for three full years, taper relief reduces the gain by 5 per cent – so 95 per cent of the gain on it is chargeable. After 10 years, taper relief rises to 40 per cent, leaving 60 per cent of the gain chargeable.

For business assets, the rate of taper relief is higher – a maximum of 75 per cent that leaves just 25 per cent of the gain chargeable. For disposals on or before 5 April 2000, this maximum is reached after 10 years, but from 6 April 2000 onwards, the time to reach the maximum falls to just four years.

Number of complete years asset owned after 5 April 1998	Non-business assets		Business assets			
			Disposal on or before 5 April 2000		Disposal on or after 6 April 2000	
	Taper relief	% of gain chargeable	Taper relief	% of gain chargeable	Taper relief	% of gain chargeable
0	0	100	0	100	0	100
1	0	100	7.5	92.5	12.5	87.5
2	0	100	15	85	25	75
3	5	95	22.5	77.5	50	50
4	10	90	30	70	75	25
5	15	85	37.5	62.5	75	25
6	20	80	45	55	75	25
7	25	75	52.5	47.5	75	25
8	30	70	60	40	75	25
9	35	65	67.5	32.5	75	25
10	40	60	75	25	75	25

Also from that date, the definition of business assets widens. Until 5 April 2000, business assets were restricted to those used for a trade (see p. 123) and shares in trading companies where you have at least 5 per cent of the voting rights as a director or employee or 25 per cent as an outside investor. From 6 April 2000, the definition of business assets is widened so it covers all employee shareholdings in traded companies, all shareholdings by non-employees in unquoted trading companies and shareholdings by non-employees in quoted trading companies who have at least 5 per cent of the voting rights.

This extension to all employee shareholdings includes part-timers. If a shareholding only became a business asset on 6 April 2000 and is disposed of less than four years after that date, part of the gain will qualify for taper relief at the rate for business assets and part for the non-business rate. Note that shares listed on the Alternative Investment Market (AIM) count as unquoted.

With assets owned before 1 April 1998, you get indexation allowance up to 5 April 1998 and taper relief for the period of ownership after 5 April 1998. If you owned the asset before 17 March 1998, you will be given one bonus year of ownership if you sold it after 5 April 1998. So if you bought the asset on 1 January 1998 and sold it on 1 July 2000, you would be treated as having owned it for three years after 5 April 1998 – the two complete years after that date plus the one bonus year. But non-business assets disposed of on or after 6 April 2000 no longer qualify for a bonus year because taper relief is enhanced for such assets.

Taper relief is calculated on the chargeable gain after deducting any losses for the tax year and previous tax years. To maximise the amount of taper relief, you can claim, losses are deducted first from the gains that qualify for least tax relief, then the next least and so on. So, for example, if you have a non-business asset that qualifies for 10 per cent taper relief and one that qualifies for 20 per cent, the losses are deducted from the first gain – if it is too small to use up all the losses, they can then be deducted from the second gain. Note that a business asset owned for just a few years qualifies for a higher rate of taper relief than a non-business asset owned rather longer, so may come behind the non-business asset in the queue for losses.

Calculating your capital gains tax bill

If there is anything left after deducting expenses, indexation allowance, losses, taper relief and the tax-free allowance, there is capital gains tax to pay.

For the tax year ending 5 April 2000, your total net tapered gains minus the tax-free allowance of £7,100 is added to your taxable income for the year. If the combined total is less than £28,000 – the upper limit for the basic rate of tax on income – the rate of capital gains tax is 20 per cent. If the combined total comes to more than £28,000, tax on the amount over that limit is charged at 40 per cent.

For the tax year beginning 6 April 2000, your total net tapered gains minus the tax-free allowance of £7,200 is added to your taxable income for the year and taxed as if it was savings income. So if the combined total comes to less than £1,520, the tax rate on the gains is 10 per cent. Any amount over £28,400, the upper limit for the basic rate of income tax, is taxed at the top rate of 40 per cent. Between the upper and lower limit for the basic rate, gains are taxed at 20 per cent.

SHARES AND UNIT TRUSTS

Shares and unit trusts are treated in the same way as other assets for capital gains tax purposes. But if you buy and sell shares in a particular company or units in a particular unit trust at different times, how do you decide which you have bought or sold when working out the gain? And there are further complications when companies merge, are taken over or otherwise reorganise their capital. This section explains the special rules for working out the gains and losses on share transactions. Help sheet *IR284 Shares and capital gains tax*, has more details.

Valuing shares

The market value of shares bought and sold on one of the Stock Exchange markets is normally the amount you paid for them or got for selling them.

But you should use the market value when valuing gifts or disposals to a connected person (see p. 105) – use the prices recorded in the Stock Exchange Daily Official List (which can be supplied by a stockbroker or bank). The market value is the lower of the following two figures, calculated using prices on the date of the gift or disposal:

- the selling price, plus a quarter of the difference between the selling price and the (higher) buying price – the quarter-up rule
- the half-way point between the highest and lowest prices of recorded bargains for the day.

With any disposal of unquoted shares, the market value must be agreed with the Share Valuation Division of the Inland Revenue. This cannot be negotiated in advance and reaching agreement can be a lengthy business. For more about the Share Valuation Division, see Inland Revenue leaflet SVD1.

Unit trusts and investment trusts

The gain on disposing of unit trusts and investment trusts is worked out in the same way as for shares. If you receive an equalisation payment with your first distribution from a unit trust, this is a return of part of your original investment and should be deducted from the acquisition price in working out your gain or loss.

Which shares or unit trusts have you sold?

If you buy one batch of shares in a company and later sell it without any other dealings in the shares, it is quite simple to calculate the gain or loss. But if you buy shares in the same company on different occasions and then sell them – together or in parcels, disposals will be matched with acquisitions in the following order:

- first, shares acquired the same day
- second, shares acquired at any time in the next 30 days (see opposite)
- third shares acquired before the day of sale and after 5 April 1998 – with the most recent acquisitions first (last in, first out, or LIFO)
- fourth, shares acquired between 6 April 1982 and 5 April 1998 – see opposite for how their initial cost and indexation allowance are calculated
- fifth, shares acquired between 6 April 1965 and 5 April 1982 – see opposite
- finally, shares acquired on or before 5 April 1965 – see opposite.

Shares acquired at any time on the next 30 days

Shares bought in the 30 days after a sale are treated as those sold in the sale before those bought earlier – to stop a practice that was known as 'bed and breakfasting'. This involved selling some shares towards the end of the tax year and buying them back the next day to realise a gain which could help use up the tax-free allowance or realise a loss for offsetting gains made on other assets.

This can no longer be done. If you sell shares and buy them back within 30 days of the sale, the shares you sell are matched to those you buy back, not shares bought earlier. So if you sell some shares for £5 each which you originally bought for £3 and then buy them back for £5 the next day, the initial value of the shares you sold will be £5 each not £3 – and there would be no gain realised.

Shares acquired before 6 April 1998 and after 5 April 1982

Share you acquired between these two dates qualify for indexation allowance, according to when the acquisition was made. If you acquired more than one batch of the same shares at different times between the two dates, they are pooled when working out the gain or loss – this means they are treated as a single asset. Each share given the average initial value of all the shares in the pool, and each is entitled to the average indexation allowance. The example overleaf shows how pooling works.

Shares bought on or before 5 April 1982

Shares owned on or before 5 April 1982 and on or after 6 April 1965 are kept in a separate pool, and treated like other assets owned before 1 April 1982:

- the gain is based on their value on 31 March 1982, unless it is to your advantage to base it on their cost when you bought them (see p. 109)
- indexation allowance runs only from March 1982.

Shares bought before 6 April 1965

Shares acquired before 6 April 1965 are kept completely separate. They are the last to be sold if you have bought batches since that date – all shares bought after that date are sold first. When you come to sell pre-April 1965 quoted shares, it is assumed the last to be bought are the first to be sold.

However, you can elect for your shares acquired before 6 April 1965 to be added to your pre-April 1982 pool. This is usually to your advantage, as their value on 31 March 1982 is likely to be higher than what you paid for them more than 17 years before.

Employee share schemes

Employee share schemes allow employees to acquire shares in their companies free or cheaply – and if they are certain types approved by the Inland Revenue, without an income tax bill. There could be a capital gains tax bill when the shares are disposed of, though from 6 April 2000 onwards the gain will qualify for the higher rates of taper relief for business assets (see p. 114).

The initial cost of the shares and when you are deemed to have received them depends on the type of scheme:

- approved savings-related share option schemes – you acquire the shares at the price paid on the day you opted to buy them
- approved profit-sharing schemes – you acquire the shares at the market value on the day they are allocated to you, even though you can't sell them for three years
- approved discretionary share option schemes – you acquire the shares at the price you pay for them on the day you exercise the option. If you paid anything for the option, this an allowable expense.

Until 6 April 1999, you could transfer up to £3,000 of shares into a single company personal equity plan (PEP) direct from approved profit-sharing and savings-related share option schemes. The shares transferred in this way are free of capital gains tax on the transfer or when they are eventually sold. There is a similar provision with individual savings accounts (see p. 77).

Help Sheet *IR287 Employee share schemes and capital gains tax* has more details.

Rights issues

If you get extra shares through a rights issue or a bonus issue, they are allocated to the relevant shares or pool. So if half your shares were bought in May 1990 and half in July 1998, the rights issue is split 50:50 between the July 1998 shares and the pool of 1982-1998 shares. Whatever you pay for the rights issue is added to the initial costs of the two lots of shares, with any indexation allowance running from the time the payment was made. Taper relief on the new shares is calculated from the time the shares they relate to

Example

Diana Nichols bought 2,000 ordinary shares in United Enterprises plc in June 1983 at a cost of £7,000. In December 1988, she added another 2,000 United Enterprises shares for £10,000. That gave her a pool of 4,000 United Enterprises shares bought before 6 April 1998 and after 5 April 1982. She works out the average cost and indexation allowance of the shares in the pool using the following figures for indexation factor:
- June 1983 – 0.917
- December 1988 – 0.474

First Diana calculates the average initial cost of the shares in the pool. The total cost is £7,000 + £10,000 = £17,000, which bought her 4,000 shares. So the average cost is:

$$\frac{£17,000}{4,000} = £4.25$$

Then she works out the indexation allowance on the 2,000 shares bought in June 1983:

$$£7,000 \times 0.917 = £6,419$$

The indexation allowance on the 2,000 shares bought in December 1988 is:

$$£10,000 \times 0.474 = £4,740$$

Total indexation allowance on the 4,000 shares is:

$$£6,419 + £4,740 = £11,159$$

Average indexation allowance for each share in the pool is:

$$\frac{£11,159}{4,000} = £2.79$$

So if she sells 1,000 shares in the pool, the initial costs is taken to be 1,000 × £4.25 = £4,250. The indexation allowance is 1,000 × £2.79 = £2,790.

were acquired, since rights and bonus issues are treated as share reorganisations.

Stock dividends and accumulation unit trusts

If you get extra shares instead of dividends, this is known as a stock dividend (or scrip dividend). The value of the new shares is the amount of dividend forgone excluding the value of the tax credit – the cash equivalent. Any indexation allowance or taper relief runs from the date of the dividend.

Accumulation unit trusts work in a similar way, with extra units allocated to the appropriate pool.

Takeovers and mergers

If you own shares in a company which is taken over, you may get shares in the new parent company in exchange for your old shares. This exchange does not count as a disposal. The new shares are assumed to have been acquired at the cost of the old ones and on the same dates.

If part of the price for the old shares is cash, this is a disposal. For example, if you get half cash, half shares, you have disposed of half the old shares.

When mutuals become PLCs

Some building societies and mutual insurance companies are converting to public limited companies or are involved in other organisational changes that may produce benefits for members. If you receive shares or cash – or both – in such circumstances, there may be a bill for income tax or capital gains tax. Ask the building society or insurance company for guidance.

Payment by instalments

If you have bought newly issued shares, you may have paid for them in instalments. Indexation allowance and taper relief on the full purchase price runs from when the shares were acquired only if all the instalments were paid within 12 months of acquisition. If instalments are paid more than 12 months after the shares were acquired, indexation allowance and taper relief on those instalments runs from when the payments were made.

However, if you paid in instalments when buying newly issued shares in a privatised state enterprise, indexation allowance and taper relief runs from the date you acquired the shares (even though you hand over some of the money months or even years later).

Monthly savings schemes

If you have invested in unit trusts or investment trusts through a monthly savings scheme, working out your gains and losses could be very complicated. You would have to work out the gain, indexation allowance and taper relief for each instalment you invested when making a disposal. If you have been investing in a monthly savings scheme since before 6 April 1998, you can opt for a simplified method of working out the initial costs and indexation allowance for instalments invested up to the end of the accounting year of the fund after that date.

For each year the simplified method applies, it assumes that all 12 monthly instalments for a year were made in the seventh month. So if you invested £100 a month in a fund with an accounting year that runs from 1 January to 31 December, you could assume that you invested 12 x £100 = £1,200 in July, the seventh month.

You may have to add in or deduct extra amounts:

- any distribution or dividend reinvested during the year is added to your investment. So a £50 dividend added to your fund in the above example would take the amount you had invested in July to £1,200 + £50 = £1,250
- extra savings over and above the regular instalments are included, provided you don't add more than twice the monthly instalment in any month – a bigger payment is treated as a separate investment
- if you increase the monthly instalments, the extra is added to the year's investment so long as the increase is in or before the seventh month (if later, it is added to next year's fund)
- small withdrawals are deducted if they are less than a quarter of the amount invested in the year by regular instalments (if withdrawals exceed this amount, the simplified calculation cannot be used).

To opt for this simplified method, you must write to your tax inspector within two years of the end of the first tax year after 6 April 1988 in which you dispose of the units or shares and any of the following applies:

- you face a capital gains tax bill
- the disposal proceeds are more than twice the amount of the tax-free band for the year (£7,100 for the tax year ending 5 April 2000, £7,200 for the tax year beginning 6 April 2000)
- your other disposals in the year create net losses.

HOW TO REDUCE OR DELAY YOUR CAPITAL GAINS TAX BILL

There are a number of ways to reduce or delay a CGT bill. For a start, it is important to claim all the allowable expenses you can (p. 106), indexation allowance (p. 108) and taper relief (p. 113). Also, take advantage of the special rules for disposing of assets owned before 31 March 1982 (p. 109). Then use the tax-free capital gains allowance you can make each year (see p. 112) and don't overlook losses which you can set off against gains (see p. 111).

These are all ways to minimise your tax bill once you have made a disposal. But there are several steps you can take before reaching a disposal to keep your tax bill down:

- take advantage of the allowances of your husband or wife (below)
- make the best use of losses (below)
- pass the tax bill for gifts of business assets and certain other gifts on to the recipient if possible, or pay it in instalments if not (opposite)
- invest the gains from any disposals in growing businesses if you don't need the proceeds immediately – you may be able to defer the tax bill by claiming reinvestment relief on buying shares in certain types of small companies (opposite)
- claim the special reliefs which can reduce your tax bill if you are disposing of a business or farm (see p. 124).

It will help in minimising your capital gains tax bill if you keep a record of the assets you have acquired which may fall into the tax net, together with relevant receipts (for example, for allowable expenses).

Husbands and wives

Husbands and wives are treated as separate individuals for capital gains tax (see p. 102). They pay tax on their own gains and can deduct their losses only from their own gains. They have their own tax-free allowances to deduct from their own net chargeable gains.

But if a married couple living together dispose of assets to each other, this is ignored for the purposes of capital gains tax. For example, if a husband buys shares worth £10,000 in June 2000 and gives them to his wife at a later date, her gain or loss when she sells them will be calculated as if she had bought them for £10,000 in June 2000. Anything they pay each other on such transfers is ignored.

A married couple is treated as living together unless legally separated or where the separation appears to be permanent. Gifts between husband and wife in the year of separation are free of capital gains tax, but after this, tax may be payable. For more about marriage and capital gains tax, see Help Sheet *IR281 Husband and wife, divorce and separation*.

> ## TAX-SAVING IDEA
>
> Since there is no capital gains tax on gifts between husband and wife, you can effectively double your tax-free band if you are married by giving assets to your spouse to dispose of. So in the tax year which began on 6 April 2000, a married couple can effectively make £14,400 of disposals.

Making the best use of losses

If your allowable losses in a tax year look likely to mean you will not be able to use the whole tax-free allowance for the year, there are two options:

- make more disposals to increase your chargeable gains – by selling some

shares that have done well, for example
- hold back on loss-making disposals to a later year when there are no gains or they can be used to reduce future gains.

Gifts

If you give away certain assets or sell them for less than their market value, you can avoid paying capital gains tax by claiming hold-over relief. This means the recipient is treated as having acquired the assets when you did and having paid the costs you paid (less anything paid to you). The recipient's agreement is necessary, since he or she is taking over the tax bill for your period of ownership.

Hold-over relief is available only for the following gifts, however:

- business assets
- heritage property
- gifts to political parties
- gifts which result in an immediate inheritance tax bill (mainly gifts to certain trusts and companies).

If the person you have made the gift to becomes non-resident without having sold or given it away, you might have to pay a capital gains tax bill.

There is no point in claiming hold-over relief if your net taxable gains for the year, including the gift, will be within the tax-free band (£7,100 for the tax year ending 5 April 2000, £7,200 for the tax year beginning 6 April 2000). There would be no capital gains tax for you to pay, but you might add to the tax the person you are making the gift to has to pay eventually.

Business assets include land or buildings used by the business, goodwill, fixed plant and machinery. For gifts made on or before 8 November 1999, shares or securities could also qualify for hold-over relief.

If you make a gift of land or certain types of shareholdings which no longer qualify for hold-over relief, you may be able to pay the capital gains tax in ten annual instalments. The shareholdings in question are a controlling shareholding in a company or minority holdings in unquoted companies. Interest is charged on the unpaid tax, except with agricultural property. For more about hold-over relief, see Help Sheet *IR295 Relief for gifts and similar transactions*.

Reinvestment relief

If you're facing a capital gains tax bill that you can't reduce by claiming losses or other reliefs, consider investing the gain in the shares of certain types of small companies. You can claim reinvestment relief which allows you to defer the tax bill.

To get the relief you have to invest in the ordinary shares of unquoted companies – companies which are not listed on the UK Stock Exchange or any other recognised stock exchange. Investments in companies quoted on the Alternative Investment Market (AIM) are eligible, provided they meet the other requirements for reinvestment relief. The main one is that the company must be trading in certain qualifying sectors or be a holding company for such trading companies. The shares must be newly issued.

You must make the investment any time between one year before and three years after the disposal that produces the gain. The amount of the gain that you reinvest will be taxed only when you eventually sell the shares – although you could then defer the tax bill again by reinvesting any gain in more qualifying shares and claiming further reinvestment relief. Otherwise, the deferred gain will be taxed only if you emigrate or the company ceases to be a qualifying one during the three years after you acquired the shares.

There's a further tax benefit for people who invest in two or more Enterprise Investment Scheme (EIS) companies. EIS shares are free of capital gains tax if owned for a minimum period (see p. 81) and they carry on their qualifying activity for three years or more. But if there is a gain when you dispose of EIS shares and you reinvest in shares in another EIS company, you can treat this as a single investment in calculating taper relief when you sell the second lot. This is designed to encourage 'serial entrepreneurs' by giving an incentive to reinvest gains on successful EIS companies in new ones.

To claim reinvestment relief, you must tell your tax inspector within five years after the 31 January in the year following the tax year in which you make the disposal or acquire the shares. So if you made the disposal and bought the shares in the tax year ending 5 April 2000, you have until 31 January 2006 to make the claim. Use the form at the end of Help Sheet *IR291 Reinvestment relief*.

Businesses and farms

If you are disposing of a business or farm, you could face an enormous tax bill on the gain. There are two important reliefs to reduce the impact on entrepreneurs and others who create small businesses:

- retirement relief when you retire from your business (opposite)
- roll-over relief if you replace business assets (overleaf).

What follows is a brief introduction to indicate their scope. But with large sums at stake, it would pay to seek professional advice on these reliefs to ensure you meet the complex requirements.

Retirement relief

Retirement relief reduces the tax bill if you dispose of a business when aged 50 or more, or less if you are retiring because of ill-health. It is being phased out since taper relief – introduced in 1998 – allows up to 75 per cent of the gain on selling business assets to be free of capital gains tax (see p. 113). But until retirement relief disappears, it is a valuable concession for businesses.

The maximum relief is for people disposing of a business owned for at least ten years. For the tax year beginning 6 April 1999, up to £200,000 of the capital gain can be tax-free and only half the gain between £200,000 and £800,000 is taxable. If you have owned the business for less than ten years, the amount on which you can get relief is reduced by 10 per cent for each year less than ten – the example overleaf shows how this works.

For the tax year beginning 6 April 2000, up to £150,000 of the capital gain is tax-free and half the gain between £150,000 and £600,000 is taxable. Similar reductions will follow each tax year thereafter, so the relief will end by the tax year beginning 6 April 2003. Over this period, the amount of gain free of tax under taper relief – which is subject to no maximum – will begin to build up.

With retirement relief, a husband and wife can each make claims if they are eligible – effectively doubling the limits for a married couple who share ownership of the business. And you do not have to retire to claim it unless you are making your claim when aged under 50.

If you are selling or disposing of your business before 50, you must be retiring because of your ill-health (which is strictly defined) to claim the relief. If you wish to claim this relief because of ill-health, you must do so on or before the second 31 January after the end of the tax year in which you dispose of the business. So if you disposed of the business in the tax year ending 5 April 2000, you can claim retirement relief on ill-health grounds up to 31 January 2002.

Retirement relief applies to business assets, and to shares in a company in which you have at least 5 per cent of the voting rights, providing you have been a full-time director or an employee of the company for the past ten years.

EXAMPLE

Harry Singh, aged 65, started a business 30 years ago and sold it in May 1999. The gain after indexation allowance was £500,000. He is entitled to the maximum retirement relief as he had the business for more than ten years.

Harry can claim full relief on the first £200,000 plus relief on half the gain between £200,000 and £800,000:

$$£200,000 + 50 \text{ per cent of } (£500,000 - £200,000)$$
$$= £200,000 + 50 \text{ per cent of } £300,000$$
$$= £200,000 + £150,000$$
$$= £350,000$$

Harry's taxable gain is:

$$£500,000 - £350,000 = £150,000$$

This £150,000 gain is Harry's only chargeable gain for the tax year and he has no losses to set off against it. But he is entitled to taper relief: one year for owning it for more than a year since 5 April 1998 and a bonus year for owning it before 17 March 1998. Two years for a business asset means only 92.5 per cent of the gain is taxable – that is, 92.5 per cent of £150,000 = £138,750.

The first £7,100 of taxable gains in the tax year ending 5 April 2000 is free of capital gains tax, so tax is charged on:

$$£138,750 - £7,100 = £131,650$$

Harry's taxable income is £45,000 on which he pays tax at the higher rate of 40 per cent. His capital gains tax bill is therefore:

$$40 \text{ per cent of } £131,650 = £52,660$$

You can still get retirement relief if you have owned several different businesses in the last ten years. Providing that each business qualifies for the relief, and the gap between each is not more than two years, you can add together the separate periods of business activity over the past ten years to calculate the total period that counts for the relief.

Roll-over relief

Roll-over relief allows you to defer the capital gains tax bill when you sell or otherwise dispose of assets from your business, providing you replace them in the three years after the sale or the one year before it. You can claim this roll-over relief even if you do not buy an identical replacement as long as you use the proceeds to buy another qualifying business asset. Assets which qualify include land or buildings used by the business, goodwill, fixed plant and machinery.

You usually get the relief by deducting the gain for the old asset from the acquisition cost of the new one. So when you come to sell the new asset, the gain on it has been increased by the gain on the old asset. However, if you replace again, you can claim further roll-over relief, and currently capital gains tax will not have to be paid until you fail to replace the business asset.

You can make a claim for roll-over relief up to six years after the end of the tax year in which you dispose of the asset or the year in which you replace it if this is later.

INHERITANCE TAX

There is no space on the 2000 tax return for inheritance tax. This is because it is largely a tax on what you leave when you die (including gifts made in the seven years before). And few people are affected by inheritance tax – just one in 45 estates currently falls in its net.

Do not ignore it, however. The tax rate is a hefty 40 per cent of anything over £234,000. There is plenty that can be done to reduce the amount paid – as long as you plan carefully. As one former chancellor said a few years ago: 'It is largely paid by people of modest means who either cannot or simply do not make careful plans to avoid it.'

This chapter tells you how inheritance tax works and how to reduce the amount that goes to the Inland Revenue. It also has some guidance on what can be done to reduce an inheritance tax bill after the event; there is some scope to ease the burden even then.

HOW INHERITANCE TAX WORKS

When you die, everything you own – your home, possessions, investments and savings – goes into your estate. So does money paid out by life insurance policies unless they are written in trust (see p. 133), and the value of things you have given away but reserved the right to use for yourself (gifts with reservation – see p. 135). Debts such as outstanding mortgages and funeral expenses are deducted from the total to find the value of your estate.

Some or all of your estate may be free of inheritance tax: anything left to your husband or wife, or to a UK charity, for example (for a full list of what is tax-free, see p. 130). These tax-free bequests and legacies are deducted from the value of your estate before the tax bill is worked out.

Then any gifts to other people in the seven years before your death which are not tax-free are added. So are gifts made to a trust for a disabled person, or to an accumulation and maintenance trust for children and grandchildren under 25.

If the resulting total exceeds a certain limit – £234,000 for deaths on or after 6 April 2000 – inheritance tax is payable on the amount over the limit at 40 per cent. (For deaths in the tax year ending 5 April 2000, the limit was £231,000.)

So if the total is £250,000, tax is payable on £250,000 – £234,000 = £16,000. This gives a tax bill of 40 per cent of £16,000, that is £6,400.

Inheritance tax due on what you leave on death is paid out of your estate. But if inheritance tax is due on a gift made before your death, it must be paid by the person you made the gift to. They may be able to reduce the amount payable if the gift was made more than three years before death by claiming tapering relief:

Years between gift and death	% of inheritance tax payable
Up to 3	100%
More than 3 and up to 4	80%
More than 4 and up to 5	60%
More than 5 and up to 6	40%
More than 6 and up to 7	20%

EXAMPLE

Angela Framing died in May 2000, leaving an estate worth £287,000 (largely the value of her home counties house). In December 1995, she had made a taxable gift of £10,000 to help a grandchild with the cost of studying for an MBA at a leading business school. Subsequently, in August 1996, she gave another grandchild a taxable gift of £5,000 to start a business.

The calculation of the inheritance tax due starts with the earliest taxable gift – the £10,000 made just over four years before her death. There is no tax to pay on this gift, since it is well below the £234,000 threshold for inheritance tax applying in May 2000 when she died. Nor is there any inheritance tax to pay on the 1996 gift of £5,000. It brought her total of taxable gifts to £15,000 – still well below the £234,000 tax threshold.

In calculating the tax due on Angela's estate, the £15,000 of taxable lifetime gifts is added to the £287,000 left on death to produce a total of £302,000. The first £234,000 of that is free of tax, leaving £302,000 – £234,000 = £68,000 on which tax is due.

Tax at 40 per cent on £68,000 is £27,200 – tax that will be entirely paid out of Angela's estate.

Inheritance tax may also have to be paid on gifts to certain types of trust made more than seven years before death. The tax, which must be paid at the time of the gift, can also affect the tax payable on death. If you are involved with such trusts, you should seek professional advice from an accountant or solicitor – this chapter does not deal with their complexities.

Gifts free of inheritance tax
Gifts that are always tax-free:

- gifts between husband and wife – even if the two are legally separated. But only the first £55,000 is tax-free if the gifts are to someone who is not domiciled in the UK (domicile reflects the individual's natural home, see p. 296)
- gifts to UK charities
- gifts to certain national institutions such as the National Trust, National Gallery, British Museum (and their Scottish, Welsh and Northern Ireland equivalents)
- gifts of certain types of heritage property such as paintings, archives, land or historic buildings to non-profit-making concerns like local museums
- gifts of land in the UK to registered housing associations
- gifts of shares in a company into a trust for the benefit of most or all of the employees which will control the company
- gifts to established political parties.

Gifts that are tax-free on death only:

- lump sums paid out on your death by a pension scheme provided the trustees of the scheme have discretion about who gets the money
- refunds of personal pension contributions (and interest) paid directly to someone else or a trust – in other words, not paid into your estate
- the estate of anyone killed on active military service in war or whose death was hastened by such service.

Gifts that are tax-free in lifetime only:

- anything given to an individual more than seven years before your death – unless there are strings attached (see p. 135)
- small gifts worth up to £250 to any number of people in any tax year. But you can't give anyone more than this limit and claim exemption on the first £250 – if you give someone £500, the whole £500 will be taxable unless it is tax-free for one of the other reasons below
- regular gifts made out of normal income. The gifts must come out of your usual after-tax income and not from your capital. After paying for the gifts, you should have enough income to maintain your normal standard of living
- gifts on marriage to a bride or groom: each parent of the bride or groom can give £5,000, grandparents or remoter relatives £2,500 and anyone else £1,000. The gifts must be made before the great day – and if the marriage is called off, the gift becomes taxable
- gifts for the maintenance of your family – an ex-husband or wife, certain dependent relatives and children under 18 or still in full-time education.

The children can be yours, stepchildren, adopted children or any other children in your care
- up to £3,000 in total a year of other gifts. If you don't use the whole £3,000 annual exemption in one year, you can carry forward the unused part to the next tax year only. You can't use the annual exemption to top up the small gifts exemption. If you give someone more than £250 in a year, all of it must come off the annual exemption if it is to be free of inheritance tax.

PLANNING FOR INHERITANCE TAX

If your estate is likely to be well below the threshold for paying inheritance tax, there is no need to worry about it. But if it looks as if you are above it, there is much you can do to reduce the tax bill. An important first step is to draw up a will which will make you think about what you own and how you want it to be disposed of after you die.

Most of the ways of minimising inheritance tax involve making gifts which are free of tax or making taxable gifts more than seven years before your death. But remember your heirs will still be better off even if tax is due on your estate. Don't give away so much that you or your spouse are left impoverished in old age, merely to cheat the Inland Revenue of every last penny of tax.

> **TAX-SAVING IDEA**
> Draw up a will. There are simple steps you can take to minimise the tax payable on your estate when you die and to reduce the complications for those you leave behind.

Tax-free gifts
If you do have some resources to spare, make as full use as possible of the tax-free small gifts, gifts on marriage and such like. And make sure your spouse has enough to make similar gifts free of inheritance tax.

If you want to make larger gifts, the earlier you make them the better – because inheritance tax may have to be paid on a gift if you die within seven years of making it. (For this reason, lifetime gifts are often described as potentially exempt transfers (PETs). They are potentially free of inheritance tax but you must survive for seven years after they are made for the tax to be avoided.)

Even if you die within seven years of making a gift, the inheritance tax paid by the person you made the gift

> **TAX-SAVING IDEA**
> Make as full use as possible of the gifts you can make which do not fall into the inheritance tax net. Gifts on marriage and those made out of normal income are tax-free.

to will be reduced by tapering relief (see p. 129) if the gift is made more than three years before your death. Note that gifts in your lifetime, other than cash, may mean a capital gains tax bill – see Chapter 10.

Share your wealth
A married couple can share their wealth – what they give to each other is free of inheritance tax. Each can then make tax-free gifts and leave a taxable estate of up to £234,000 without paying inheritance tax.

In practice, it may not be easy to split your worldly goods and give them away during your lifetime. It may make more sense to pass all or most of them on to the survivor so he or she has enough to live on. But this principle of estate-splitting is a basic strategy to be followed where possible.

Your home
Your home is almost certainly your most valuable possession – and may be the main reason why your estate ends up over the threshold for paying inheritance tax. But it is one of the hardest assets to remove from the tax net – assuming you intend to go on living in it until you die.

For example, you can't make a lifetime gift of it to your children on condition you can continue to live in it. That would count as a gift with reservation (see p. 135), and the home would be treated as yours.

EXAMPLE
Veronica McGrath wants to give away as much as possible free of inheritance tax before she dies.

First, she gives £1,000 a year to each of her three children – taking advantage of the £3,000 a year annual exemption. Then she makes £250 gifts every year to each of her ten grandchildren – a total of £2,500 a year free of inheritance tax as small gifts. She also gives the maximum £2,500 to any of her grandchildren who get married.

She can afford to pay the premiums on insurance policies on her own life out of her normal income. So she takes out policies written in trust (see p. 000) for each of her three children. The premiums come to £60 a month each and will be tax-free as regular gifts made out of normal income (when she dies, the money from the insurance policies will be paid straight to the children without being taxable).

Overall, Veronica manages to give away almost £7,000 a year free of inheritance tax. This is nearly £50,000 in a seven-year period, and even if she dies within seven years of starting this programme of gifts there will be no inheritance tax to pay on them.

You might be able to reduce the size of your estate somewhat by sharing the ownership of the house. If your home is jointly owned with someone under a joint tenancy, your share automatically goes to the survivor when one of you dies. But if you jointly own your home with someone else as a tenancy in common, you can bequeath your half-share to anyone you please.

For example, if you had a tenancy in common with your spouse, you could bequeath half of your half-share to your spouse and the other half to the next generation. This would reduce the size of your spouse's estate but leave him or her in control of the home.

There is no inheritance tax to pay if you leave part or all of a home to your spouse, since gifts between husband and wife are always tax-free. But a gift to anyone who is not your husband or wife is taxable.

Life insurance

If you want to make sure there is enough money to pay an inheritance tax bill on a home or business, you can take out a term life insurance policy which pays out if you die within seven years of giving it away. And if you plan to leave a large asset on death, whole life insurance policies pay out whenever you die, again providing cash to pay the inheritance tax.

Make sure you have any such policies written in trust to the person you want to have the money. The proceeds will then be paid directly to that person on your death and be free of inheritance tax. If the policy is not written in trust, the money will be added to your estate and inheritance tax charged on it (there will also be a delay before your heirs can get their hands on it until probate is granted).

The premiums for a policy written in trust count as gifts, but will be free of inheritance tax if the policy is for your spouse. And if you pay the premiums

> ## EXAMPLE
>
> Alan and Meg Riordan realise they are going to face a hefty inheritance tax bill when they die, since most of their assets are in Alan's name. They decide to start an active programme of making tax-free gifts and estate-splitting.
>
> They adopt a similar approach to Veronica McGrath in making gifts. Since each of them can make these tax-free gifts, they are soon passing on around £100,000 to their children and grandchildren every seven years.
>
> They also divide their assets between them, and bequeath a further £200,000 each to their children in their wills, with the rest to each other. When the first dies, the £200,000 bequest to the children will be below the threshold for inheritance tax.
>
> The second to die will thus leave £200,000 less to fall into the tax net. And the Riordans will have saved £100,000 from inheritance tax for each seven years of the lifetime gifts programme.
>
> By starting 15 years before their deaths, the Riordans manage to pass on £400,000 more without tax than if they had left it all in Alan's name. This saves their heirs £160,000 in inheritance tax.

out of your normal spending, they will be tax-free whoever benefits.

Shares

The market value of any shares left on death (or given away in the previous seven years) must normally be included in your estate in working out the inheritance tax bill. But some sorts of shares qualify for business relief, which reduces the value for inheritance tax purposes – or even removes them from the calculation altogether:

- shares in a listed company which form a controlling interest – for gifts made on or after 10 March 1992 and inheritance tax bills which arise out of deaths on or after that date, the value of the shares is halved
- shares quoted on the Alternative Investment Market (AIM) – no inheritance tax provided they have been held for at least two years
- unquoted shares and those traded on the Over the Counter (OTC) markets are also eligible for business relief on the same basis as AIM shares.

Your own business or farm

If you own or have an interest in a small business or a farm, seek professional advice on inheritance tax, since there are substantial concessions which can reduce or eliminate the tax:

- business relief means there will be no inheritance tax to pay on business assets such as goodwill, land, buildings, plant, stock, patents and so on (reduced by debts incurred in the business)
- agricultural relief can mean no inheritance tax on the agricultural value of owner-occupied farmlands and farm tenancies (including cottages, farm buildings and farm houses). There are also reliefs for landowners who let farmland.

Estate freezing

Estate freezing is a way of freezing some of the value of your wealth now so the increase in value in future years benefits someone else.

A simple way of doing this is by investing in an endowment or unit-linked life insurance policy written in trust for your children or grandchildren (see Life insurance, above). Any growth in its value accumulates in the policy free of inheritance tax. Some unit trust managers can do something similar with investments in unit trusts.

A more ambitious approach is to set up an accumulation and maintenance trust for your children or grandchildren. You put some capital in and any income from it is either reinvested or used for the maintenance, education or benefit of the beneficiaries at the discretion of the trustees. When the beneficiaries reach the age of 25, either the capital is shared out or they become entitled to the income from it. If you live for more than seven years after making gifts to such trusts, there is no inheritance tax to pay.

If you are thinking of setting up a family trust, consult a professional tax adviser such as a solicitor or accountant.

INHERITANCE TAX PLANNING PITFALLS

You might think that there are some rather obvious wheezes that will help you avoid inheritance tax. It is unlikely that the Inland Revenue will not have thought of them and blocked their use.

Gifts with strings attached

If you give something away but reserve the right to use it, it counts as a gift with reservation – and is treated as remaining your property. The gift would not be recognised for inheritance tax purposes and its value would be added to your estate when you died.

For example, if you give your home to a child on condition that you can go on living in it until your death, this would count as a gift with reservation. This could apply even if there was no formal agreement that you go on living in the home. If the gift was made after 17 March 1986, it counts as subject to a reservation if you go on using it.

Associated operations

If you try to get round the inheritance tax rules by making a series of gifts, the Inland Revenue is allowed to treat them as associated operations which form a single direct gift.

For example, you might think you could give an extra £5,000 to an adult child by making ten tax-free gifts of £500 to friends which they pass on. The taxman will treat this as a single £5,000 gift, however – and one subject to inheritance tax.

Related property

In working out the value of a bequest or gift, the Inland Revenue treats as yours property which it reckons is related to yours – in particular, anything owned by your husband or wife. This means you can't reduce its value by splitting it up with your spouse.

Suppose, for example, you own 30 per cent of the shares in a company and your spouse owns another 30 per cent. The Inland Revenue will value your 30 per cent as worth half the value of a 60 per cent controlling interest, which is generally higher than the value of a 30 per cent minority interest.

Property will also be treated as related if it has been owned at any time in the previous five years by a charity, political party or national institution to which you or your spouse gave it.

PAYMENT OF INHERITANCE TAX

Inheritance tax is due six months after the end of the month in which the death happened. In practice, it can often take longer for the executors or personal representatives to sort out the will and tidy up the dead person's affairs. As part of the process of seeking probate, they must submit an Inland Revenue account, listing the value of the dead person's property (including property owned jointly with anybody else) and the amounts of any debts. Probate will not be granted until the tax has been paid.

Interest is charged if the tax is paid after the six-month deadline, running from the time the tax was due. Likewise, if you pay too much inheritance tax, you will get interest on the over-payment from the Inland Revenue.

If you take out a loan to pay inheritance tax before probate is granted, you can get tax relief on the interest on it for up to 12 months.

Payment by instalments
You can spread the pain of paying inheritance tax over ten equal yearly instalments with two sorts of assets:
- land and property
- a business, including certain holdings of unquoted shares.

This option is allowed only with bequests on death and lifetime gifts where the recipient still owns the property when the death occurs. Interest has to be paid on the delayed tax with land and property, unless it is business property or agricultural land.

If you want to pay in instalments, tell the Inland Revenue before the normal payment date for the tax. The first instalment is due on the date the whole tax would have been payable.

Reducing the tax on bequests that have fallen in value
If you inherit investments or land and buildings which fall in value after the

death of the person who bequeathed them, you might be able to reduce your inheritance tax bill.

For investments, this applies to quoted shares (including those quoted on the AIM) and authorised unit trusts which fall in value or become worthless in the year after death:

- if sold during this period for less than they were worth on death, the sale price can be used to value them for inheritance tax purposes instead of their value on death
- if cancelled without replacement, they are treated as having been sold immediately before the date of cancellation for the nominal sum of £1
- if suspended and remaining suspended a year after the death, their value at the first anniversary can be used for inheritance tax purposes instead of their value on death.

When this relief is claimed, however, all such investments sold in the year after death are revalued in this way. So if some shares or unit trusts have been sold for more than they were worth on death, this would offset any loss made on other shares or unit trusts.

For land or buildings, you can ask for the inheritance tax bill to be recalculated if you sell them within four years of the death for less than their probate value. The inheritance tax bill will be worked out on the actual sale proceeds instead. Again, if this relief is claimed, all land or property sold during the four-year period is revalued for inheritance tax purposes at what it was sold for, rather than what it was worth on death.

Facing a second inheritance tax bill within five years?

If you inherit something that has only recently been subject to inheritance tax, the tax due on this second change of ownership is reduced by what is known as quick succession relief. Provided the death which led to the first payment was within five years of the death that has led to a second tax bill, the second bill can be reduced by a fraction of the first bill.

If the first death was within one year of the second death, the second bill is reduced by the following fraction of the first bill:

$$\frac{\text{Value of inheritance at the time of first transfer}}{\text{Value of inheritance at transfer + tax paid on first transfer}}$$

If the first death was more than one year before the second death, the fraction is reduced by 20 per cent for each complete year between the two. The example, right, shows how quick succession relief works.

Changing inheritances after a death

If you are facing an inheritance tax bill, one option to reduce it is to vary the inheritances covered. Whether or not there is a will, those who are entitled to a share of a dead person's estate can agree to vary the way the estate is divided up. For example, the variation could direct some of the estate towards tax-free bequests – from the children to the dead person's husband or wife, for example.

The procedure is to draw up a deed of variation in writing, which must be signed within two years of the death by all those who will lose out. If it increases the amount of tax, the personal representatives of the dead person must also sign it. A variation can be carried out only once, so it is important to get it right. A solicitor can advise on drawing up the document – if children under 18 and unmarried are involved, it will be necessary to obtain a court order.

EXAMPLE

Maurice Thornton inherits a half-share of his mother's estate, worth £150,000. Inheritance tax of £16,000 is due on this share.

However, Maurice's mother had inherited £80,000 from her father only two and a half years earlier – an inheritance on which tax of £20,000 had been paid. Because Maurice's legacy is within five years of his mother's own legacy, he is entitled to reduce the inheritance tax on his legacy by a fraction of what was paid on hers.

The fraction of the tax bill on his mother's legacy which can be taken into account is worked out as follows:

$$\frac{£80,000}{£80,000 + £20,000}$$
$$= \frac{£80,000}{£100,000}$$
$$= \frac{4}{5}$$

This, expressed as a decimal, is 0.8, which is reduced by 20 per cent for each complete year between Maurice's mother's legacy and her death. Since this period was two and a half years, the 0.8 is reduced by 2 x 20 per cent = 40 per cent. Forty per cent of 0.8 is 0.32.

Thus the tax on Maurice's estate is reduced by 0.8 – 0.32 = 0.48 of the tax due on the legacy when he got it (£20,000), that is, £9,600. This results in a tax bill of £16,000 – £9,600 = £6,400.

HOW TO FILL IN YOUR TAX RETURN

When you receive your tax return for the tax year ending 5 April 2000, this is what you should have:

- an eight-page booklet entitled Tax Return. We show you how to complete these pages in Chapters 13 to 15
- a Tax Calculation Guide
- supplementary pages for the tax return to cater for your individual circumstances – there are nine sets of supplementary pages (see below). If your tax office knows that a supplement is relevant to you it may be bound into your tax return. We explain how to complete these pages in Chapters 16 to 24
- a Tax Return Guide. This consists of 31 pages which explain how to complete the eight pages of the tax return (see above) plus extra pages on how to fill in any supplements bound into your tax return.

What you should do next
Step 1
Make sure you have the correct supplementary pages.

Step 2
If one or more of the supplementary pages you need are missing, contact the Inland Revenue. The Orderline is open every day from 8 am to 10 pm, except on Christmas Day. The phone number is 0645 000 404, fax number is 0645 000 604, the e-mail address is saorderline.ir@gtnet.gov.uk or you can write to PO Box 37, St Austell, PL 25 5YN.

Step 3
Gather together all your records and supporting documentation, which you need to fill in the tax return.

Step 4
Fill in your supplementary pages FIRST, using the advice in Chapters 16 to 24 of this Guide. The Inland Revenue has a helpline number for general

advice: 0645 000 444.

Step 5
After filling in the supplementary pages, complete the tax return.

Step 6
If you are not going to work out your tax bill yourself, send in your tax return and supplementary pages by 30 September 2000.

Step 7
If you want to calculate your own tax – and we recommend that you don't – use your Tax Calculation Guide or the free software you can use if your tax affairs are simple (see p. 13).

Step 8
If you are an employee and the tax you owe is £1,000 or less, choose to send in your tax return, supplementary pages and tax calculation by 30 September. Then you can ask to pay your tax bill through the PAYE system on a monthly basis starting in April 2001.

Step 9
Otherwise send in your tax return, supplementary pages and tax calculation by 31 January 2001, and send your final tax payment for the tax year ending 5 April 2000 at the same time. If you pay tax by making payments on account (see Chapter 25), you must also make your first payment for the tax year ending April 2001 at this time.

THE SUPPLEMENTARY PAGES

On page 2 of the basic tax return you are asked nine questions. You have to answer yes or no to each of these questions. If you answer YES to a question you will need to fill in the corresponding supplementary page. If you have not been sent that page or pages automatically you will need to ask for it from the Orderline (see p. 139).

Employment

Q1 Were you an employee, or office holder, or director, or agency worker or did you receive payments or benefits from a former employer (excluding a pension) in the year ended 5 April 2000?   NO ☐   YES ☐   EMPLOYMENT YES ☐

You are required to fill in the Employment supplementary pages if you answer YES to this question. The Inland Revenue will regard you as an employee even if you work on a part-time or casual basis. There are more guidelines on who counts as an employee in Chapter 16 (p. 195).

Share schemes

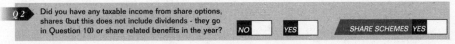

Q 2 Did you have any taxable income from share options, shares (but this does not include dividends - they go in Question 10) or share related benefits in the year? NO ▢ YES ▢ SHARE SCHEMES YES ▢

If you receive shares or options under one of the special approved schemes which are tax-free and you kept to the rules of scheme, you aren't required to complete this supplementary page. You will have to fill it in if in the tax year ending 5 April 2000 you have received shares or options in any other way or you have broken the rules of an approved scheme. Chapter 17 on p. 215 gives a lot of background information on share schemes and guides you through the completion of this supplementary page.

Self-employment

Q 3 Were you self-employed (but not in partnership)? (Tick 'Yes' if you were a Name at Lloyd's) NO ▢ YES ▢ SELF-EMPLOYMENT YES ▢

If you carried on a trade, profession or vocation as a self-employed person during the tax year ending on 5 April 2000 you need to complete this supplementary section. Chapter 18 on p. 225 has guidelines on who counts as self-employed.

If you are in partnership you need to complete a different set of supplementary pages (see below).

Partnership

Q 4 Were you in partnership? NO ▢ YES ▢ PARTNERSHIP YES ▢

If you are in business with one or more partners, you should answer YES to this question and complete a set of supplementary pages. There is a short version and a long version. You will find guidance on which version you should complete in Chapter 19 (p. 251).

Land and Property

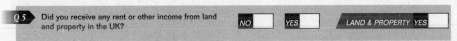

Q 5 Did you receive any rent or other income from land and property in the UK? NO ▢ YES ▢ LAND & PROPERTY YES ▢

You need to complete these supplementary pages if you receive income from land and property, furnished holiday accommodation, or providing furnished accommodation in your home during the tax year ending 5 April 2000. However, if you provide additional services, such as meals, you will need to complete the Self-employment supplementary pages, as you are considered to be carrying on a trade. You can get more guidance by turning to Chapter 20 (p. 253).

Foreign

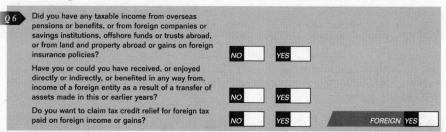

There are five supplementary pages which have space to give details about your foreign savings, pensions and benefits, gains on foreign life policies, property income and other investment income from abroad. Ask for it if you received any such income or benefit in the tax year ending 5 April 2000 or if you answered yes to any of the three questions above. If you turn to Chapter 21 (p. 266) you will find more information on what is foreign income and how it is taxed.

Trusts etc

You need to complete this supplementary page if you were a beneficiary, a settlor or had income from the estates of someone who had died. You can find more information and guidance on filling in the supplementary page in Chapter 22 (p. 274) A beneficiary of a bare trust enters the income in the basic tax return, see p. 147.

Capital gains

You must complete these supplementary pages if you have made a capital gain (with some exceptions – see below) or you wish to claim an allowable capital loss for the tax year ending 5 April 2000.

You won't need to return the supplementary page if your gains were less than £7,100 (which is the tax-free slice for the year). Nor do you need to fill it in

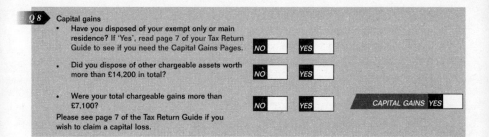

if any gain was from selling your home (and it is free of tax) and the other assets which you disposed of (leaving out assets on which gains are tax-free) were less than £14,200 altogether for the year. For more information on which gains are tax-free and guidance on whether the gain on selling your home will be taxable or not, see Chapter 10 (p. 99).

Non-residence etc

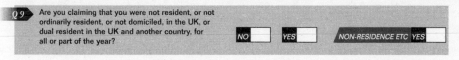

For the tax year ending 5 April 2000, if you consider yourself to be not resident in the UK, or not ordinarily resident (or not for part of the year), or not domiciled or resident but resident in a country with which the UK has a double taxation agreement, then you will need to complete this supplementary page. Chapter 24 (p. 295) will give you guidance.

COMPLETING THE TAX RETURN

You can fill in the first six pages of the tax return, using Chapters 13-15 of this guide. Chapter 15 completes the Income pages, Chapter 14 explains the Reliefs page and Chapter 15 deals with the Allowances page.

In the last two pages of the tax return, you are asked for some miscellanous information about your tax bill, repayments and refunds.

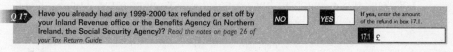

If NO, go direct to Q18.

If YES enter the amount you were refunded, either directly from your tax office (including repayments of tax deducted from dividends or other investments) or from your Benefits Agency (such as refunds of tax deducted from jobseeker's allowance). You should also include similar amounts which, rather than being repaid directly to you, have been set against payments of tax you owe.

Enter the amount refunded for the tax year ending 5 April 2000 in box 17.1.

Tick YES if you intend to work out your own tax bill, although we recommend that you send in your return by 30 September to let the Inland Revenue work out the sum for you.

If you are not going to work out your own tax bill, tick NO and go to Q19.

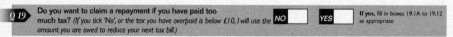

Tick YES.

In box 21.4, you need to give your date of birth if you are self-employed, or if you are claiming higher age-related personal and married couple's allowances, tax relief on investments in a venture capital trust or relief for pension contributions.

Give the information asked for in boxes 22.1 to 22.5.

If you are on PAYE and owe tax of less than £1,000, it will normally be collected through the PAYE system. You are asked to tick box 22.2 if you do not want this to happen, but do not do so without some thought. PAYE spreads out and delays the payment of your tax.

Tick box 22.2 if you do **not** want any tax you owe for 1999-2000 collected through your tax code.   22.2

In box 22.3, you have to say whether any of the figures are provisional. If they are, don't delay sending in your tax return. In the Additional information box, explain which figures are provisional (including the box numbers), why they are provisional and when they will be finalised. If you know you are not going to be able to give reliable figures, because you have lost information or have had to estimate a valuation, for example, explain what they are and how you have arrived at the estimates.

Tick box 22.3 if this Tax Return contains figures that are provisional because you do not yet have final figures.
Page 27 of your Tax Return Guide explains the circumstances in which Tax Returns containing provisional figures may be accepted and tells you what you must enter in the box below.

22.3

Be warned that, if you negligently submit a provisional figure which is inaccurate or unnecessary, you may be liable to a penalty.

And finally
Tick any additional pages you are sending with the basic tax return. And don't forget to sign the declaration. One of the commonest mistakes made by taxpayers is to forget to sign the tax return. If you are signing for someone else, state in what capacity you are doing this.

INCOME

The first stage in working out your income tax bill for the tax year ending 5 April 2000 is to find your taxable income. Pages 3 and 4 of the basic tax return set out various different types of income, such as income from savings and investments, pensions and benefits, maintenance income received and other bits and pieces. You should complete this income section to tell your tax inspector what types of income and how much of each type you received. You may find it helpful to read Chapter 8.

This is not the only way in which your tax inspector will find out about your income. There are also supplementary pages, including Employment, Self-employment and Land and property, where you must give details of other sorts of income. And these should be filled in before you tackle the basic tax return.

You don't need to enter in the tax return any income which is tax-free. A comprehensive list is given in Appendix A (see p. 309).

INCOME *for the year ended 5 April 2000*

When entering your income in the tax return, you should enter the amount you received in the year ending on 5 April 2000 (although in a few cases there are special rules for what counts as received). If you receive income of the same type from more than one source – for example, you have several savings accounts – enter the overall total for each type, but keep records for each separate account in case your tax office asks to see them.

When you enter amounts of income, round any odd pence down to the nearest £. When you enter amounts of tax credits or tax already deducted, round any odd pence up to the nearest £. If you are entering the total of income or tax from several sources (several savings accounts, say), add up each amount including the pence and round just the total.

SAVINGS AND INVESTMENT INCOME

You can get an income from your investments or savings in the form of interest, dividends or distributions (which are treated in the same way as dividends); for example, interest on a building society account, dividends from shares or distributions from unit trusts. Although the income from these sources can be paid out to you, this is not always the case. For example, interest can be added to your account rather than paid out, and with distributions from unit trusts it can be reinvested if you choose. It counts as income whether it is paid out to you or not. If you have any investment income (unless it is tax-free, see p. 149), you should tick the YES box at Q10 and fill in boxes 10.1 to 10.26.

Only enter details of investments you own. If you own an investment jointly, you need to enter only the amount in the tax return which is your share. If you are married, the income from a jointly-owned investment will be split equally. But if you own an investment in a different proportion, the income can be split to reflect ownership (see p. 45).

There are many opportunities for tax saving and tax planning with investments. Turn to Chapters 5 and 8 which should help you maximise your tax-efficient investing.

> ### TAX-SAVING IDEA
> Take advantage of the many ways you can save which are free of tax: pensions, ISAs and many National Savings products. These are especially helpful if you are a higher rate taxpayer. If you are a basic rate taxpayer, check to see that any expenses, for example on managing an ISA, are not more than the saved tax.

If you are the beneficiary of a bare trust, that is one in which you have an immediate absolute title to (a share of) the capital and income, you should enter the amount of your share of the income on page 3. Your trustee will be able to give you the details of your share.

Your income from investments includes income from investments which you have given to your children aged 18 or less and unmarried. You need to enter details if the amount of income for the tax year is more than £100 before tax. This tax treatment now applies even to a bare trust you have set up for your child, where the trust was set up on or after 9 March 1999. If you make additional gifts on or after that date to an existing trust, income from the extra gifts is also treated in the same way.

Which investment income should not be included on page 3 of your tax return?

You shouldn't include in your tax return any investment income which is tax-free (see box on right). If all your investment income is tax-free, tick the NO box at Q10.

These other types of income may be taxable but should go elsewhere in the tax return. They include:

- income from an annuity under a personal pension plan or retirement annuity contract or trust scheme. These should be included on page 4 under Q11
- gains on UK life insurance policies or life annuities or capital redemption policies. These should be included on page 4 under Q12
- a share of any partnership investment income should be entered in the Partnership supplement
- annual payments from UK unauthorised unit trusts should go on page 4 under Q13.

The documents you need
Get together all your dividend and distribution tax vouchers, interest statements, tax deduction certificates and trust vouchers. Keep them safe; don't send with your tax return.

EXAMPLE
Sidney Barrow has the following investments and accounts: National Savings Certificates, a stocks and shares ISA, a TESSA account and a bank current account which pays interest on credit balances. If he didn't have the bank current account he could tick the NO box. But the interest payable on his bank current account means that he has to tick the YES box.

TAX-SAVING IDEA
Couples, where one person pays tax at the higher rate and the other does not, can adjust their investments between them, so that more investments are in the name of the lower taxpayer. Thus less of the return will be taxed at the higher rate. Couples, where one pays tax at the starting rate and the other pays at the basic or higher rate, can save tax in the same way by shifting interest-earning investments (but not shares or unit trusts) to the lower taxpayer.

TAX-FREE INVESTMENT INCOME

Some investment income is free of income tax. This income does not have to be entered in the tax return. Income from the following investments is tax-free:

- prizes from premium bonds, National Lottery and gambling
- an ISA (individual savings account)
- a TESSA account (tax exempt special savings account), but not if you closed your account before the five years was up
- a PEP (personal equity plan), but not if you withdraw more than £180 in interest
- SAYE schemes
- National Savings Ordinary account (but only up to the first £70 of interest)
- National Savings Certificates, including the index-linked ones
- National Savings Children's Bonus Bonds
- Ulster Savings Certificates, if you normally live in Northern Ireland and you bought the certificates or they were repaid while you were living there
- dividends on shares in venture capital trusts (up to £100,000 for each tax year).

There are other less obvious forms of investment income which are also tax-free and don't need to be entered in the tax return:

- interest awarded by a UK court as part of a claim for damages for personal injury or death. There is an extra-statutory concession which means that this can also apply to awards from a foreign court
- adoption allowances paid under the Adoption Allowance Regulations 1991 (or the Scottish equivalent)
- if you are a trustee, before-tax interest which is paid out direct to beneficiaries from the payer, but through your authority. But beneficiaries should declare this income

INTEREST

Banks and building societies

- Interest from UK banks, building societies and deposit takers

Most saving income is now paid with tax deducted and the current rate of tax is 20 per cent. Income from most accounts in UK banks, building societies, finance houses, organisations offering high-interest cheque accounts and other licensed deposit takers is paid after deduction of tax. There is no further tax bill to pay if you pay tax at the basic rate only on your income, which applies to most taxpayers. If you pay tax at the higher rate, there will be extra tax to pay, at the rate of 20 per cent (see p. 62). If your top rate of tax is the starting rate, tax due on your savings income is reduced to 10 per cent – you can claim back the excess tax already deducted. If you are a non-taxpayer, you can claim back all of any tax already deducted. If you expect to carry on being a non-taxpayer, you should register to receive your interest before any tax is deducted – see Chapter 8 (p. 61).

You may have received interest from your bank or building society paid gross, that is without tax deducted. The most common circumstance where this might apply is if you have registered to receive interest gross because you are a non-taxpayer (see p. 64).

Add up all the interest you have received without tax deducted from your bank, building society or deposit taker in the tax year ending 5 April 2000 and enter it in box 10.1.

If you are a beneficiary of a trust and you are entitled to income as it arises, you should include in box 10.1 any untaxed interest paid direct to you because the trustee has authorised the payer to do so.

Don't include National Savings interest here (it goes in box 10.8).

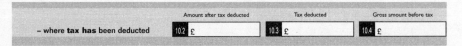

You can get the information for these boxes from your statements or pass books or ask your bank, building society or deposit taker direct to give you a tax deduction certificate. Enter the totals for all three figures in the boxes.

If your statement only shows the after-tax figure, you will need to gross it up, see Appendix B on p. 312.

You may have received cash or shares when two or more building societies have merged or a building society has converted to a company or been taken over by a company. You may have to pay either income or capital gains tax and your building society should be able to tell you this. If you have received a cash payment on which you should pay income tax, put the details in boxes 10.2 to 10.4. If you don't know whether you have to pay income tax, put the details under Q13 on page 4, but also tick box 22.3 on page 8 and explain the situation in the Additional information box. Any capital gain should be entered in the Capital gains supplementary pages. If you have received shares, you may need to supply details only when you dispose of the shares – ask your tax office.

Unit trusts

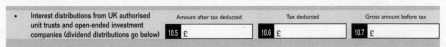

Some types of unit trusts and open-ended investment companies pay interest rather than dividends. These include unit trusts which invest in British Government stocks and other fixed-interest distributions. In these cases, 20 per cent tax has been deducted from the income before you get it in the same way as for bank or building society interest (see left) and you will get a tax voucher telling you the amount paid. You may be able to claim some or all of it back, or you may have to pay more tax in the same way as for bank or building society interest.

The interest may not be paid out to you but automatically reinvested in accumulation or other units. However, you still have to enter the interest in your tax return.

Add up all the interest you receive after tax has been deducted and enter the total in box 10.5. Put the tax deducted in box 10.6. Then add together boxes 10.5 and 10.6 and enter the sum in box 10.7 (gross amount before tax). If you received interest without any tax deducted, enter nil in boxes 10.5 and 10.6 and enter the before-tax amount in box 10.7.

When you buy units in a unit trust, part of the purchase price includes an amount of income which the trust has received but not yet paid out. The first payment you receive will include an equalisation payment, which is not income, but a refund of part of the original purchase price you paid. It is not taxable, so do not enter it here. (Note that it is deducted for CGT purposes).

Don't enter dividend distributions from unit trusts here, but in boxes 10.18 to 10.20.

National Savings
You will receive interest paid before deduction of tax from the following National Savings investments:

- Ordinary Account

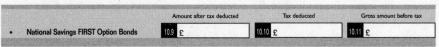

	Taxable amount
National Savings (other than FIRST Option Bonds and the first £70 of interest from a National Savings Ordinary Account)	10.8 £

- Investment Account
- Deposit Bonds
- Income Bonds
- Capital Bonds
- Pensioners' Guaranteed Income Bonds

Tot up the before-tax interest you received (or added to your account) in the tax year ending 5 April 2000. You don't include the first £70 of interest on a National Savings Ordinary Account, as this is tax-free (as are many other National Savings investments – see box on p. 149).

Enter the total amount you received in box 10.8.

	Amount after tax deducted	Tax deducted	Gross amount before tax
National Savings FIRST Option Bonds	10.9 £	10.10 £	10.11 £

You receive interest after tax at the savings rate has already been deducted, if you invest in:

- FIRST option bonds
- Fixed rate savings bonds. These bonds went on sale from October 1999. You will only have income to declare here if you have opted to receive the interest monthly.

Enter in box 10.9 the amount you received, in box 10.10 the amount of tax deducted and in box 10.11 the amount of interest before tax. Include details for fixed rate savings bonds here even though the tax form only mentions FIRST option bonds.

British Government stock and other interest-paying investments

	Amount after tax deducted	Tax deducted	Gross amount before tax
Other income from UK savings and investments (except dividends)	10.12 £	10.13 £	10.14 £

There is a hotch-potch of interest from other investments which should be entered here. Depending on the nature of the interest, it may be paid without tax being deducted or after tax is deducted. Tot up the relevant amounts and enter in boxes 10.12 to 10.14. If no tax has been deducted, put the interest in box 10.14 only and put nil in boxes 10.12 and 10.13. If tax has been deducted fill in all the boxes.

Here are examples of the investments to include:

- certificates of tax deposit when the certificate is applied to payment of a tax bill
- British Government stock (see below)
- other loan stocks, such as local authority loans and stocks
- permanent interest bearing shares (PIBS) of building societies
- loans to an individual or organisation
- income from credit unions or friendly societies
- interest from Enterprise Zone trusts
- discount on relevant discounted securities (enter in box 10.14)
- discount from gilt strips (enter in box 10.14)
- income from securities to which you have sold or transferred the right to the income, but not the security – even if you have not received the income (enter in box 10.14)
- purchased life annuities (see below).

British Government stock

Tax at the rate of 20 per cent for the tax year ending 5 April 2000 may have been deducted from the interest on your British Government stocks (or gilts) before you receive it. Note that you can arrange to have the interest paid in future without tax deducted.

If tax has been deducted, your interest payment should be accompanied by a tax voucher which lets you know how much tax has been paid. If you are a non-taxpayer, you should be able to claim back the amount deducted. If you are a basic rate taxpayer, there is no more tax to pay. Enter the appropriate amounts in the three boxes 10.12, 10.13 and 10.14.

If you own fixed-interest securities with a nominal value in excess of £5,000, and you buy or sell them, there are special tax rules designed to stop tax avoidance by turning income into capital gains. Ask your tax inspector to send you Inland Revenue leaflet *IR68 Accrued Income scheme*.

Annuities

An annuity is an investment made with a life insurance company. You invest a lump sum and in return the insurance company will pay you an income. Sometimes this could be for a particular period, say ten years, or it could be until you die. The income which you receive is considered to be in two parts: some of it is your original investment being returned to you. There is tax to pay on only the interest.

The annuity payment is made to you with tax at the rate of 20 per cent of the interest part already deducted. The tax voucher which accompanies the payment will tell you how much tax has been deducted. If you are a non-tax-payer you can claim back the tax deducted.

With an annuity which you buy as part of your pension, the tax treatment is different. Tax will be deducted from the whole payment through the PAYE system. Details of annuities bought under personal pension schemes or retirement annuity contracts should be entered on page 4 of the tax return under Q11.

DIVIDENDS

You will receive share dividends from UK companies and distributions from authorised unit trusts with no more basic rate tax to pay because you also receive a tax credit. The payments are accompanied by a tax voucher which sets out the amount of the tax credit (10 per cent for the year ending 5 April 2000). You work out the gross amount of dividend by adding together the net dividend and the tax credit (see p. 65).

For the tax year ending 5 April 2000 onwards, non-taxpayers cannot claim back the tax credit. Starting rate and basic rate taxpayers have no further tax to pay, but higher rate taxpayers must pay extra bringing the rate they pay up to 32.5 per cent (see p. 66).

If you are a beneficiary of a trust and you are entitled to income as it arises, include in these boxes any dividends or distributions shown on your trust voucher.

Shares in UK companies

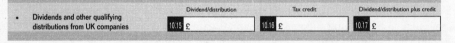

	Dividend/distribution	Tax credit	Dividend/distribution plus credit
• Dividends and other qualifying distributions from UK companies	10.15 £	10.16 £	10.17 £

Your dividend voucher should show the amount of the dividend and the tax credit. Put these in boxes 10.15 and 10.16 and add them together to enter the sum in box 10.17. Note that scrip dividends are included below in boxes 10.21 to 10.23.

Companies can make other kinds of distributions as well as dividends, for example, payment in kind. A distinction is drawn between qualifying and non-qualifying distributions (see right). Qualifying distributions should be entered in boxes 10.15 to 10.17; explain how you got it in Additional information on page 8 of the tax return. (Non-qualifying distributions are entered below in boxes 10.24 to 10.26).

Unit trusts

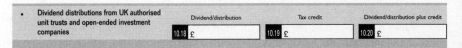

Distributions from most authorised unit trusts are treated in the same way as dividends (see p. 65). If you have invested in an accumulation unit trust, you don't receive the income but the unit trust managers reinvest it for you in more units. However, for tax purposes this is treated in exactly the same way as if you received the cash. You will receive a tax voucher with a tax credit.

Your dividend vouchers show the amount of the dividend and the tax credit. If you own units in more than one unit trust, add up the distributions and tax credits and enter the totals for each in boxes 10.18 and 10.19. Add them together to get the entry for box 10.20. Don't enter any equalisation payments (see p. 151).

Scrip dividends

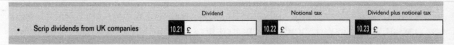

If you received new shares instead of cash as a dividend, this is known as a scrip dividend. The value of the scrip dividend is known as the cash equivalent and is the amount of cash dividend forgone. It should be shown on your dividend statement as the appropriate amount of cash. This is what you enter in the dividend box. For the tax year ending 5 April 2000, you are treated as having received the cash equivalent grossed up at 10 per cent.

Enter in box 10.21 the appropriate amount of cash. In box 10.22 enter the notional tax (11.11 per cent of the cash equivalent).

Enter this figure in box 10.22. Add together boxes 10.21 and box 10.22, and enter the sum in box 10.23.

Non-qualifying distributions

A non-qualifying distribution is broadly one which gives a future rather than a current claim on the company's assets, such as a bonus issue of redeemable shares. The amount of the distribution is the nominal value of the securities you received less any consideration (for example, cash) you paid.

Enter the amount of the distribution in box 10.26. Multiply box 10.26 by 10 per cent to get the amount of notional tax to enter in box 10.25. Leave box 10.24 blank.

For loans written off, contact your tax adviser or tax office.

PENSIONS AND SOCIAL SECURITY BENEFITS

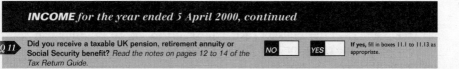

If you received none of these, tick the NO box and go to Q12.

But if you received one or more of these, you will need to find out whether what you received should be entered here in your tax return. Some pensions and benefits are not taxable.

What pensions and benefits should not be included in your tax return

If you received any of the following, you do not need to give details here in the tax return because they are tax-free:

- additions to your state pension or social security benefits which you get because you have a dependent child
- attendance allowance
- child benefit
- child's special allowance (only payable to those already claiming before 6 April 1987)
- Christmas bonus for pensioners and winter fuel payment
- council tax benefit
- disability living allowance
- disability working allowance
- family credit and childcare allowance
- guardian's allowance
- home renovation and repair grants
- housing benefit (rent rebates and allowances)
- incapacity benefit for the first 28 weeks (but not taxable after that time if you were receiving invalidity benefit before 13 April 1995 unless there

is a break in your claim; incapacity benefit replaced invalidity benefit)
- industrial disablement benefit
- jobfinder's grant, most YT training scheme allowances, employment rehabilitation and training allowances
- maternity allowance
- most income support
- pensions and benefits for wounds or disability in military service or for other war injuries
- school uniform grants
- severe disablement allowance, including age-related addition
- social fund payments
- student grants, scholarships and loans
- war orphan's benefit
- war widow's pension and some pensions paid to other dependants of deceased Forces and Merchant Navy personnel. Ask the Orderline for Help Sheet *IR310 War Widow's and Dependant's pensions*
- widow's payment.
- similar benefits to those above paid by foreign governments

What pensions and benefits should be entered in your tax return
Details of the following should be entered here:

- income withdrawals from a personal pension plan where the purchase of an annuity has been delayed
- industrial death benefit
- invalid care allowance
- jobseeker's allowance (this has replaced unemployment benefit and income support if you are out of work)
- old person's pension for people aged 80 or over
- pension for injuries at work or for work-related illnesses
- pension from a former employer or a pension from your late husband or wife's employer
- pension from a free-standing additional voluntary contribution
- pension from a personal pension scheme or retirement annuity contract or trust scheme
- pension from service in the armed forces
- state retirement pension, the basic pension, state earnings related pension and graduated pension
- statutory sick pay and statutory maternity pay paid by the DSS
- taxable incapacity benefit
- widowed mother's allowance
- widow's pension.

If you receive any of the above pensions or benefits, tick the YES box in answer to Q11.

Refunds of surplus additional voluntary contributions are not entered here. Details should be put in boxes 12.13 to 12.15. Overseas pensions and taxable benefits paid under the rules of another country should be entered in the Foreign supplementary pages (covered in Chapter 21).

The documents you need
You will need to gather together certain information such as the details of your state pension and your P60, which your pension payer may have given you, or any other certificate of pension paid and tax deducted. Details of any taxable amounts of social security benefits, such as jobseeker's allowance, incapacity benefit or any other taxable state benefits will also be required – ask your benefit office for Form BR735 for pensions and either Form P60U or Form P45U for jobseeker's allowance.

State pensions and benefits

■ *State pensions and benefits*

Enter the amount of pension or benefit you were entitled to for the tax year ending 5 April 2000, whether or not you actually received that amount in the year. You should enter the total of all the weekly amounts which you were entitled to in the year, even if you chose to receive your pension or benefit monthly or quarterly.

State retirement pension

	Taxable amount for 1999-2000
• State Retirement Pension (enter the total of your weekly entitlements for the year)	11.1 £

The state retirement pension is taxable but paid without tax deducted. So if you have other income you will find that tax on your state retirement pension might be collected from your other income.

In box 11.1, you should enter the amount you were entitled to receive in the tax year ending 5 April 2000, but excluding any amount paid for a dependent child, the Christmas bonus and winter fuel payment.

A married woman might receive a pension which is based on her husband's contributions and not her own (but not any dependency allowance which he receives for her before her 60th birthday). She can claim a personal allowance to deduct from her pension and the pension should be entered in her tax return, not her husband's.

Widow's pension

• Widow's Pension	11.2 £

Enter the full amount you were entitled to receive in the tax year ending 5 April 2000, including any earnings-related additional pension, in box 11.2. For more information on the benefits available to widows, ask for leaflet *NP45 A guide to widow's benefits* from your local Benefits Agency office.

Widowed mother's allowance

• Widowed Mother's Allowance	11.3 £

You should include in box 11.3 the flat rate basic allowance which you were entitled to and any earnings-related increase. But don't include any child dependency increase.

Industrial death benefit

• Industrial Death Benefit Pension	11.4 £

In box 11.4 you should enter the yearly pension you are entitled to receive under the industrial death benefit scheme. But do not include industrial death benefit child allowance which is tax-free.

Jobseeker's allowance

• Jobseeker's Allowance	11.5 £

Jobseeker's allowance is taxable but paid without any tax deducted. There are two kinds of allowance, one based on your National Insurance contribution record and one means-tested. There is a limit on the overall amount that is treated as taxable.

The benefit office will usually have given you a statement of the total jobseeker's allowance paid and the taxable portion (either Form P60U or Form P45U). You should enter the taxable amount in box 11.5. If you haven't received a statement, tell your tax office. You have 60 days to check your statement to see if it is correct.

Invalid care allowance

•	Invalid Care Allowance		11.6 £

Enter the amount you were entitled to receive in the tax year ending 5 April 2000. Include any addition for a dependent adult, but exclude any additional amount for a dependent child, because this is tax-free.

Statutory sick pay and statutory maternity pay

•	Statutory Sick Pay and Statutory Maternity Pay paid by the Department of Social Security		11.7 £

Generally, these are paid by your employer and taxed under the PAYE system (see p. 83). They will be included in your P60 or P45. Details should be entered in the Employment supplementary pages.

But if your employer didn't pay you, and the Department of Social Security did so instead, enter the total received here in box 11.7.

Taxable incapacity benefit

		Tax deducted	Gross amount before tax
•	Taxable Incapacity Benefit	11.8 £	11.9 £

Some incapacity benefit is tax-free. You will not pay tax on it when you receive it during your first 28 weeks of incapacity or you are receiving it for a period of incapacity which began before 13 April 1995, and for which invalidity benefit used to be payable.

The Department of Social Security will give you a form showing you whether your incapacity benefit is taxable or not. If it is taxable, enter the amount of the benefit in box 11.9 and any tax that has been deducted in box 11.8.

Other pensions

■	*Other pensions and retirement annuities*

Apart from the state pension, you can get a pension from your employer, from what you have paid into a personal pension scheme or a retirement annuity contract.

You should enter here details of pensions paid to you by someone in the UK who is not paying on behalf of someone outside the UK. Pensions received from abroad will be entered in the Foreign pages (see p. 266).

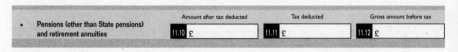

You should total the amount you receive from all your pensions (excluding state pension) and put it in box 11.10. You should include in the total:

- annuity payments from a personal pension scheme
- if you have taken advantage of the ability to defer buying the annuity, perhaps because annuity rates were low, the income withdrawals which you receive during the deferred period
- any annual payments from a retirement contract or trusts scheme.

Put the amount of tax deducted in box 11.11. The information about an employer's pension should be on Form P60 and for other pensions from a certificate given to you by the pension payer. Adding up boxes 11.10 and 11.11 should give you the total for box 11.12, unless you have received some non-cash benefit. If you have, you'll need to ask your tax office what to do.

There are some special pensions which can be partially free of UK tax:

Tax-free pensions
Part of your pension may be tax-free if you receive it as a former employee who was awarded a pension on retirement because you were disabled by injury on duty or a work-related illness. If that pension is more than the amount you would receive if you had retired at the same time on the grounds of ordinary ill-health, the extra amount is free of tax. You should not enter any tax-free amounts in the tax return.

10 per cent deduction

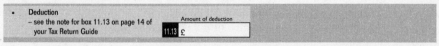

This applies to some UK pensions for service for certain overseas governments. Only 90 per cent of the pension is taxed.

Enter the full pension received in box 11.12 and the 10 per cent deduction in box 11.13.

OTHER INCOME TO BE ENTERED HERE

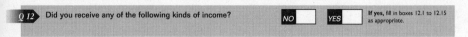

The income includes taxable maintenance or alimony, gains on UK life insurance policies, life annuities or capital redemption policies or refunds of surplus additional voluntary contributions.

If you tick the NO box you should go to Q13.

Maintenance income

		Income receivable	Exempt amount	Income minus exempt amount
•	Taxable maintenance or alimony	12.1 £	12.2 £	12.3 £

Maintenance you receive could be taxable. It depends on whether your maintenance agreement was made under the old rules or the new rules.

If you receive maintenance under the new rules you do not pay tax and you do not need to enter the amount in your tax return. Even if you remarry and carry on receiving maintenance from your former husband or wife, for example, for your child, the maintenance received will be tax-free.

A maintenance agreement is made under the new rules if:
- it was made on or after 15 March 1988 (unless it merely alters or replaces an arrangement to which the old rules apply)
- it was made before 15 March 1988, but you didn't tell your tax inspector about it in writing by 30 June 1988
- it is a court order which was applied for after 15 March 1988
- it was a court order made after 30 June 1988 (unless it is merely altering or replacing an arrangement to which the old rules apply)
- it is assessed by the Child Support Agency
- the person paying the maintenance has opted for it to be taxed under the new rules.

If the maintenance you receive is made under a legally-binding agreement not in the list above, it will be taxed under the old rules. This means that you may have to pay income tax on it and will need to enter the details in boxes

12.1 to 12.3.

Under the old rules, the first £1,970 in the tax year ending 5 April 2000 is tax-free. Anything else you receive above this is taxed at your top rate of tax, except that, if what you receive in maintenance has increased since the tax year ending 5 April 1989, you pay no tax on this extra bit. If you remarry and you carry on receiving maintenance, the first £1,970 will no longer be tax-free.

If your child receives maintenance under the old rules paid direct to him or her, rather than to you for his or her benefit, there is no tax-free band. What he or she receives, up to the amount received in the tax year ending 5 April 1989, counts as taxable income, but the child can set his or her personal allowance against it (giving a tax-free band of £4,335 in the tax year ending 5 April 2000).

If you are receiving maintenance from your parents and are over 21, you do not have to pay tax on it.

If your maintenance is taxable, you have to pay tax on the lower of:

- the amount you were due to receive and did receive between 6 April 1988 and 5 April 1989, or
- the amount you were due to receive and did receive between 6 April 1999 and 5 April 2000.

In box 12.1 put in the lower of these two amounts. If you receive maintenance from more than one source under the old rules, treat each maintenance payment separately when working out the taxable amounts. Add together the taxable amounts and put the total in box 12.1.

EXAMPLE

Patricia Smith receives maintenance from her ex-husband. The agreement was made in 1986 and is taxed under the old rules. The agreement was that she would receive £5,000 a year. This is what she was paid in the tax year ending 5 April 1989. For the tax year ending 5 April 2000 she received £4,500 as her former husband was having difficulty meeting the payments. In box 12.1 she puts the lower of the amounts she received in the tax years ending 5 April 1989 and 5 April 2000. This was the £4,500 she received in the tax year ending 5 April 2000. In box 12.2 she puts the lower of what she entered in box 12.1 or £1,970. She enters £1,970. She will be taxed on £4,500 minus £1,970, that is £2,530.

The first £1,970 for the tax year ending 5 April 2000 is tax-free if:

- you received it from your separated or former husband or wife; and
- it is for yourself or for the support of a child aged under 21 of whom you are both the parents, or whom you have treated as part of the family; and
- you have not remarried; and
- you did not, during the tax year ending 5 April 2000, live again with your separated husband or wife who pays the maintenance.

If all these apply to you, you can claim your tax-free bit of maintenance. In box 12.2 put the lower of the taxable maintenance you received (the figure in box 12.1) or £1,970.

Deduct box 12.2 from box 12.1 and enter the difference in box 12.3.

There is more information in Chapter 6.

Life insurance policies
Gains on life insurance policies, contracts for life annuities or capital redemption policies are treated as investment income and may be taxable.

The tax treatment of life insurance policies depends on whether they are qualifying or non-qualifying. Most types of life insurance which involve you paying regular premiums are qualifying; if you pay just a single premium, it will almost certainly be a non-qualifying policy, which has less favourable tax treatment.

Taxation of qualifying policies
The life insurance company will have paid tax on the income and gains which its life fund makes as they arise. And so, with qualifying policies, there is not usually any income or capital gains tax to pay when the policy matures – that is, it comes to the end of its agreed period or the person insured by the policy dies.

The exception to this is if you cash in or make a policy paid up before the end of the agreed period. A policy might be treated as non-qualifying if this happens before ten years or, if this is less, three-quarters of its term.

Taxation of non-qualifying policies
The tax treatment of non-qualifying policies is less favourable than for the qualifying ones and it is possible that income tax might be due when you receive the proceeds. Most insurance policies are treated as having already paid basic rate tax, but the basic rate tax is notional only and cannot be reclaimed by a non-taxpayer or starting rate taxpayer.

But if you are a higher rate taxpayer, or become one when you add the proceeds of your policy to your other taxable income, there will be higher rate
tax due on it. There may also be a loss of age allowance (see p. 4).

The proceeds are treated as a chargeable gain and the amount of the gain is
usually what you receive less what you have paid during the life of the
policy. If the person insured has died and the policy pays out, the gain is
taken as the cash-in value of the policy, if this is less than you receive.

You may be able to draw an income from your non-qualifying policy by
cashing part of it. These withdrawals won't be taxed at the time as long as
you have not cashed in more than 5 per cent of what you paid for each year
of the policy. But at the end of the policy, the amount you have withdrawn
will be added to the gain to work out the tax due. If you don't cash the full
5 per cent each year, you can carry forward the unused amount, meaning
that you might be able to cash more than 5 per cent in a later year without
paying tax at the time. However, you will eventually be taxed on what you
have received during the life of the policy, unless you are no longer a higher
rate taxpayer when it comes to an end (see below). Selling a non-qualifying
policy is treated the same as a policy maturing or being cashed in.

The gain on a non-qualifying policy is added to your taxable income for the
year. But there is no basic rate tax due. For the tax year ending 5 April 2000,
there will be higher rate tax to pay if your taxable income and the gain come
to £28,000 or more.

If the policy is treated as having had basic rate tax deducted, the rate of tax
to pay is $40 - 23 = 17$ per cent for the tax year ending 5 April 2000. This
could still mean a large tax bill in the year of the gain. But you may be able
to benefit from top-slicing relief which spreads the gain you make over the
years of the policy. Broadly, you work out the average gain for each year you
have held the policy, calculate the amount of tax that would be due if the
average gain was added to your income and multiply this by the number of
whole years the policy was held. The tax return asks you to enter the number of years so that top-slicing relief can be worked out.

Although most gains from UK insurances are treated as having had basic rate
tax deducted, gains from certain life annuities and friendly societies' tax
exempt policies are not treated in this way, that is, there is no notional tax
paid. Your insurance company should be able to tell you how your gain is
treated. And you may have received a chargeable event certificate showing
your gains and the other information you need to fill in your tax return.

• Gains on UK annuities and friendly societies' life insurance policies where no tax is treated as paid	Number of years 12.4		Amount of gain(s) 12.5 £

If you have made a gain and it is not treated as having had basic rate tax deducted, put the amount of the gain in box 12.5 and the number of complete years since the insurance was made in box 12.4.

• Gains on UK life insurance policies etc on which tax is treated as paid - read page 15 of the Tax Return Guide	Number of years 12.6	Tax treated as paid 12.7 £	Amount of gain(s) 12.8 £

If you have made a gain and it is treated as having had basic rate tax deducted, put the amount of the gain in box 12.8 and the notional tax in box 12.7 (23 per cent of the amount in box 12.8). Enter the number of complete years in box 12.6.

Where you have made more than one sort of gain, or you hold a cluster of policies, things become complex. You will probably need to put additional information in the section on page 8 of the tax return. Ask the Orderline (see p. 139) for a copy of Help Sheet *IR320 Gains on UK life insurance policies*. Consult your tax office or tax adviser for more guidance.

• Gains on life insurance policies in ISAs that have been made void	Number of years 12.9	Tax deducted 12.10 £	Amount of gain(s) 12.11 £

Normally, gains on life insurance policies held within an ISA are tax-free and you do not include them in your tax return. But there are strict rules on the types of policy which qualify to be held through an ISA. If it's found that the life policy you hold does not qualify or has ceased to qualify, the policy may come to an end and there may be tax to pay on any gain. Tax is worked out as for a non-qualifying policy – see previous page. Your ISA manager will give you the information you need. Enter the amount of gain in box 12.11, the number of complete years the policy ran in box 12.9 and tax already paid by the ISA manager in box 12.10.

Corresponding deficiency relief

Corresponding deficiency relief	Amount 12.12 £

If you had a life insurance policy on which you made a loss on final surrender, you may be able to claim a relief to ensure that the amount treated as income is not more than the total gain made under the policy. Ask for Help Sheet *IR320 Gains on UK life insurance policies.*

Repayment of additional voluntary contributions

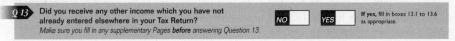

Additional voluntary contributions are extra payments you can make to your employer's or your own free-standing additional voluntary contribution scheme (see p. 70). A condition of the contributions is that they cannot buy you pension benefits greater than the maximum limits set by the Inland Revenue for approved schemes. If you inadvertently contribute so much in additional voluntary contributions that the benefits would exceed the limits, the excess will be paid back to you at retirement, with a deduction to cover the tax relief the contributions have enjoyed.

Your certificate from your pension scheme provider should show you the amount of surplus contributions and the tax refunded to you. Enter the total amount in box 12.15, the amount actually repaid to you in box 12.13 and the tax deducted in box 12.14.

Any other income

Q 13 Did you receive any other income which you have not already entered elsewhere in your Tax Return? NO YES If yes, fill in boxes 13.1 to 13.6 as appropriate.
*Make sure you fill in any supplementary Pages **before** answering Question 13.*

You should have already filled in the appropriate supplementary pages for income from employment, self-employment, trusts, abroad and so on. You may have other odd bits of income not yet entered. For example:

- freelance or casual income
- profits from the odd literary or artistic activity
- income received after you close a business (post-cessation receipts). This could include money which you have recovered from a bad debt or royalties arising after the business ceased from contracts made before it ceased. You can claim to have this treated as income for the year in which the business ceased (tick box 22.5 on page 8 of the tax return). Or you can enter the total here
- any recovery of expenses or debts for which you claimed relief as post-cessation expenses
- sale of patent rights if you received a capital sum
- receipts from covenants entered into for genuine commercial reasons which are in connection with the payer's trade, profession or vocation.

Losses cannot be set against this income
- rental from leasing equipment you own
- income from guaranteeing loans, dealing in futures and some income from underwriting
- accrued income on the transfer of securities (but not if the nominal value of securities in the tax year ending 5 April 2000 was £5,000 or less)
- annual payments received in the year including annual payments received from UK unauthorised unit trusts, and annual payments paid by former employers which do not count as a pension. Expenses and losses cannot be deducted from this income.

You should also enter in this section any cashbacks or other incentives which you received to take out a mortgage if there is tax to pay. Ask the person who gave you the incentive or check with your tax office to find out if it is taxable. Include it in box 13.3.

Some part of income received under a permanent health insurance policy may be taxable and should be entered here. This does not include income from a policy which you paid for yourself, as that is tax-free. Income from your employer for sickness and disability should go on the Employment pages. But if you have left your employer and you are still receiving benefits because you are covered by your former employer's scheme, you should enter that amount here (part might be tax-free if you contributed to the cost of the scheme). Check with your tax office if you are not sure how much is taxable, and ask for leaflet *IR153 Tax exemption for sickness or unemployment insurance payments*.

If you received any other income which should be taxed but which you have not put anywhere else, you should tick the YES box at Q13.

You need to keep careful records of the income and the expenses.

If you are self-employed and make losses in your business, one option available to you is to deduct the loss from any other income which you have in that year or the next year. See p. 247 for your other options. You can deduct the losses from all the income listed above except from the covenant income received, the annual payments and benefits from a permanent health insurance policy.

Enter the amount of income after any tax deducted and after any allowable expenses or capital allowances in box 13.1. If you made a loss put nil. In box 13.2, put the amount of tax deducted from the payments you received. Add together boxes 13.1 and 13.2, to find the figure for box 13.3.

• Other income (read page 16 of your Tax Return Guide if you made losses)	Amount after tax deducted	Tax deducted	Amount before tax
	13.1 £	13.2 £	13.3 £
		Losses brought forward	Earlier years' losses used in 1999-2000
		13.4 £	13.5 £
		1999-2000 losses carried forward	
		13.6 £	

If you made a loss in box 13.3, you can deduct it from some other income in a future year. Put it in box 13.6.

If you have made losses in earlier years, either from your business or other income, enter the amount of unused allowable losses brought forward in box 13.4. If you have any income in box 13.3, and unused losses brought forward in box 13.4, you can deduct the losses from box 13.3, reducing it to nil (and thus cutting your tax bill). Put in box 13.5 the amount of losses you are using this year. Note that you only use these pages for losses from your business if you haven't used the supplementary pages.

If you have several types of other income, the calculation can become complex. Help Sheet *IR325 Other income* has a worksheet to help you.

RELIEFS

You can pay less tax by spending more money on things the government wants to encourage – and thus gives tax relief on – such as pensions and training. In some instances you can get tax relief at your highest rate of tax, which could be 40 per cent. Assuming that you want to spend the money, buying any of these things could be highly advantageous. You claim for them on page 5 of the basic tax return.

You get your tax relief in different ways. Frequently you get basic rate tax relief by deducting it from what you spend. Any higher rate tax relief that is due you will claim here in the tax return and give yourself the relief when you are working out your tax bill. Or you could get higher rate relief through your PAYE code. Non-taxpayers will not have to repay the tax deducted, except in the case of covenants and Gift Aid.

If you don't get basic rate relief by deducting it from what you pay, you will claim the relief here in the tax return and get it by deducting the amount from the tax you owe on 31 January or through your PAYE code.

The documents you need
You must gather together all the supporting documents you need to be able to prove to your tax inspector that you are entitled to the relief you are claiming (but keep the documents safe, don't send them with your tax return). These could include:

- certificates of premiums paid from your pension provider
- receipts of payments paid for vocational training
- certificates of interest paid on loans
- maintenance agreements, court order, Child Support Agency assessments
- share certificate in a venture capital trust
- Forms EIS3 or EIS5 (for Enterprise Investment Scheme)

> ## TAX-SAVING IDEA
> You can go back six years to claim deductions which you forgot to claim at the time or didn't know you were able to. You will get tax relief at the rate you should have got it if you had claimed the deduction at the right time.

- details of covenants paid or lump sums to charity under Gift Aid.

What deductions can you claim?

You can claim here for:

- pension contributions
- additional voluntary contributions to a pension scheme
- vocational training payments
- interest paid on qualifying loans
- maintenance payments
- investments in growing business (venture capital trusts or Enterprise Investment scheme)
- payments to charities (through covenants or Gift Aid)
- post-cessation expenses for a business and losses on relevant discounted securities
- certain payments to a trade union or friendly society.

PENSIONS

For the tax year ending 5 April 2000, you can get tax relief at your highest rate of tax on contributions to a pension scheme. If you are an employee, your employer can also make contributions to an approved pension scheme for you, and these would also get tax relief (and not count as a fringe benefit for you). There are more details about saving for your pension in Chapter 8.

You can save for a pension through an employer's pension scheme or a personal pension scheme if you are an employee, and through a personal pension scheme if you are self-employed or a partner.

EXAMPLE

Tony Jabot is wondering which is the best way to save for his retirement. He considers a tax-free investment, an ISA (see p. 76), or taking out a personal pension plan. The tax treatment of investments held in an ISA or pension fund is similar, except the pension fund pays tax on share dividends and similar income. The pension plan benefits from tax relief on money paid in but the ISA does not. However, the proceeds of the ISA are tax-free whereas the eventual pension will be taxable. What gives pension plans the edge is that usually about a quarter of the pension fund can be taken at retirement as a tax-free lump sum – so this part of the savings benefits from tax relief on the way in and on the way out. Jason opts for the pension plan. He pays in £1,000 in the tax year ending 5 April 2000, but this costs him just £770 because he is a basic rate taxpayer and gets 23 per cent tax relief.

Q 14 **Do you want to claim relief for pension contributions?**
*Do not include contributions deducted from your pay by your employer to their pension scheme because tax relief is given automatically. But **do include** your contributions to personal pension schemes and free-standing AVC schemes.*

NO ☐   YES ☐   **If yes,** fill in boxes 14.1 to 14.17 as appropriate.

With an employer's pension scheme, you are likely to get tax relief on your contributions deducted at source (they will be deducted from your salary before your employer works out your income tax through the PAYE system). If this is the only way you are saving for a pension, you can tick the NO box and go on to Q15. Obviously, if you are not saving at all for a pension, you should also tick the NO box.

What you should claim for

In the tax return you can claim tax relief for payments into two different types of pension scheme:

- retirement annuity contracts (new contracts not available from 1 July 1988)
- personal pension plans (not available before 1 July 1988)

If you started saving for a pension before 1 July 1988, unless you converted it into a personal pension, your scheme will be a retirement annuity contract. If you started saving for a pension on or after 1 July 1988, you will be saving in a personal pension plan. You could have started a personal pension plan in addition to a retirement annuity contract.

Although it is possible for you to have both a retirement annuity contract and a personal pension scheme, you cannot get double the tax relief. The tax relief for the retirement annuity contract is always given before the relief for the personal pension scheme. Relief for a retirement annuity contract reduces the relief for the personal pension. The Inland Revenue has produced Help Sheet *IR330 Pension payments* which has an explanation and working sheets.

Retirement annuity contracts

Under the heading of Retirement annuity contracts you need to give information about your payments in the tax year ending 5 April 2000, about any you wish to carry back to an earlier year, and about any payments you have made since 5 April 2000 which you want to bring back to get tax relief in this tax return.

In Box 14.1, enter the amount of payments which you have made to a retirement annuity in the year ending 5 April 2000. You will be entering gross figures (before deduction of tax).

Qualifying payments made in 1999-2000	14.1 £	1999-2000 payments used in an earlier year	14.2 £	Relief claimed
				box 14.1 *minus* (boxes 14.2 and 14.3, but not 14.4)
1999-2000 payments now to be carried back	14.3 £	Payments brought back from 2000-2001	14.4 £	14.5 £

You are allowed to carry back pension payments (see p. 74). You may have already claimed tax relief on some of the amount in box 14.1, for example, for the year ending 5 April 1999. If you have done so, enter the amount used in an earlier year in box 14.2.

If you now want to carry back some of what you paid in the year ending 5 April 2000 to the previous tax year (or possibly the one before that, see p. 74), put this amount in box 14.3. On this amount you will get tax relief at the rate of tax you paid in the previous year.

Between 5 April 2000 and the date you are filling in your tax return, you may have made some pension payments. If you want these to be included in your tax return for the year ending 5 April 2000 (see p. 74), enter the amount in box 14.4.

The amount of relief you are claiming for your retirement annuity contract payment for the tax year ending 5 April 2000 will be worked out in box 14.5 (box 14.1 minus box 14.2 minus box 14.3). If the amount you are claiming for this year is greater than the percentage limit (see p. 72), you may have unused relief from the previous six years to set against the excess.

EXAMPLE

Paul Taylor has a retirement annuity contract. For the year ended 5 April 2000, he earned £20,000 and is aged 37. He can save £3,500 within the limits of 17.5 per cent of his net relevant earnings. He made payments of £3,000 and enters this figure in box 14.1. However, £1,000 of his pension contributions were made before he returned his tax return for the last tax year and he had asked for them to be carried back to the year ending 5 April 1999. He enters that amount in box 14.2. He chooses now to carry back a further £1,000 to the last tax year as he was a higher rate taxpayer and this would mean he would get more tax relief. The figure of £1,000 is entered in box 14.3.

The amount of contributions on which he is now claiming tax relief in the year ended 5 April 2000 is box 14.1 minus box 14.2 minus box 14.3, that is £3,000 minus £1,000 minus £1,000. He is claiming relief on pension contributions of £1,000 for the year ended 5 April 2000.

There is no place on the tax return to claim unused relief carried forward from earlier years. Simply enter the pension contributions actually made, but keep your workings in case the Inland Revenue queries your payments. Use the working sheets which come with Help Sheet *IR330 Pension payments*.

For more information on retirement annuity contracts, see p. 71.

see p. 71.

Personal pension plans

■ *Self-employed contributions to personal pension plans*

Qualifying payments made in 1999-2000	**14.6** £	1999-2000 payments used in an earlier year **14.7** £
		Relief claimed
		box 14.6 *minus* (boxes 14.7 and 14.8, but not 14.9)
1999-2000 payments now to be carried back **14.8** £	Payments brought back from 2000-2001 **14.9** £	**14.10** £

If you are self-employed and contributing to a personal pension plan, you claim your tax relief in boxes 14.6 to 14.10.

Under the heading of Personal pension plans, you need to give information about your payments in the tax year ending 5 April 2000, about any you wish to carry back to an earlier year, and about any payments you have made since 5 April 2000 which you want to bring back to get tax relief in this tax return.

In Box 14.6, enter the amount of payments which you have made to a personal pension scheme in the year before 5 April 2000. The self-employed pay before-tax amounts to the pension provider, so you will be entering gross figures (before deduction of tax).

You are allowed to carry back pension payments (see p. 74). You may have already claimed tax relief on some of the amount in box 14.6, for example, for the year ending 5 April 1999. If you have done so, enter that amount used in an earlier year in box 14.7.

If you now want to carry back some of what you paid in the year ending 5 April 2000 to the previous tax year (or possibly the one before that, see

p. 74), put this amount in box 14.8. On this amount you will get tax relief at the rate of tax you paid in the previous year.

Between 5 April 2000 and the date you are filling in your tax return, you may have made some pension payments. If you want these to be included in your tax return for the tax year ending 5 April 2000, enter the amount in box 14.9.

The amount of relief you are claiming for your personal pension scheme will be worked out in box 14.10 (box 14.6 minus box 14.7 minus box 14.8). If the amount of relief you are claiming for this year is greater than the percentage limit (see p. 72), you may have unused relief from the previous six years which could be set against the excess. There is no place for this on the tax return. You claim it and the Inland Revenue has to ask you for your workings. Use Help Sheet *IR330 Pension Payments*.

For more information on self-employed contributions to personal pension plans, see p. 71.

■ **Employee contributions to personal pension plans** (include your gross contribution - see the note on box 14.11 in your Tax Return Guide)

Qualifying payments made in 1999-2000	14.11 £		1999-2000 payments used in an earlier year	14.12 £		Relief claimed
						box 14.11 *minus* (boxes 14.12 and 14.13, but not 14.14)
1999-2000 payments now to be carried back	14.13 £		Payments brought back from 2000-2001	14.14 £	14.15 £	

Employees pay their contributions into a personal pension plan after deducting basic rate tax. So you will need to adjust the figures you paid to enter the gross amount here. For the year ending 5 April 2000, divide the amount you paid by 0.77.

In Box 14.11, enter the gross amount of payments which you have made to a personal pension scheme in the year before 5 April 2000.

You are allowed to carry back pension payments (see p. 74). You may have already claimed tax relief on some of the amount in box 14.11, for example, for the year ending 5 April 1999. If you have done so, enter that amount used in an earlier year in box 14.12.

If you now want to carry back some of what you paid in the year ending 5 April 2000 to the previous tax year (or possibly the one before that, see

p. 74), put this amount in box 14.13. On this amount you will get tax relief at the rate of tax you paid in the previous year.

Between 5 April 2000 and the date you are filling in your tax return, you may have made some pension payments. If you want these to be included in your tax return for the tax year ending 5 April 2000, enter the amount in box 14.14.

The amount of relief you are claiming for your personal pension scheme for the tax year ending 5 April 2000 will be worked out in box 14.15 (box 14.11 minus box 14.12 minus box 14.13). If the amount of relief you are claiming for this year is greater than the percentage limit (see p. 72), you may have unused relief from the previous six years which could be set against the excess. There is no place for this on the tax return. You claim it and the Inland Revenue has to ask you for your workings. Use Help Sheet *IR330 Pension Payments*. If you do not get a tax return, you need to claim using Form PP42 (from your pension scheme administrator or tax office).

For more information on employee contributions to personal pension plans, see p. 71.

Contributions to an employer's scheme

■ *Contributions to other pension schemes and free-standing AVC schemes*

• Amount of contributions to employer's schemes **not deducted** at source from pay | 14.16 | £

Contributions to your employer's scheme are usually deducted from your salary by your employer and these are not included here. Put here (box 14.16) any contributions which have not been deducted from your salary before tax, for example, additional voluntary contributions paid late in the tax year.

Additional voluntary contributions

• Gross amount of free-standing additional voluntary contributions paid in 1999-2000 | 14.17 | £

If you are going to qualify for less than the maximum permitted amount of an employer's pension and want to improve the benefits you will get, you can get tax relief on additional voluntary contributions (see p. 70).

Instead of paying additional voluntary contributions into your employer's scheme, you can choose to invest in the fund of a pension provider, such as a life insurance company or unit trust manager. These are known as free-standing additional voluntary contributions.

When you made your payment to the pension provider, you would have made it after basic rate tax was deducted. But in box 14.17, you have to enter the gross amount. Take the amount you paid and divide it by 0.77 to give the gross figure. Using the tax return you will be able to claim higher rate tax relief if you are entitled to it.

OTHER RELIEFS YOU CAN CLAIM

Q15 Do you want to claim any of the following reliefs?   NO   YES   If yes, fill in boxes 15.1 to 15.12, as appropriate.

Your tax return on page 5 lists out the possible reliefs you might be able to claim. If you are entitled to any of these deductions from your income, put a tick in the YES box. Otherwise tick the NO box and go to Q16.

Vocational training

- Payments you made for vocational training (read the box 15.1 note on page 20 of your Tax Return Guide)   Amount of payment   15.1 £

You can get tax relief at your highest rate of tax for fees you paid for training which would count towards the National Vocational Qualifications and Scottish Vocational Qualifications. If you are aged 30 or over, you can also get tax relief on fees for full-time vocational courses lasting between four weeks and a year, whether or not they lead to the qualifications.

Relief at the basic rate is normally deducted from the payments you make so you can benefit even if unemployed. You cannot get higher rate tax relief on vocational training for the tax year ending 5 April 2000.

Enter at box 15.1, the amount of the payment you have made for the tax year ending 5 April 2000, that is after the deduction of basic rate tax.

You are entitled to relief only if you are not receiving or entitled to receive financial assistance for a course under a government scheme. Nor can you claim if you are doing the course mainly for your own recreation.

Loan interest

You can get tax relief on interest you pay on loans of £30,000 or less to buy your only or main home (or to improve it but only if the loans were taken out on or before 5 April 1988 – see p. 54).

The rate of tax relief is 10 per cent in the tax year ending 5 April 2000. So every £1 of interest you pay within the £30,000 limit will be reduced by tax relief to 90p. The rate has been consistently cut over the years and from 6 April 2000 this relief will be abolished altogether.

Most taxpayers get their tax relief through MIRAS (mortgage interest relief at source). Under this system, you make reduced payments to your lender. Your lender receives the amount of tax relief direct from the Inland Revenue. And you get the relief whether you pay tax or not. If your mortgage is in MIRAS, put nothing in box 15.2.

If your mortgage is **NOT** in MIRAS, claim here for tax relief. You will need a certificate of interest from your lender (but do not send this with your tax return unless your tax office asks to see it). If your mortgage is for more than £30,000 or if your home is used partly for business, you will have to work out what proportion of the interest you can claim (see pp. 51 and 55).

You also qualify for tax relief on mortgage interest if before 9 March 1999 you took out a loan on your only or main home in order to buy an annuity and you are aged 65 or more. This is commonly known as a home income scheme (see p. 52). The tax relief on such loans is usually given through the MIRAS system. If it is not, it also needs to be claimed here. These loans qualify for tax relief at the basic rate of tax, so you need to adjust the amount you enter here in order to produce the right result when taken into the calculations together with other (less favourably treated) mortgages. Help Sheet *IR340 Relief on loans not in MIRAS* will guide you through the calculations.

Home income schemes taken out on or after 9 March 1999 do not qualify for tax relief. If you took out your scheme before that date, you will continue to get tax relief for the lifetime of the loan and you will not lose that relief if you move home or switch the mortgage to another lender.

Interest on other qualifying loans

	Amount of payment
• Interest eligible for relief on other qualifying loans	15.3 £

Claim here for tax relief on the interest for a variety of loans, including loans to buy:

- a share in or putting capital into a co-operative partnership (but not if you are a limited partner)
- plant or machinery for use in your job if you are an employee or partner (if you are self-employed you claim in the Self-employment supplementary pages)
- shares in a close company (see below). To be eligible you should own more than 5 per cent of the company or be a shareholder and work for most of your time in the business.

A close company is one which is controlled by a small number of people. Broadly, it should have five or fewer 'participators', such as shareholders, or it should be controlled by shareholder directors.

You may also be able to claim relief here if you are an employee and get a low-interest or interest-free loan from your employer which counts as a taxable benefit (see p. 96).

Don't enter here to claim tax relief on the interest on a loan for a self-employed business (use box 3.47) or to buy a property you let (use box 5.4). Nor should you enter overdraft or credit card interest, which does not qualify for tax relief here.

Maintenance payments

	Amount claimed under 'new' rules	
• Maintenance or alimony payments you have made under a court order, Child Support Agency assessment or legally binding order or agreement	15.4 £	
	Amount claimed under 'old' rules up to £1,970	Amount claimed under 'old' rules over £1,970
	15.5 £	15.6 £

You may be entitled to tax relief on payments you make to your former or separated spouse and your children, but not if these are voluntary payments (that is you can't be forced to make them). And you can't get tax relief on payments made to or for your children if they are over 21.

Payments on which you can get tax relief include those made under:

- a court order

- a Child Support Agency assessment
- a written agreement
- a verbal agreement made before 15 March 1988, if written details were received by your tax inspector by 30 June 1988.

There are different rules about tax relief on maintenance payments depending on when the agreement was made. Chapter 6 explains the distinctions between the old and new rules and gives tax-saving ideas.

What to enter if your maintenance comes under the new rules

If your payments come under the new rules what you should enter in box 15.4 is the lower of £1,970, which is the maximum payments each year on which you can get tax relief under the new rules, and the amount you paid in the year ending 5 April 2000. If your former husband or wife has remarried during the tax year ending 5 April 2000, you are not entitled to tax relief on any payments made after he or she remarried. If what you paid before the date of marriage is less than £1,970, enter that amount.

You can get tax relief on maintenance payments only up to a total of £1,970, no matter how many ex- or separated husbands or wives you have.

You will need to give the dates of the court order, agreements and so on in the section headed Additional information on page 8 of the tax return.

You do not get tax relief at the rate of tax you pay. This is a fixed-rate relief and is 10 per cent for the year ending 5 April 2000.

What to enter if your maintenance comes under the old rules

You can get tax relief on the amount of maintenance payments which you paid and got tax relief on in the tax year ending 5 April 1989, unless you were due to pay less and did pay less in the tax year ending 5 April 2000. If the lower of these two amounts is less than or equal to £1,970, enter it in box 15.5. If it is more than £1,970, put £1,970 in box 15.5 and the excess in box 15.6. You have to split up the payments like this because tax relief on the first £1,970 is only 10 per cent, but on the excess you get relief at your

> ### EXAMPLE
>
> Peter Smith pays maintenance to his ex-wife and child. The agreement was made in 1992, so it comes under the new rules. In the year ending 5 April 2000 he paid £5,000. He is entitled to tax relief on the lower of what he paid (£5,000) or £1,970. He puts £1,970 in box 15.4.
>
> He is entitled to tax relief on his maintenance payments at the rate of 10 per cent. On the £1,970 which he can claim under the new rules he will get tax relief of 10 per cent of £1,970, which is £197.

top rate of tax.

You can get tax relief on maintenance payments to more than one
former husband or wife under the
old rules. Maintenance payments for
two agreements under the old rules
must be looked at separately. You
can get tax relief on the sum of the
lower of the two amounts for each
agreement. If the sum of the two
amounts is less than or equal to
£1,970, enter it in box 15.5. If it is
more than £1,970, put £1,970 in box
15.5 and the excess in box 15.6.

> ### Example
> Jane Spires was divorced from her
> husband in 1987. Ever since, she
> has paid him the same amount of
> maintenance, £2,500 a year under a
> written agreement. In the year end-
> ing 5 April 2000, she paid him the
> amount he was entitled to. She can
> get tax relief on the full £2,500 a
> year because it is paid under the old
> rules. She enters £1,970 in box 15.5
> and the difference (£2,500 minus
> £1,970 equals £530) goes in box
> 15.6.

If you make two lots of maintenance payments, one under the old rules and
one under the new rules, you may be able to get tax relief under both sets of
rules. Work out the amount on which you can get tax relief under the old
rules and put the figures in boxes 15.5 and 15.6 (as instructed above). If the
figure in box 15.5 is less than £1,970 for the tax year ending 5 April 2000,
you can claim under the new rules for maintenance payments which come
within those rules. Deduct the figure in box 15.5 from £1,970 and put in box
15.4 the lower of that figure and the amount of maintenance payments you
made in the year ending 5 April 2000 under the new rules.

Investing in growing businesses

There are some schemes which encourage investment into growing businesses which require risk capital. These types of investments can carry a high
degree of risk and to compensate investors for carrying this extra risk element,
there is a broad range of tax incentives. For more details, see Chapter 8.

Venture capital trusts

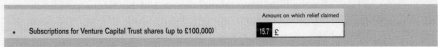

Amount on which relief claimed
* Subscriptions for Venture Capital Trust shares (up to £100,000)   15.7 £

If you invest in a venture capital trust, you are not investing directly in these
companies but in a fund like an investment trust which is quoted on the
Stock Exchange.

When you buy new ordinary shares in a venture capital trust, you can get
income tax relief at 20 per cent on your investment up to £100,000 for the

year ending 5 April 2000, as long as you hold your shares for five years. If you are reinvesting the gain made from selling some other asset, you can also claim capital gains tax reinvestment relief on that gain (that is, you can put off paying the capital gains tax until you dispose of your new asset, in this case the shares you hold in the venture capital trust).

Any dividends paid out by the venture capital trust and gains you make on the shares in the trust are all free of tax.

In box 15.7, put the amount you have invested in venture capital trusts, up to a maximum of £100,000.

Enterprise Investment Scheme

	Amount on which relief claimed
• Subscriptions under the Enterprise Investment Scheme (up to £150,000)	15.8 £

You can get tax relief of 20 per cent on investments (not more than £150,000 in the tax year ending 5 April 2000) made in the shares of unquoted trading companies. Any gain you make on the shares will be free of capital gains tax. There are a lot of detailed rules about which companies are eligible and whether you yourself are eligible.

If you have invested in shares eligible for the Enterprise Investment Scheme after 5 April, but before 6 October 2000, you can ask for half the investment up to a maximum of £25,000 to be deducted from your income for the year ending 5 April 2000.

You can claim here in this tax return for an investment only if you have received Form EIS3 from the company in which you invested (Form EIS5 for an investment made through a fund). This form certifies that the company qualifies for the scheme.

Enter in box 15.8 the total investments (up to £150,000) for which you are claiming relief in the tax year ending 5 April 2000. If you have made an investment for which you have not yet received Form EIS3, or form EIS5, don't enter it here. You can either claim before 31 January 2001 by asking your tax office to amend this tax return or you can claim using the form in EIS3 after 31 January 2001.

Enter details of each investment for which you are claiming relief in the section headed Additional information on page 8 of the tax return.

Giving to charity

As well as making donations in the street or in other ways, you can make more formal donations and use the tax system to reduce what it costs you to make the donation. With either a covenant or Gift Aid, you can get tax relief at your highest rate of tax.

> ### TAX-SAVING IDEA
> If you are giving to charity, try to arrange to do so either with a covenant or through the Gift Aid scheme. The charity you support can receive more by reclaiming the basic rate tax on what you give.

Covenants

Enter in box 15.9 the amount you actually paid to the charity (not the gross amount which you agreed to pay). You can get tax relief at your highest rate of tax on payments you make to registered charities if you make them under a deed of covenant. This is a legally binding agreement to make a series of payments and to get the tax relief on payments to charity; they should be capable of continuing for more than three years. You won't get the tax relief if you get significant benefits from the payments, but you will get tax relief if you are allowed access to the charity's property as a benefit of membership. This includes subscriptions to charities such as the National Trust and those which conserve wildlife for the public benefit, even though you get free or reduced-price entry to the property.

When you make the payment to the charity, you will often agree to pay a gross amount, for example, £100 a year. But when you make the payment, you always pay only the net amount, because you deduct tax at the basic rate. For the tax year ending 5 April 2000, the basic rate tax is 23 per cent, so you would have handed over to the charity £77, not the £100 you agreed to pay. The charity reclaims the £23 of basic rate tax which you deducted from the Inland Revenue. So the charity receives £100, but it costs you £77. And you can get higher rate tax relief if you pay tax at 40 per cent.

If you don't pay tax at the basic rate, but at the starting rate of 10 per cent, or if you are a non taxpayer, you may have to hand money back to the Inland Revenue. If you pay tax at the starting rate for the year ending 5

> ### TAX-SAVING IDEA
> If you are a couple and want to donate to charity using a covenant, make sure that the covenant is made by whichever of you has the highest rate of tax.

April 2000, and you had agreed to make a gross payment of £100, handing over £77 to the charity, you will have to repay £13 to the Inland Revenue (this is taken into account when working out your overall tax bill).

It depends on the exact wording of the covenant, but unless you agreed to hand over a fixed net amount, if the basic rate of tax changes you will need to alter how much you pay to the charity. For example, in the tax year ending 5 April 2001, the basic rate falls to 22 per cent. For a gross amount of £100, you will need to pay £78.

You can get more information about charitable covenants from the Charities Aid Foundation, King's Hill, West Malling, Kent ME19 4TA.

Annuities and covenants entered into for full value, for genuine commercial reasons in connection with the payer's trade or profession, are also eligible for tax relief at the highest rate, but covenants paid to individuals don't get any tax relief.

EXAMPLE

Julia West is a higher rate taxpayer. She has agreed to donate to her favourite charity, the Cricketers Benevolent Foundation, £200 a year. This is the gross amount entered in the covenant. But before she pays over the donation each year she deducts basic rate tax. In the year ending 5 April 2000, she deducted £46 and sent £154 by standing order. The charity reclaimed the £46 from the Inland Revenue. Because she is a higher rate taxpayer, she is entitled to more tax relief and claims it through her tax return. In box 15.9, she enters the amount she actually paid, £154 (not the gross amount of £200 which she agreed to pay). She gets her higher rate tax relief when she works out her tax bill and the amount she has to pay or can claim as a refund on 31 January 2001.

Gift Aid

	Amount of qualifying payments
• Gift Aid and Millennium Gift Aid	15.10 £

Enter in box 15.10 the total amounts you actually paid to the charity under these two schemes.

Under the Gift Aid scheme, in the tax year ending 5 April 2000 you can get tax relief at your highest rate of tax on single one-off gifts to a charity of £250 or more. There is no upper limit. You make the payment by agreeing to pay a gross amount, for example, £1,000. You actually hand over to the charity £1,000 less the amount of basic rate tax. For the tax year ending 5

April 2000, this would be £1,000 less £230 giving a payment of £770.

If you pay tax at less than the basic rate, you are a starting rate taxpayer or a non-taxpayer, you will have to pay back to the Inland Revenue some of the tax you have deducted. For example, a starting rate taxpayer who had deducted £230 from a gross amount of £1,000 in the tax year ending 5 April 2000 will have to pay £130 to the Inland Revenue.

> **TAX-SAVING IDEA**
>
> If you are a couple and want to make a donation to charity under Gift Aid, make sure that whichever of you pays the highest rate of tax makes the donation.

Millenium Gift Aid is tax relief for cash gifts made by individuals up to 31 December 2000. Each single gift must be £100 or more (or a series of gifts to one charity must come to £100 or more). The gifts you make are treated as having basic rate tax deducted.

Closing a business

	Amount of payment
• Post-cessation expenses, pre-incorporation losses brought forward and losses on relevant discounted securities etc	15.11 £

Even after you have closed a business, you may find that there are certain obligations and expenses which you have to meet. For example, you may need to put right some defect in work which you carried out.

You can deduct some expenses from any other income and gains you have in the year in which the business expense arises, if you have no income from your closed business. The relief is available for expenses incurred within seven years after the business closure. You must claim for the relief by 31 January in the second year after the tax year in which you incurred the expense. So for an expense which you met in the tax year ending 5 April 2000, you must claim by 31 January 2002.

The expenses which qualify for this special relief are:

- costs of putting right defective work you did or faulty goods or services which you supplied and the cost of paying any damages as a result
- premiums for insurance against claims due to defective work or faulty goods and services
- legal and other professional expenses you incur in defending yourself against accusations of defective work or providing faulty goods or services
- debts owed to the business which you included in your accounts but which have subsequently turned out to be bad debts
- cost of collecting debts owed to the business and included in its accounts.

Expenses which don't qualify for post-cessation relief can only be set against future income which comes from the closed business. There are some special rules about unpaid expenses. Ask your tax adviser or your tax office for help.

Enter in box 15.11 the amount of expenses which you want to deduct from your income in the tax year ending 5 April 2000 (and in box 8.5 of the Capital Gains pages the amount you want to deduct from your capital gains). If you are later reimbursed for any expenses or bad debts entered in this section, remember to enter the amount recovered under Any other income (box 13.3 of the tax return – see p. 167).

If you used to run a business on a self-employed basis but have converted the business to a company, you may be able to claim relief for losses made while you were self-employed against your income from the company. You must previously have opted to carry forward the losses to set against future profits (see page 247), you must have transferred the self-employed business solely or mainly in exchange for shares in the new company and you must meet certain other conditions. Enter the loss you are claiming in box 15.11.

You also claim in box 15.11 for losses on relevant discounted securities (formerly deep discount bonds and deep gain securities), including a newish investment called gilt strips. A loss incurred in the tax year ending 5 April 2000 can be deducted only from the income in the same tax year.

Payments to a trade union or friendly society

	Half amount of payment
• Payments to a trade union or friendly society for death benefits	15.12 £

Friendly societies supported their members before the arrival of the welfare state by paying sickness benefit, unemployment benefit and widow's pensions. Some continue in existence and you can get tax relief on premiums you pay on certain combined sickness and life insurance policies they offer. The tax relief is at half your top rate of tax on the life part of the premium; you can also get the same tax relief on part of your trade union subscription if it includes pension, funeral or life insurance benefits. With the friendly society policy, to be eligible for tax relief the premiums must be £25 or less a month and 40 per cent or less of the premium should be for the death benefit.

Ask your friendly society or trade union to tell you how much of the premium was for pension, life insurance, funeral or death benefit. Enter in box 15.12 half that amount.

ALLOWANCES

Another way of reducing the amount of income tax you have to pay is to claim any allowances to which you are entitled. These are deducted from your income, along with reliefs (deductions), to make your taxable income smaller – and so also your tax bill.

Personal allowances

Everyone gets a personal allowance. It comes automatically; you don't have to claim it in the tax return.

Age-related personal allowances

However, people aged 65 or over during the tax year beginning 6 April 1999, can claim a higher allowance. There is one level of age-related allowance if you were 65 or over during the tax year beginning 6 April 1999 and a still higher rate if

> ### TAX-SAVING IDEA
> You can go back six years to claim an allowance which you forgot at the time or didn't know you were entitled to. You get tax relief at the rate of tax which would have applied if you claimed the deduction at the right time.

you were 75 or over. On the tax return it says if you were born before 6 April 1935, enter your date of birth in box 21.4 to claim the age-related allowance. Box 21.4 is at the bottom of page 7 of the return.

ALLOWANCES *for the year ended 5 April 2000*

Q16 You get your personal allowance of £4,335 automatically. **If you were born before 6 April 1935, enter your date of birth in box 21.4** – you may get higher age-related allowances.

Do you want to claim any of the following allowances?　　NO ☐　YES ☐

If yes, please read pages 23 to 26 of your Tax Return Guide and then fill in boxes 16.1 to 16.28 as appropriate.

Blind person's allowance

Anyone registered as blind with a local authority can claim blind person's allowance. The amount of the allowance for the tax year ending 5 April 2000 is £1,380. A registered blind person must be unable to perform any work for which eyesight is essential. The partially sighted cannot claim the allowance.

	Date of registration (if first year of claim)	Local authority (or other register)
■ **Blind person's allowance**	16.1 / /	16.2

In box 16.1, enter the date you were registered blind if this is the first year you are claiming, and enter the name of the local authority in box 16.2.

If you are not registered until after 5 April 2000 but before 6 April 2001, you can still get the allowance for the tax year ending 5 April 2000 if you can show that you were blind at that date, for example, with an ophthalmologist's certificate.

The requirement for Scotland and Northern Ireland is different. You don't need to be registered. You can claim blind person's allowance if you are not able to perform any work for which eyesight was essential. To claim, write Scotland claim or Northern Ireland claim in box 16.2.

If your income is less than your allowances, including blind person's, and you are married and living with your husband or wife, you can transfer the unused part of this allowance to your partner (see pp. 44 and 194). If both of you are blind, you can claim two allowances.

Transitional allowance

■ *Transitional allowance* (for some wives with husbands on low income if received in earlier years).

• Tick to claim and give details in the 'Additional information' box on page 8
(please see page 23 of your Tax Return Guide for what is needed) 16.3 ☐

• If you want to calculate your tax, enter the amount of transitional allowance you can have in box 16.4 16.4 £

Transitional allowance is for some wives with husbands on low income which was introduced to ease the changes to the allowances available for married men when independent taxation was introduced. To get this allowance for the year tax ending 5 April 2000 you must be:

• a married woman, and
• have received transitional allowance in the tax year ending 5 April 1999, and
• lived with the same husband in the tax year ending 5 April 2000 as you were for the whole of the year ending 5 April 1999.

Your husband must have been UK-resident for the year ending 5 April 2000, and have written to his tax office asking for the allowance to be given to you.

To claim the allowance tick box 16.3. You will need to enter details about your husband in the Additional information box on page 8 of the return – his name, address, tax reference, National Insurance number and tax office.

If you are working out your own tax bill, you will need to know the amount of the allowance and put it in box 16.4. You can ask either your husband or your tax office for the figure. It should be the amount of transitional allowance you received in the year ending 5 April 1999, less any increase in your allowances in the year to 5 April 2000, or, if lower, the amount of your husband's unused allowances (excluding blind person's and married couple's allowance).

Married couple's allowance

This is an allowance which can be claimed when you marry. There are more details of it in Chapter 6.

The amount of the married couple's allowance for those aged under 65 for the tax year ending 5 April 2000 is £1,970 and higher levels can be claimed by the 65 or over and 75 or over age groups (see p. 42). Whichever amount you qualify for, the allowance is restricted to 10 per cent.

Married couple's allowance is automatically given to the husband but if you asked before 6 April 2000 it can be split between the two of you or used 100 per cent by the wife. Note, though, that if one of you is 65 or over during the tax year, and entitled to a higher level of married couple's allowance, only the basic amount (£1,970 for the tax year ending 5 April 2000) can be allocated between the two of you. The extra bit always goes to the husband.

Married men

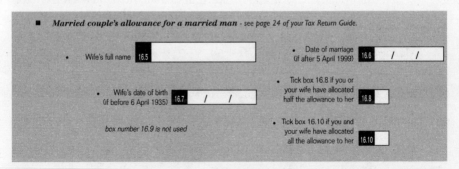

■ *Married couple's allowance for a married man* - see page 24 of your Tax Return Guide.

• Wife's full name 16.5

• Date of marriage (if after 5 April 1999) 16.6 / /

• Wife's date of birth (if before 6 April 1935) 16.7 / /

• Tick box 16.8 if you or your wife have allocated half the allowance to her 16.8

box number 16.9 is not used

• Tick box 16.10 if you and your wife have allocated all the allowance to her 16.10

A married man can claim married couple's allowance if he was married and living with his wife for at least part of the tax year. He can also claim it if he was separated from his wife before 6 April 1990 but was maintaining her voluntarily (and not able to claim tax relief on the payments) from separation to 6 April 1999.

Fill in boxes 16.5 to 16.10. Claim married couple's allowance by entering:

- your wife's full name in box 16.5
- her date of birth in box 16.7, if before 6 April 1935.

Tick box 16.8 if you and your wife have decided to split the allowance equally between the two of you. Tick box 16.10 if you and your wife have decided to transfer the whole of the married couple's allowance to your wife.

If you married during the tax year ending 5 April 2000 and want to claim all or part of the married couple's allowance (see p. 44), put the date of your marriage in box 16.6. You get one-twelfth of the full married couple's allowance for each month (or part-month) of your marriage (see Chapter 6).

However, there may be two other options open to you:

- if this is a second or later marriage, you may already be claiming married couple's allowance for a previous marriage. If you want to carry on doing this (because you would be able to claim more of the allowance), don't enter anything in box 16.6. And in boxes 16.5, 16.7 and 16.9 fill in the information about your former wife
- or if you have a child living with you, you can claim additional personal allowance instead of married couple's allowance. If you can claim only part of married couple's allowance, you would be better off doing this as you could be entitled to the whole of additional personal allowance (unless you are sharing it or qualify for a higher, age-related married couple's allowance). This would reduce your tax bill. If you make this choice don't enter anything in boxes 16.5 to 16.10, but fill in the additional personal allowance section instead.

Married women

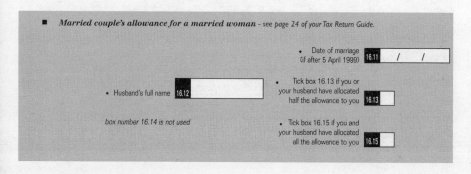

■ *Married couple's allowance for a married woman* - see page 24 of your Tax Return Guide.

- Date of marriage (if after 5 April 1999) 16.11 / /
- Husband's full name 16.12
- *box number 16.14 is not used*
- Tick box 16.13 if you or your husband have allocated half the allowance to you 16.13
- Tick box 16.15 if you and your husband have allocated all the allowance to you 16.15

You should fill in boxes 16.11 to 16.15. You can claim married couple's allowance only if you and your husband have agreed to transfer it, but you can demand for it to be split equally between the two of you without his agreement. You must have lived with your husband for all or part of the tax year ending 5 April 2000.

If you have agreed to split the allowance, tick box 16.13. If you have agreed to transfer the whole allowance to you, tick box 16.15. Fill in your husband's full name (box 16.12).

If you have married since 5 April 1999, enter the date of the marriage in box 16.11 if you want to claim married couple's allowance. If you are still receiving all or your share of the allowance for a previous marriage, don't enter anything in box 16.11 and give details of your former husband in boxes 16.12 and 16.14.

If your husband died in the tax year ending 5 April 2000, you can use only the part of the married couple's allowance which is not used up against your husband's income. This applies even if you had agreed to allocate it differently. If this is the case, do not tick boxes 16.13 or 16.15. Tick instead box 16.26. And if you are filling in a tax return for your husband who has died, do not tick boxes 16.8 or 16.10 because the allowance has first to be deducted from your husband's income.

Additional personal allowance

If you are a single parent, there is an allowance you may be able to claim if the child lives with you. This allowance is known as additional personal allowance. The amount of the allowance is the same as the married couple's allowance (£1,970 for the tax year ending 5 April 2000). The amount of the relief for the tax year ending 5 April 2000 is restricted to 10 per cent.

You may be able to claim this allowance if at some time in the tax year you are:

- single
- a widow or widower
- divorced
- married but separated (and so not entitled to the married couple's allowance if a man)
- married, but your wife or husband is totally unable to look after him- or herself throughout the tax year. If this is the case please tick box 16.16A.

You can also claim the allowance instead of the married couple's allowance if you got married or reconciled during the tax year.

To get the allowance you must have a child (either your own or someone else's) living with you for the whole or part of the tax year. You can only claim for a child aged 16 or over at the start of the tax year if the child is in full-time education at university, school or college or training full-time for at least two years for a trade or profession. If the child is not yours, you cannot claim if the child is 18 or over at the start of the tax year. If the child is yours, there is no age limit on claiming. Your child includes a step-child, adopted child or legitimated child.

It is possible that two people could claim the allowance for the same child because the child lives with each of them for part of the year (who has custody is not the deciding factor). If this applies to you, you can agree with the other what proportion each claims. If you cannot agree, the allowance will be divided up according to the amount of time the child lives with each of you during the tax year. If there are two or more children, you may be able to claim a full allowance each.

If you are living with someone as husband and wife, but are unmarried, you and your partner can claim only one additional personal allowance between the two of you and only for the youngest child. The allowance can be divided up as you wish. If you are not entitled to the allowance for the youngest child, you can't claim it at all.

To claim the allowance, you need to give the name of the child claimed for in box 16.16 and the child's date of birth in box 16.17. Tick box 16.18 if the child lives with you. Fill in box 16.19 if you are claiming for a child over 16 years old.

If you and someone else want to share the allowance, you will need to fill in

> ## EXAMPLE
>
> Nicky White is a single parent with two children living with her. Her income is £15,000. She can't claim the married couple's allowance, but she can claim the additional personal allowance (which is the same amount). The allowance is restricted to relief of 10 per cent of £1,970, that is £197 for the tax year ending 5 April 2000. Her tax bill is as follows:
>
> | | |
> |---|---:|
> | Income | £15,000 |
> | less personal allowance | £ 4,335 |
> | | |
> | Taxable income | £10,665 |
> | | |
> | Tax bill: | |
> | £1,500 at 10 per cent | £150 |
> | £9,165 at 23 per cent | £2,108 |
> | | £2,258 |
> | | |
> | less tax relief on additional personal allowance | £197 |
> | | |
> | Tax for the year ended 5 April 2000 | £2,061 |

boxes 16.20 to 16.23. Enter the name and address of the other person claiming the allowance in box 16.20 and the percentage of the allowance you are claiming in box 16.21. If you cannot agree the percentage for each of you, you will have to give the further information in boxes 16.22 and 16.23 and the Inland Revenue will decide your share.

Widow's bereavement allowance

■ *Widow's bereavement allowance*	• Date of your husband's death	16.24 / /

You can claim widow's bereavement allowance in the tax year you are widowed and the following tax year (see p. 49). The allowance is £1,970 for the tax year ending 5 April 2000. This is restricted to 10 per cent, as it is with the married couple's and additional personal allowances.

To claim the allowance, enter the date your husband died in box 16.24.

Transfer of surplus allowances

You can transfer any unused amount of married couple's or blind person's allowance to your wife or your husband if you did not have enough income in the year to use up the allowance and you lived with your wife or husband for at least part of that year.

In certain limited circumstances, if a husband cannot use up all his personal allowance, his wife can receive a transitional allowance (see p. 188).

If you want your wife or husband to have the surplus of married couple's and blind person's allowances or transitional allowance, tick box 16.25. In the Additional information box on page 8 of your tax return, give your spouse's name, address, tax reference, National Insurance number and tax office.

If you want to claim and use your spouse's unused allowances, tick box 16.26. Give your spouse's name, address, tax reference, National Insurance number and tax office in the Additional information box on page 8.

If you are working out your own tax bill, enter in boxes 16.27 and 16.28 the amount of the surplus allowances. You can ask your tax office for help if you are not sure of the amount.

EMPLOYMENT

 Were you an employee, or office holder, or director, or agency worker or did you receive payments or benefits from a former employer (excluding a pension) in the year ended 5 April 2000? NO ☐ YES ☐ EMPLOYMENT YES ☐

It is usually easy to tell whether or not you are an employee. There are some grey areas, however, where the Inland Revenue will seek to tax you as an employee even if you think of yourself as self-employed:

- if you are a company director (even if you own the company)
- if you work on a freelance or consultancy basis, but have to work closely under the control of your boss, working a set number of hours at an hourly rate, say, and at a particular location
- if you work on a casual, part-time basis
- if you work as a temp through an agency. This includes, for example, locum doctors; but it does not apply to entertainers or models working through an agency, or to people who work solely from home
- you have more than one job: you may be classed as an employee for one job, even if you are clearly self-employed in another.

The key significance of being an employee is that in most cases your employer will have to operate PAYE (see Chapter 3) on your earnings from that job and deduct tax and National Insurance before paying you. Exceptionally, the Inland Revenue has agreed that most actors can count as employees for National Insurance purposes but as self-employed for income tax.

For many employees, the advantage of being paid under PAYE is that the right amount of tax on all their income should be deducted from their earnings and so they do not have to worry about paying a separate tax bill. If their income from their job is their only income many also do not need to fill in a tax return. But you may still have to fill one in if:

- you are a higher rate taxpayer and get taxable perks such as a company car or receive investment income
- you have other income which is paid out before tax is deducted, such as some types of investment income

- your tax affairs are complex for any other reason.

If you are an employee and are sent a tax return, you need to tick the YES box at Q1 of the basic tax return and fill in a separate Employment page for each job you have. If you are not sure of your status, check with your tax office.

Your employer

Details of employer

Employer's PAYE reference – may be shown under 'Tax office number and reference' on your P60 or 'PAYE reference' on your P45

1.1

Employer's name

1.2

Date employment started (only if between 6 April 1999 and 5 April 2000)

1.3 / /

Employer's address

1.5

Date finished (only if between 6 April 1999 and 5 April 2000)

1.4 / /

Tick box 1.6 if you were a director of the company

1.6

and, if so, tick box 1.7 if it was a close company

1.7

Postcode

TAX-SAVING IDEA

A disadvantage of being an employee is that you cannot deduct as many expenses from your taxable income as you could if you were self-employed. So if you are setting up on your own, check that you will meet the Inland Revenue's conditions for self-employment.

So that your tax office can tie up the information on your tax return with that provided by your employer, give your employer's name, address and PAYE reference (shown on the P60 or P45). If the employment started or ended during the tax year ending 5 April 2000, you also need to give the start or end dates of the job, the length of time you worked there, whether or not you are a director (box 1.6) and if it is a close company (box 1.7). This may affect how your perks and benefits are taxed.

What is taxed

Broadly speaking, the Inland Revenue seeks to tax any benefit you get from being employed, even if you get it from someone other than your employer. The tax return organises your remuneration into the following categories:

- money (including earnings from working abroad)
- benefits (taxable perks given by your employer) and expenses payments (either flat-rate allowances or reimbursement for expenses you have incurred)
- lump sums received on retirement, redundancy or death.

Not all of these will actually be taxable. But in general, you have to put it all down first, and the tax return then guides you to enter the various tax reliefs which you can deduct, for example, tax relief for expenses incurred in doing your job.

One thing you do not have to enter anywhere on your tax return is details of your National Insurance contributions as an employee. These should all be sorted out for you by your employer.

The date income is taxable
As a general rule, you are counted as receiving income from employment from the earlier of:

- the date you get it
- the date you are entitled to it, even if you do not actually get it till later on.

So if, for example, you are entitled to payment on 15 March 2000, but do not actually receive it until 15 April, you must still include it in your tax return for the tax year ending 5 April 2000. If you receive payment early – on 15 March 2000, for work not completed until 15 April, for example – it is taxable from the date you received it, that is 15 March.

If you are a director, your earnings for a particular period may be decided on one date, credited to you in the company accounts on another date, but not paid out till much later. It is the earliest date that counts, unless the earnings for a particular period were decided before that period ended. In this case, you are treated as receiving them on the last day of the period to which the earnings relate.

The documents you need
Most of the information you need will be on Forms P60, P11D or P9D.

Your P60 is a form your employer must give you by 31 May after the end of the tax year (that is, by 31 May 2000 for the tax year ending 5 April 2000). The P60 is a summary of how much you have been paid, and how much tax has been deducted. If you haven't got a P60, you should be able to find the information from your pay slips. If you left a job during a tax year, the information will be on your P45.

Your employer has to declare to the Revenue any taxable benefits or expenses you receive and the cash equivalent on form P11D or form P9D. Which form you get depends on how much you earn. You should get a copy from your employer by 6 July after the end of the tax year, that is by 6 July 2000 for the tax year ending 5 April 2000.

Note that if you leave a job, you will not automatically be given a form, but your ex-employer must give you one if you ask for it within three years after the end of the tax year in which you left. Your employer has 30 days from receiving your request in which to supply the form (if this is after the normal 6 July deadline).

Your P11D or P9D should be the starting point of all the expenses payments you have received. But you also need to keep receipts or documentation to back up your claim to deduct allowable expenses, particularly if they were not reimbursed by your employer and so did not appear on your P11D or P9D.

If you receive a lump sum from your employer, for example, when you left your job, it may be included on your P60, your P11D, or your P45, or you may just have a letter from your employer. Remember to include only payments that were made because of the change or job loss in the relevant tax year, even if they were actually paid in a different tax year. Your employer should be able to help you decide which category a payment falls within. If there is any doubt, employers can get advance decisions from their tax office, so it is worth talking about the tax consequences with your employer before any payment is made.

MONEY FROM EMPLOYMENT

Income from employment

- *Money* - see Notes, page EN3

		Before tax
• Payments from P60 (or P45 or payslips)	1.8	£

You should enter as money:

- salaries, wages, fees, overtime, bonuses, commission and honoraria (after deducting money you have donated to a payroll giving scheme, or contributed to your employer's pension scheme, see right)
- amounts voted to you as a director and credited to an account with the company, even if you cannot draw the money straight away
- voluntary payments and gifts, whether from your employer or anyone else, such as tips and Christmas boxes (excluding some small gifts and personal gifts such as long-service awards, see Tax-free fringe benefits on

p. 83)
- incentive awards (but see below)
- profit-related pay (excluding any tax-free amount – see overleaf)
- the taxable value of shares withdrawn early from an approved profit-sharing scheme
- sick pay, including statutory sick pay and statutory maternity pay (see overleaf)
- holiday pay
- various payments to do with your employment which are not strictly pay. Examples are golden hellos paid to entice you to join the company; a loan written off because you satisfied or completed an employment condition; payments made to recognise changes in your conditions of service or employment; payments made if you leave a job and agree, in return for a lump sum, not to compete with your employer.

P60 forms vary slightly in design. The figure to look for is your pay 'for tax purposes' or 'this employment pay'. Enter the figure from Form P60 in box 1.8, but check that it does not include employer's contributions to a pension scheme or what you give under a payroll giving scheme (see below). If you were unemployed during the year, your P60 may give details of any jobseeker's allowance you received. Do not enter this in your Employment page – enter it instead in box 11.5 in the basic tax return.

Contributions to an employer's pension scheme
You can get tax relief on contributions you make to your employer's pension scheme, up to a maximum of 15 per cent of your taxable income from the job. This tax relief is given by deducting your contributions from your pay before tax is worked out on it, so giving you relief at your top rate of tax. The figure you enter as taxable pay in box 1.8 should be the figure after deducting pension contributions.

Payroll giving schemes
You can get tax relief on charitable donations of up to £1,200 a year through the payroll giving scheme (the biggest scheme run by the Charities Aid Foundation is called Give As You Earn, or GAYE) run by your employer. The money is deducted from your pay each week or month and passed straight to the charity by your employer. The donations are deducted from your pay before your tax is worked out on it, in the same way as contributions to an employer's pension scheme, so remember to check that what you enter in box 1.8. is your pay after payroll giving donations.

Incentive awards
Broadly speaking, these are taxable whether you receive them from your

employer or from someone else in connection with your job; for example, a car sales representative may receive prizes from the car manufacturer. However, the person paying the award may pay the tax for you, through a taxed award scheme. In this case, the award still counts as part of your income, but the tax paid on your behalf will reduce your tax bill. Whoever makes the award should give you a Form P443 stating the value of the award and how much tax has been paid on it, unless the figures have been included on your P60. You should include the amount of the award in box 1.10 and the tax already paid in box 1.11.

Suggestion scheme awards are tax-free and need not be entered, provided that there is a formal scheme open to all employees, and the suggestion concerned is outside your normal job. If the suggestion is not taken up, the maximum award is £25; if it is implemented, the maximum award is 50 per cent of the first year's expected net benefit, or 10 per cent of the benefit over five years, with an overall maximum of £5,000.

Profit-related pay

If you are in a registered scheme, your profit-related pay is tax-free, up to a ceiling of £1,000 for profit periods beginning between 1 January 1999 and 31 December 1999, or (if lower) 20 per cent of your total pay in the profit period to which the profit-related pay relates. Any profit-related pay above the limit is taxable in the normal way. Your employer should take into account any tax relief when working out the taxable pay shown in your P60. You do not need to enter details of the scheme or tax relief itself in the tax return or the Employment page.

Tax relief on profit-related pay is being abolished. There is no relief for profit periods beginning on or after 1 January 2000.

Sick pay and maternity pay

If you are off work through illness or on maternity leave, any payment made to you by your employer, including statutory sick pay (SSP) or statutory maternity pay (SMP), is taxable. It will be taxed before you get it and shown on your P60 or P45 in the same way as other income, and you enter it with your other taxable pay in box 1.8. There are two exceptions to this rule:

- occasionally, SMP or SSP may be paid directly to you by the Department of Social Security. In this case, the benefit is still taxable, but tax is not deducted before it is paid to you and rather than enter it under Employment you should enter it in box 11.7 on page 4 of the basic tax return
- if you pay part or all of the premiums for an insurance policy taken out

by your employer to meet the cost of employees' sick pay. In this case, the proportion of the sick pay which arises from your contributions is tax-free and need not be entered on the tax return. Any sick pay arising from your employer's contributions is taxable. Put it in box 1.8.

Tips and other payments

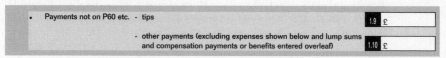

Boxes 1.9 and 1.10 are there to catch any income which does not appear on your P60 (for example, because it is paid by people other than your employer) and for which there is no other place on the Employment page.

Tax deducted

	Tax deducted
• UK tax deducted from payments in boxes 1.8 to 1.10	1.11 £

The tax your employer has deducted under PAYE is set against your tax bill. Enter it in box 1.11, together with any other tax deducted (for example, under a taxed incentive scheme). Occasionally, your employer may have given you more tax back as a refund than was actually deducted. If so, remember to enter the amount in brackets.

FRINGE BENEFITS AND EXPENSES

> ■ **Benefits and expenses** - see Notes, pages EN3 to EN6. If any benefits connected with termination of employment were received, or enjoyed, after that termination and were from a **former** employer you need to complete Help Sheet IR204, available from the Orderline. Do not enter such benefits here.

Many employers give their employees non-cash fringe benefits, such as a company car or free medical insurance (see Chapter 9). Generally, you are taxed on the cash equivalent of these benefits (and the same applies, as for pay, if the benefit or expense is paid to you by someone other than your employer). Benefits for your family or household are regarded as a payment to you. However, some types of benefits are tax-free, and others are taxable only for higher-paid employees.

Expense payments you receive are yoked together with benefits in this section and sometimes the dividing line between them can be a fine one; for example, a company car may be a way of covering your travelling costs for work, as well as a perk of the job.

Payments you do not need to enter

There are three sorts of payments which you can ignore when filling out the benefits and expenses section of the Employment supplementary page.

Dispensations

You do not need to enter in your tax return expenses payments which are covered by a dispensation. A dispensation is a special permission from the Revenue which means that your employer does not have to include on your P11D or P9D expenses which would be tax-free anyway. Dispensations are usually given for things like travelling and subsistence expenses on an approved scale: they do not generally cover fringe benefits.

PAYE Settlement Agreements

The tax on some of your expenses and benefits may already have been paid by your employer under a PAYE Settlement Agreement (PSA). This is a voluntary agreement between an

> **TAX-SAVING IDEA**
> Remember – you do not need to enter items covered by a dispensation or PAYE Settlement Agreement.

employer and the Inland Revenue under which the employer undertakes to pay the tax due on some types of benefits and expenses. The advantage for your employer is the saving of paperwork; the advantage for you is that you do not need to enter the payments on your return and they are effectively tax-free in your hands. Only some types of benefits and expenses can be covered by this sort of agreement, for example, minor expenses such as taxi fares and one-off payments such as parties for employees.

Tax-free fringe benefits

You do not need to enter the details of any fringe benefits which are tax-free (see p. 83 for a list). Note that there are conditions to be met before most of these benefits can be tax-free. Fuller information is given in Help Sheet *IR207 Non-taxable payments or benefits for employees*.

Payments you need to enter

There are some benefits which are always taxable and need to be entered on the tax return. They are assets which are transferred to you (including payments in kind), vouchers and goods paid for by credit cards, living accommodation (with a few exceptions) and mileage allowance.

You may receive other benefits. But if you earn at a rate of less than £8,500 a year and are not a director they will be tax-free and you do not need to enter them on the tax return. Chapter 9 gives much more detail. It helps you work out whether you are paid at the rate of £8,500 a year or not and helps you work out the taxable value of benefits which you need to enter here.

Assets transferred to you and payments made for you

Payments in kind may be taxed in a number of ways, depending on how much you earn and whether you have the alternative of cash instead (see p. 86 to find out the taxable value). You should be able to get the amount to enter in box 1.12 from your P11D. If you earn less than £8,500, the taxable value is the second-hand value. But if you earn £8,500 or more, the taxable value is the larger of the second-hand value or the cost to the employer of providing the asset.

Payments your employer makes for you, like your phone bill, should also be entered in box 1.12. But don't put assets which remain the property of your employer and which you merely have the use of, or to services supplied by your employer – these go in box 1.22, unless there is a more specific box.

Vouchers and credit cards

You may be given a voucher for a particular service (for example, a season ticket), a credit token or a company credit or charge card. If so, you are taxed on their cash equivalent unless they appear in the list of tax-free fringe benefits on p. 83 (for example, luncheon vouchers, gift vouchers which count as a small gift). Cash vouchers worth a specified amount of cash should already have been taxed under PAYE, so you will not usually have to enter them here as a benefit. If you used vouchers or your company credit card to settle expenses of your job (such as train fares), include the full value of the vouchers or card bill here, but claim a deduction for 'Expenses you incurred in doing your job' on the back of the Employment page.

For vouchers and cards which count as a taxable fringe benefit, broadly speaking you pay tax on the expense incurred by the person who provided them, less any amount that you have paid yourself. You will not have to pay tax on any annual card fee or interest paid by your employer.

Company credit cards and charge cards are often provided as a convenient way of paying business expenses. If so, you still have to enter the value of any vouchers or goods or services obtained with a credit card or credit token in box 1.13. You can claim any allowable business expenses back in boxes 1.32 to 1.35. For more information see Help Sheet *IR201 Vouchers, credit cards and tokens.*

Living accommodation

The basic taxable charge for any living accommodation (unless it counts as a tax-free fringe benefit, see p. 83), and the extra charge if applicable, should be entered in box 1.14. However, if you have the alternative of getting cash instead of accommodation, and the cash alternative comes to more than the taxable value of the accommodation, you should enter the extra cash in box 1.12 as well as the taxable value in box 1.14. This applies even if you have decided to live in.

There is Help Sheet *IR 202 Living Accommodation* if you want to work out the taxable value in all these situations.

Mileage allowances

If you use your own car for work, most employers pay you a mileage allowance of so many pence per mile. Quite often this is generous enough to allow you to make a profit on it. Any such profit needs to be entered as a benefit in box 1.15. Any loss should be entered in box 1.32.

Which method?
There are three different methods (exact, quick and Fixed Profit Car Scheme) for working out your profit, see p. 88. You do not have to stick with the Fixed Profit Car Scheme, even if your employer operates it, but using the scheme's scales is much simpler than keeping full records. Keep records for a few months to see how similar your actual cost per mile is to the Fixed Profit Car Scheme scale. Then:

- if your car happens to be more expensive to run than average, choose the exact method (but you must keep records of all your expenses)
- if its running costs are average, or cheaper than average, choose the Fixed Profit Car Scheme if your employer runs one, or the Quick method

- if you find that your mileage allowances come to less than the amount of your actual business expenses, do not enter anything in box 1.15 but remember to enter your loss in box 1.32.

Company cars

A company car is taxable only if you earn at the rate of £8,500 a year or more (see p. 90). Put in box 1.16 the cash equivalent of cars made available to you (or to members of your family or household) for private use. Check the figure with your employer or on your form P11D. Chapter 9 and Help Sheet *IR203 Car benefits and car fuel benefits* will be useful.

Fuel for company cars

If you have a company car, you may get free fuel for private use as well. This is taxed according to a fixed scale of charges added to your taxable income (see p. 95) and only taxable if you earn at the rate of £8,500 a year or more.

Enter the amount in box 1.17.

Vans

A van is only taxable if you earn at the rate of £8,500 a year or more (see p. 90). The basic taxable value of a van is £500, but there may be reductions (see p. 95). Enter the adjusted taxable amount in box 1.18.

Interest-free and low-interest loans

Free or cheap loans are only taxable if you earn at the rate of £8,500 a year or more. The basic rule is that you have to pay tax on the difference between the interest you pay and the interest worked out at an official rate set by the Inland Revenue. But there can be exceptions (see p. 96).

In box 1.19, you should put the cash equivalent (your employer should tell you what this is).

- Interest-free and low-interest loans

Amount
1.19 £

If the loan is for a qualifying purpose (for example, a mortgage to buy a home) you should claim tax relief in box 15.2 or box 15.3.

If the loan is eventually written off, you pay tax on the amount written off. Include the amount with the taxable value of any other loans in box 1.19. There is no box 1.20.

Private medical or dental insurance

- Private medical or dental insurance

Amount
1.21 £

This is taxable only if you earn at the rate of £8,500 a year or more. Enter the taxable amount, which you should find on Form P11D, in box 1.21. For more explanation, see p. 97.

Other benefits

- Other benefits

Amount
1.22 £

This is a box to sweep up any other taxable perks which you have not already entered elsewhere. Remember, though, that it applies only if you earn at a rate of £8,500 or more. The figures should be shown on your P11D. The main types of benefits you may have to enter here are listed on p. 97.

Expenses payments and balancing charges

- Expenses payments received and balancing charges

Amount
1.23 £

You should enter here all expenses payments and expense allowances you received, whether or not they are tax-free. You can deduct tax-free expense payments later on in boxes 1.32 to 1.35. The only expenses which you should not enter either here or later on are those for which your employer has a dispensation.

Your expenses payments should be shown in your P11D or P9D. In your P11D they will be broken down into the gross amount received, any contributions you made or amounts on which tax has already been deducted, and the taxable amount. Enter the taxable amount in box 1.23.

Balancing charges are not something you will see on your P11D or P9D. They apply only if you claimed capital allowances on something that you bought for your work and that you have now disposed of (see p. 243).

LUMP SUMS AND COMPENSATION

Income from employment continued

■ *Lump sums and compensation payments or benefits including such payments and benefits from a former employer*
Note that 'lump sums' here includes any contributions which your employer made to an unapproved retirement benefits scheme

You must read page EN6 of the Notes before *filling in boxes 1.24 to 1.30*

You may have something to enter here if:

- you received a lump sum when you left a job, such as redundancy pay
- you retired and received a lump sum from a non-approved retirement scheme (that is, anything other than an Inland-Revenue approved, foreign government or other statutory pension scheme)
- your employer (or ex-employer) paid you a lump sum which you have not already entered as pay (for example, in box 1.8 or box 1.10).

You will need Help Sheet *IR204 Lump sums and compensation payments* in order to work out what to enter in each of the boxes. It is important to enter the right bit in the right category because each is taxed under different parts of tax legislation. You can get various types of tax relief on some categories, but not on others. One payment might be made up of several different types. They may also affect your overall tax calculation.

	Tax deducted
. Tax deducted from payments in boxes 1.27 to 1.29	1.30 £

Your employer may deduct tax from any taxable sums you get before paying you. If so, make sure you enter it in box 1.30, so that it is taken into account when working out your tax bill.

Payment expected under the terms of your employment
Lump sums that you should enter here include:

- any payment that you receive under the terms and conditions of your contract, or where the expectation that you would get it is firm enough for it to be regarded as part of your contract – for example, a payment based on length of service which it is your employer's established policy

to make when a job ends
- payments received in return for you undertaking not to carry out certain actions, sometimes called a restrictive covenant (if not already entered with other pay in box 1.8 or 1.10)
- bonuses on leaving a job (for example, for doing extra work in the period leading up to redundancy). Do not enter redundancy payments themselves in this category – they go in box 1.29, after deducting various reliefs.

All these payments are taxable in full. For tax purposes, they are treated just like the rest of your pay.

Payments from non-approved retirement schemes

Most pension schemes are approved by the Inland Revenue or statutory schemes, and the lump sums you receive from them are tax-free (within limits). Payments from a non-approved scheme are also tax-free if:
- they arose because of an accident you suffered at work, or
- they were funded by a contribution from your employer on which you have already paid tax, or
- they arose from your own contributions.

If you have any tax-free payments, the total should go in box 1.26. Any taxable payments you receive should be entered in box 1.28.

Other payments
Some payments are tax-free altogether if:
- you get them as a result of accident or chronic illness which meant that you couldn't do your job (or they are payments to your family because of your death)
- 75 per cent of your service in the job was foreign service, or if you worked abroad for least ten out of the last 20 years (and 50 per cent of your time in the job, if longer than 20 years). If you can't meet these conditions, you may still get some relief – see Help Sheet *IR204 Lump sums and compensation payments.*

Enter these payments under reliefs in box 1.25.

•	£30,000 exemption	1.24	£

•	Foreign service and disability	1.25	£

•	From box R of *Help Sheet IR204*	1.29	£

The first £30,000 of the following payments are also tax-free:

- redundancy pay (either statutory or at the employer's discretion)
- pay in lieu of notice which is not included in your terms and conditions of employment
- any other payments on leaving a job which were not part of your terms and conditions, and not 'expected' or received as payment for work done.

Enter the first £30,000 (or total received) under reliefs in box 1.24. Anything over £30,000 is taxable and should be entered in box 1.29.

FOREIGN EARNINGS

The broad principle of the UK tax system is that you are taxed on foreign earnings if you are resident or ordinarily resident in this country, even if your permanent home (your domicile) is elsewhere. A full explanation of all these terms is included in Chapter 24. If you think you may be able to claim non-residence you should read that chapter first.

You should include foreign earnings in boxes 1.8 to 1.10 (your employer may already have included foreign earnings in your P60). But if you are a UK resident, or a British citizen, a Crown employee or a citizen of some other countries you can claim personal allowances to set against your income. You may also be able to claim deductions in boxes 1.31, 1.37 and 1.38 which make the possibility of tax on foreign earnings a less fearsome prospect.

Foreign earnings not taxable in the UK

■	*Foreign earnings not taxable in the UK in year ended 5 April 2000* - see Notes, page EN6	1.31 £

In some cases, foreign earnings can be free of UK tax if:

- you were prevented from bringing the earnings into the UK by law, government action, or shortage of foreign currency in the country where they were earned, or
- you are resident but not ordinarily resident in the UK, or

- you are resident and ordinarily resident, but not domiciled in the UK, and the job is carried out wholly outside the country (except for incidental duties such as attending a directors' meeting in the UK).

This is called the remittance basis. You may be able to claim a deduction on these grounds even if you were non-resident for only part of the year, or if you have included in your tax return income for a different year (for example, if you have only just been able to bring into this country income earned in an earlier year). Help Sheet *IR211 Employment – Residence and Domicile issues* helps you through the calculations to see how much you should enter in box 1.31.

Foreign earnings deduction

The foreign earnings deduction can only be claimed for the tax year ending 5 April 2000 by seafarers. You can get information on this from Help Sheet *IR205(S) Foreign Earnings Deduction: Seafarers*.

Foreign tax

If you work abroad, you may be liable to two lots of tax: tax charged by the country in which you earn the money and UK tax. You have two options for avoiding this double taxation:

- claiming tax credit relief (if you are a UK resident)
- deducting the foreign tax from your foreign earnings.

Because tax credit relief can wipe out all or part of the foreign tax, it is usually the best option, but it is not always available. There are various Inland Revenue working sheets which may help you decide which is the best option for you (see Chapter 21 for more details). If you decide to claim tax credit relief, leave box 1.38 blank and complete the Foreign supplementary page. Otherwise, enter the amount of foreign tax in box 1.38.

EXPENSES INCURRED IN DOING YOUR JOB

You should already have entered all the expenses payments and allowances you received in box 1.23. However, not all these expenses will be taxable, and there may be expenses for which you were not reimbursed and on which you can claim tax relief. So you should enter all your tax-allowable expenses, whether or not you were reimbursed, in boxes 1.32 to 1.36.

The only exception is expenses for which your employer has a dispensation (see p. 202). These should not be entered anywhere on your tax return, unless your allowable expenses came to more than the amount covered by the dispensation (in which case you should enter the extra). Your employer should be able to tell you what dispensations exist.

The overall rule is that only those expenses which are expended wholly, exclusively and necessarily in doing your job are allowable, except for travel and related meal and accommodation expenses, which must be necessarily incurred. In both cases, necessarily means that it would be necessary for anybody doing the job, not just necessary for you.

There is no neat list of definitions in tax law, and much depends on previous court judgements. In practice, a lot comes down to agreement with your tax inspector and you should keep all the evidence you have (receipts, mileage details and so on) to back up your claims. However, the main tax-allowable expenses are listed below.

Travel and subsistence costs

. Travel and subsistence costs £

These include:

- business travel costs, for example fares. If you use your own car for work, the taxable amount of any mileage allowance should already have been entered in box 1.15. However, if you do not get a mileage allowance, or your mileage allowance does not cover the full cost of your business travel, you can enter the costs you bear here. You can claim either the exact amount of your expenses in line with your business mileage (method 1 on p. 89) or a fixed number of pence per mile (method 2 on p. 89). You may also be able to claim capital allowances on the cost of the car, but enter these in box 1.35, not here
- meals and accommodation costs (subsistence) incurred in making the journey
- other business expenses arising because of the journey, for example telephone costs. You cannot deduct personal expenses, such as phone calls home, daily newspapers and personal laundry – but in practice, you may

not have had to include these in box 1.23 in any case, since small amounts of personal expenses are tax-free (see p. 84).

The tax treatment of business travel changed from 6 April 1998 onwards. You can claim the full cost of travelling you are required to incur in the performance of your duties (travel 'on the job'), or travelling to or from a place that you have to attend for your job – so long as attendance is a requirement of your duties, rather than just a matter of personal convenience. You cannot claim the costs of ordinary commuting or private travel.

TAX-SAVING IDEA

If your journey counts as business travel, don't forget to include the cost of any meals and accommodation which are attributable to the journey (other than the usual expenses you incur when at your normal place of work).

Ordinary commuting is defined as travel between your home and your permanent workplace. A workplace counts as 'temporary' if you go there for a limited duration or for a temporary purpose, but it loses its temporary status if you spend at least 40 per cent of your working time there over a period which lasts (or is likely to last) for more than 24 months. You do not need to have, or return to, a permanent workplace.

The rules can be interpreted in a number of different ways depending on the facts of the case. If you are unsure what you can claim, the Inland Revenue guide *Employee Travel – a Tax and NICs Guide for Employers* (to which your employer should have access) gives the full rules and useful examples.

Add together all the allowable travel costs incurred, including the excess of your mileage allowance (see previous page), the accommodation and meal costs on business journeys and any other expenses of business journeys (such as busness phone calls, but not personal items like phone calls home). Enter the total in box 1.32. If this box includes expenses of travelling between home and a permanent workplace, tick box 1.36.

Fixed deductions for expenses

• Fixed deductions for expenses	1.33 £

The Inland Revenue has agreed flat-rate expenses with various trade unions and other bodies to cover the costs of providing equipment and special clothing which is not provided by employers. For example, carpenters and joiners in the building trade can claim a flat-rate £105, uniformed bank employees can claim £40. Ask your union or other staff body if you are covered. You do not have to claim the flat-rate deduction – if you spend more, you can claim more, but if so, you should enter the amount in box 1.35, under other expenses, not here.

Professional fees and subscriptions

| • Professional fees and subscriptions | 1.34 £ |

You may pay for membership of a particular body or society which is relevant to your work. You can claim it in box 1.34 as an allowable expense provided that:

- membership of the organisation, or registration with it, is a condition of your job, for example, as a dentist, optician or solicitor
- the organisation is approved by the Revenue as being a non-profit body which exists for a worthy purpose such as to maintain professional standards, and membership is relevant to your work.

Any such organisation should be able to tell you whether it is on the Revenue's list of approved bodies.

Other expenses and capital allowances

| • Other expenses and capital allowances | 1.35 £ |

These must be wholly, necessarily and exclusively incurred for work. This means that you cannot claim expenses which merely put you in a position to do your job – for example, a journalist's expenditure on newspapers, employment agency fees, childcare. There are special rules for business entertaining – check with your employer whether these affect you. The expenses you should be allowed are:

- the costs of providing and maintaining tools and special clothing which you have not already claimed a fixed deduction for in box 1.33. Special clothing does not cover clothes which you could wear outside work, even if you would never choose to do so
- the cost of special security needed because of your job – you can claim this only if your employer paid for the security or reimbursed you, and you have already entered the appropriate amount as a benefit
- costs and expenses if you are held liable for some wrongful act as an employee, or insurance premiums to cover you against such costs
- training expenses for which you are not reimbursed, providing that your employer requires or encourages you to attend the course and gives you paid time off to do so, it is full-time (or virtually so) and lasts for at least

four weeks. The expenses allowed are fees (unless you have already had tax relief on these) and the cost of essential books. You may also be able to claim some accommodation or travel costs if you count as being temporarily absent from your normal workplace (see p. 212)

- if you are required to work at home (and do not do so merely from choice) a proportion of the heating and lighting costs, and, for a room used exclusively for work, council tax.

You may also be able to claim capital allowances in this section if:

- you buy equipment such as a computer which is necessary (as defined on p. 211) for your job. You cannot claim an allowance if your employer would have provided the equipment had you not chosen to do so
- you buy a car or other vehicle for use in your job. This does not have to be necessary (as defined on p. 211) and what's more, if you can claim allowances, you can also claim the interest on any loan to buy the car. However, you can claim only the proportion of your capital allowance and loan interest that arises from your use of the car for work.

When you finally dispose of an asset on which you claimed capital allowances there may be a balancing charge to add to your taxable income. (See Chapter 18 for how to work these out).

SHARE SCHEMES

 Did you have any taxable income from share options, shares (but this does not include dividends - they go in Question 10) or share related benefits in the year? NO ☐ YES ☐ SHARE SCHEMES YES ☐

Part of your payment from a job may come in the form of shares (or share options – the right to buy shares at a set price at some point in the future) in your employer's company. However, there are special approved schemes under which you can get your shares or options tax-free. You only have to tick the YES box and complete this supplementary page if your shares or share options are not received through an approved scheme, or if you are in a scheme but breach its rules in some respect. You have to complete the back of the supplementary page before the front and you need to fill in a separate page 2 (or a photocopy) for each taxable event arising from a share scheme.

The benefit you get from share schemes may come in the following forms:
- a gift of the shares themselves, or a discount on the purchase price
- an option to buy a set number of shares, at a set price, at a particular time in the future
- dividends from the shares once they become your property
- a capital gain (or loss) arising from movements in the share price once the shares become your property.

The share dividends are taxed like the dividends from any share you own and you enter them at Q10 of the basic tax return (see Chapter 13). The same is broadly true for the capital gains, except that some special rules may apply, for example when deciding what allowable expenditure can be deducted (see p. 217). You give details of capital gains on the Capital gains supplementary pages. The Share scheme supplementary pages apply only on the gift (or discounted purchase) of the shares themselves, or an option to buy them, and to any associated advantages. Occasionally, with some unapproved schemes, they may also apply when you sell the shares themselves.

DIFFERENT TYPES OF SHARE SCHEMES

For tax purposes, share schemes fall within three broad categories:

- approved profit-sharing schemes
- share option schemes – either approved savings-related schemes or discretionary share option schemes (that is, company share option plans and executive share option schemes), or unapproved schemes
- cheap or free gifts of shares through an unapproved scheme (sometimes called share incentive schemes).

You may have come across Employee Share Ownership Trusts (ESOTs) – these are a special type of trust set up to acquire shares in the company and distribute them to employees. For the employee, the shares are taxable in the same way as shares received through an unapproved scheme.

The government has announced plans to introduce a new employee share scheme under which employers can give shares tax-free to employees and employees can use part of their before-tax pay to buy shares. The scheme is expected to be available from 6 April 2000.

> **TAX-SAVING IDEA**
>
> As an employee, you do not often have a choice of scheme, since employers are likely either to have just one scheme, or to have one scheme that is open to all employees and another which is open to a select few. But if you know that your employer is considering a scheme, try to make your voice heard so that the scheme which is chosen is one which suits you.

If you received shares or share options which are taxable in the tax year ending 5 April 2000, you will need to declare them on the Share schemes supplementary page, unless they have already been taxed under PAYE or have been included on Form P11D. If under PAYE, you should put the taxable value of the benefit in box 1.8 of the Employment page, and the tax in box 1.11. If on Form P11D, the taxable value goes in box 1.22.

The documents you need

You should have some correspondence from your employer concerning your scheme, including (where relevant) a share option certificate and a copy of the exercise note. You will also need to know the market price of the shares at various dates – if your employer cannot help, ask your local reference library. If the company is not quoted on the Stock Exchange, the market value has to be agreed with the Inland Revenue.

Approved profit-sharing schemes

These are a way of transferring free shares in a company to its employees via a special trust. As long as you stick to the rules, shares you receive under an approved profit-sharing scheme will be tax-free and you will not need to enter them on the Share scheme pages.

The shares will be taxable only if you sell them within three years of being allocated them. However, there is an exception if the shares are sold before the three years are up and the job ended because of an injury, disability, redundancy or death or reaching a specified age (between 60 and 75). In this case, tax is due on only 50 per cent of the market value of the shares when allocated.

Working out the tax

If tax is due, the taxable value is the lesser of:

- the initial market value of the shares at the date when they were allocated to you (occasionally, an earlier date may be used) or
- the actual proceeds of selling them, minus your expenses of selling, for example, stockbrokers' commission. If you give them away, the market value at the time of the gift will be used.

Your employer should work out the taxable value for you and deduct the right amount of tax before passing on the proceeds. If you have left the company, the trustees will work out the taxable value and deduct basic-rate tax: enter the taxable amount at box 1.8 and the amount deducted at box 1.11 in the Employment supplementary page. For more information, see Inland Revenue leaflet IR95.

Share option schemes

There are three key events in the life of an option:

- when you are first granted the option
- when you exercise your right to buy (you may decide not to)
- if you cancel the option in return for some benefit.

If you receive your options through an approved scheme, you will never have to pay tax on the grant of the option. You have tax to pay on the exercise of the option only if you fail to meet various conditions. But you will always be taxed if you agree not to use your option in return for some benefit.

> **TAX-SAVING IDEA**
> When you take your shares out of an approved profit-sharing scheme or savings-related share option scheme, you can transfer them into an ISA plan (see p. 76), providing you do so within 90 days.

To work out the taxable amount (if any), you need to keep records of:

- the date on which each key event takes place
- the number of shares involved
- the share price – both the price you actually have to pay, and the market value at the time of each event
- any cash you contributed for the option, or any cash (or other benefit) you received for cancelling it.

You have to give this information on page 2 of the Share Schemes supplementary pages for each occasion on which your options are taxable (photocopy the form if necessary or ask the Orderline – see p. 139 – for extra copies).

Approved savings-related share options

Share options					
Read the Notes, pages SN1 to SN5 **before** filling in the boxes					
■ *Approved savings-related share options*				Tick if shares unlisted	
		Name of company and share scheme			Taxable amount
• Exercise	2.1		2.2		2.3 £
• Cancellation or release	2.4		2.5		2.6 £

These schemes give you the right (or 'option') to buy a set number of ordinary shares in your employer's company at some point in the future, at a price fixed now, but you must do so using savings in a Save-As-You-Earn (SAYE) plan. If you meet the various conditions laid down by the Revenue, you will get your shares tax-free (see Inland Revenue leaflet IR97).

Among other conditions you must agree to:

- save a set amount each month, with a minimum of £5 a month and a maximum of £250
- save for a set period – three years, five years or seven years (the three-year option applies only if you join the scheme on or after 30 April 1996).

The price of the shares (the subscription price) is fixed when you are granted the option, but cannot normally be less than 80 per cent of their market value at that time (or up to 30 days before). So if, for example, shares in Horridges' plc stand at 400 pence, the lowest subscription price is 320 pence. You have no tax to pay when the option is granted to you. You will not have tax to pay when the option is used unless:

- you exercise your option when your company is taken over or sold, and you have not yet had them for three years. In this case, fill in the Exercise column on page 2 of the Share schemes supplementary page (boxes 2.32 to 2.40) and carry the taxable amount to boxes 2.1 to 2.3 on page 1 (see p. 222 for the calculation)

- you benefit from the option in any way other than using it to buy shares – for example, if you receive compensation for not using or agreeing not to use your option. Fill in the Cancellation/release column on page 2 (boxes 2.34, 2.38 and 2.41) and then carry the taxable amount to boxes 2.4 to 2.6 on page 1.

Approved discretionary share options

■ *Approved discretionary share options*				
	Name of company and share scheme			
• Exercise	2.7	2.8	2.9	£
• Cancellation or release	2.10	2.11	2.12	£

Discretionary schemes may be restricted to groups of employees. Their original name was executive share option schemes, replaced in 1995 by company share option schemes. Broadly, options received under both these schemes are tax-free as long as you exercise them within strict time limits (see below).

Unlike savings-related share option schemes, the price at which you can buy the shares under your option must not be less than the market value of the shares when the option is granted (or up to 30 days before). However, you may have been granted a discount of up to 15 per cent of the market value if you:

- were granted options in an Executive Share Option Scheme after 1 January 1992 and before 17 July 1995, and
- your company already had an approved savings-related share option scheme or approved profit-sharing scheme.

If you did receive a discounted option after those dates, this becomes an unapproved share option and you will be taxed on the grant of the option, as well as when it is exercised.

> ## TAX-SAVING IDEA
> Whether or not you will benefit from a savings-related share option scheme depends on the option price and the share price when you exercise your option.
>
> You do not have to exercise your option if you would make a loss and the return on SAYE schemes is tax-free. So if you are a higher rate taxpayer, or are optimistic that you will make some profit on the shares, joining the scheme is worthwhile.

You only have to pay tax on other options if:

- you give up the right to exercise the option in return for some benefit, or
- the scheme had ceased to be approved by the time you exercised your options, or
- you exercise the option within three years of being granted it, or
- you exercise the option more than 10 years after being granted it, or
- it is less than three years since you last exercised an option

under *any* Executive Share Option Scheme or Company Share Option Scheme (other than SAYE).

If the first point applies, fill in the Cancellation/release column on page 2 of the Share schemes supplementary page (boxes 2.34, 2.38 and 2.41) and then fill in boxes 2.10 to 2.12 on page 1. If any of the other conditions apply, fill in the Exercise column on page 2 (boxes 2.34 to 2.40) and then fill in boxes 2.7 to 2.9 on page 1.

Unapproved share options

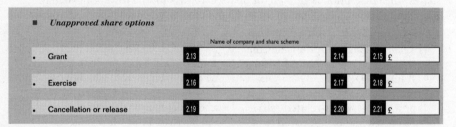

With unapproved schemes, income tax may be payable on both the grant and exercise of an option, or if it is given up in return for some benefit. However, there is no income tax to pay if the option is exercised by your legal representatives after your death, or if the option is not a long option.

A long option is one which can be exercised more than seven years after the date on which it was granted. You pay tax at the time it is granted on the market value of the shares at that time, less the price at which you can exercise the option, less anything you pay for the option. So there will be no tax to pay if the option is to buy shares at the market value at the time the option was granted. You may have further tax to pay when you finally exercise the option, but you can set against the tax due any income tax you paid when the option was granted.

An option which must be exercised within seven years is not taxable at the time it is granted (except for some non-residents).

How to work out the taxable amount

Whatever type of share option scheme you have, and whether it is approved or unapproved, if the event (the grant, exercise or cancellation) is taxable, the taxable amount is worked out as in the box on the right. You enter the amounts in the right-hand column of page 1 headed Taxable amount.

EXAMPLE

In 1991 Edward Brough is granted an option which can be exercised at any time between 1 January 1996 and 1 January 2001. This counts as a long option, so he had to pay tax when it was granted. The market value of the shares in 1991 was £3. Edward has the option to buy 1,000 shares at £2. The market value of the shares over which he has the option is £3 x 1,000 = £3,000: he has the option to buy them at £2 x 1,000 = £2,000. The taxable amount is £3,000 – £2,000 = £1,000. As a higher-rate taxpayer, Edward paid £1,000 x 40 per cent = £400 tax on this.

In October 1999 Edward exercised his option. This cost him £2 x 1,000 = £2,000. Since the market price had risen to £3.50, the market value of the shares was £3.50 x 1,000 = £3,500. The taxable amount is £3,500 – £2,000 = £1,500, incurring tax at £1,500 x 40 per cent = £600. However, Edward can set against this the tax he has already paid, so he only actually has to pay £600 – £400 = £200.

Free or cheap shares through an unapproved scheme

Employers have many reasons for offering cheap or free shares. These count as part of your payment from the job. The exact tax treatment depends on whether the shares are counted as your earnings (and entered under Shares acquired from your employment in boxes 2.22 to 2.24), or treated as a fringe benefit (and entered under Shares as benefits in boxes 2.25 to 2.27), unless these have already been shown under Earnings from employment.

TAX ON THE EXERCISE OF AN OPTION

Step 1: take the market value of the share at the date the option was exercised (which you should have entered in box 2.40) and multiply by the number of shares you actually bought (entered at box 2.36). This gives you the market value of all the shares you have bought.

Step 2: take the price at which you exercised the option (in box 2.37) and multiply by the number of shares you bought (at box 2.36). This is the actual price.

Step 3: deduct the actual price (at Step 2) from the market value (at Step 1). If you paid anything for the option, you can deduct that too. The result is the taxable amount to enter on page 1 of the Share schemes supplementary page in box 2.3, 2.9, or 2.18 as appropriate.

The grant of an option

This is taxable only for an unapproved share option which can be exercised more than seven years after it was granted. The method is the same as if you were exercising the option, except that you start with the market value at the time the option is granted. Fill in the Grant column on page 2 of the Share schemes supplementary page and carry the taxable amount to box 2.15 on page 1.

The cancellation of an option

If you get anything in return for not exercising your option, the taxable amount is what you received, less anything you paid for your option. Fill in the Cancellation column on page 2, and boxes 2.19 to 2.21.

The distinction is fine, but significant: whereas with shares which count as earnings you are taxed on the difference between the market value of the shares and the price at which you acquired them, with shares which count as benefits you are taxed as if you received an interest-free loan from your employer (see p. 96). In some circumstances, this may mean no tax to pay.

You should enter under Shares as benefits (see right):

- shares you are allowed to pay for in instalments (partly-paid shares)
- shares which you buy but where part of the purchase price is deferred, for example, when a particular profit target is met
- any other exceptional cases in which cheap or free shares do not count as earnings.

All other free or cheap shares should go under Shares acquired from your employment (see opposite above). Even after you have acquired the shares, you may be considered to receive further taxable benefits from them, for example, an increase in their value when a restriction is lifted. You should enter these under Post acquisition charges in boxes 2.28 to 2.30.

Shares acquired from your employment

You may get some benefit tax-free if the company for which you work decides to sell shares to the public and offers shares on special terms to its employees. You have to distinguish between:

• a discounted price offered to employees
• a priority allocation of the shares.

The discounted price is taxable: you pay tax on the difference between the price you pay and that paid by the general public. Enter the taxable amount under Shares acquired from your employment. However, the benefit of the priority allocation itself is tax-free and need not be entered unless:

• it is reserved for directors or higher-paid employees, or those who are entitled to it do not all get it on similar terms, and
• the shares reserved for employees in their priority allocation are more than a certain percentage of the overall shares on offer – normally, more than 10 per cent of the total shares on offer.

The calculation is very straightforward. Take the market value of the shares at the time you acquired them. Deduct anything you paid for them. The result is the taxable amount.

Example

Linden works for Good Holdings, which has just been offered for sale to the public. Using the priority allocation for employees, Linden bought 500 £1 shares, at the discounted staff price of 80p. Linden is not taxed on the benefit of the priority allocation. However, the discounted price is taxable. The market value of the 500 shares was £1 x 500 = £500, but Linden only paid 80p x 500 = £400. She is taxed on £500 – £400 = £100.

Shares as benefits

Anything entered under this category is treated as an interest-free loan. The loan is the difference between what you paid and the market value. The loan is taxable only if:

- you count as earning at a rate of £8,500 or more or are a director (see p. 86 for how this is worked out)
- the total amount of all the cheap or interest-free loans from your employer outstanding in the tax year comes to more than £5,000 (see p. 96).

If tax is payable, it will be spread out over the whole life of the loan.

The taxable value of the loan is the theoretical interest you would have paid had you been charged interest at an official rate set down by the government.

Post-acquisition charges or lifting of risk of forfeiture

• Post-acquisition charges or lifting of risk of forfeiture	2.28	2.29	2.30 £

You are charged tax on any further benefit from cheap or free shares. This applies even if you have since left the company. There is no charge if the shares were on offer to the public generally (and you did not buy them through a special offer for employees). Otherwise, you may have further tax to pay on:

- an increase in value when rights or restrictions attached to the shares are changed – for example, if you gain the right to dividends
- an increase in value if the shares are in a subsidiary company. Tax is chargeable on the seventh anniversary of acquiring the shares, or when they are sold, if earlier
- other benefits reserved only for insiders (that is, which are not available to at least 90 per cent of all the shareholders), such as bonus or rights issues of shares, cash, vouchers or tokens.

You need to enter these in boxes 2.28 to 2.30 on page 1 of the Share schemes supplementary page, giving the details on page 2.

There are also certain circumstances when you may be taxed if you receive shares which can become forfeit if certain conditions are not met. Ask the Orderline for Help Sheet *IR219: Shares acquired from your employment.*

SELF-EMPLOYMENT

Q3 Were you self-employed (but not in partnership)?
(Tick 'Yes' if you were a Name at Lloyd's)

NO ☐   YES ☐   SELF-EMPLOYMENT YES ☐

If any of your income for the tax year ending 5 April 2000 came from running your own business as a self-employed person, answer YES to Q3 on the basic tax return. You'll need to fill in a separate set of Self-employment supplementary pages for each business you have.

Self-employed people are able to claim more income tax reliefs than employed people and they usually pay less in National Insurance, so you might need to prove to your tax office that you really are self-employed. In general, you'll count as self-employed provided you can answer yes to all of the following questions:

- do you control how your business is run? For example, do you decide what work you take on, where you do the work, what hours you keep?
- is your own money at risk in the business? For example, have you had to pay for your own premises, do you have to finance the lag between incurring costs and receiving payments?
- do you have to meet any losses as well as keeping any profits?
- do you provide the major equipment necessary for your work – for example computer and photocopier for office-based work or machinery for an engineering business? It's not enough that you provide your own small tools – many employees do this too
- are you free to employ other people to help you fulfil the contracts you take on? Do you pay your employees yourself?
- if a job doesn't come up to scratch, do you have to redo it or correct it in your own time and at your expense?

Usually, it will be obvious whether you are an employee or self-employed. But sometimes it's not so clear – for example, if you are newly in business doing work for just one client, perhaps working at a former employer's premises on a freelance basis. Beware if you work through an agency – for example as an agency carer or temporary secretary. Even if you choose whether or not to take on a particular job, you will almost certainly count as an employee rather than self-employed.

If you pay tax and National Insurance as if you are self-employed, but later your tax office decides you are really an employee, you could face a large bill for back taxes, so it is important to get your status straight right from the start. If you're in any doubt, you can ask your tax office for a written decision about your employment status. If you don't agree with the decision, you can appeal.

BUSINESS DETAILS

Business details

Name of business

3.1

Description of business

3.2

Address of business

3.3

- Tick box 3.6 if details in boxes 3.1 or 3.3 have changed since your last Tax Return 3.6

The first part of the supplement simply deals with basic details – the name and nature of your business and the address from which you trade.

Your accounting year

Accounting period - *read the Notes, page SEN2 before filling in these boxes*

Start 3.4 / /

End 3.5 / /

You also need to give the start and finish dates of the accounting period for which you are giving details. Normally, an accounting period is a year long, with the new accounting year starting immediately the previous year ends.

But in the first and last year or two of your business, your accounting year might be longer or shorter (see below).

You may already have given information about your latest set of accounts in last year's return (for example, if your accounting periods overlap). If so, you do not need to give all the information again: you can leave boxes 3.11 to 3.60 and 3.93 to 3.109 blank, but tick box 3.5A (see below). Similarly, if your accounts do not run from the last accounting date, explain why in the Additional information box and tick box 3.7 (see below).

- Tick box 3.5A if you entered details for all relevant accounting periods on last year's Tax Return and boxes 3.11 to 3.70 and 3.93 to 3.109 will be blank (read step 3 on page SEN2) — **3.5A** [ ]

- Tick box 3.6 if details in boxes 3.1 or 3.3 have changed since your last Tax Return — **3.6** [ ]

- Tick box 3.7 if your accounts do not cover the period from the last accounting date (explain why in the 'Additional information' box below) — **3.7** [ ]

- Tick box 3.8A if your accounting date has changed (only if this is a permanent change and you want it to count for tax) — **3.8A** [ ]

- Tick box 3.8B if this is the second or further change (explain why you have not used the same date as last year in the 'Additional information' box) — **3.8B** [ ]

- Date of commencement if after 5 April 1996 — **3.9** [/ /]

- Date of cessation if before 6 April 2000 — **3.10** [/ /]

What profits are taxed

This section of the self-employment pages establishes which profits form the basis of your tax bill for the year ending 5 April 2000, and what information you need to give the Revenue about them. In most cases, your tax bill for the year ending 5 April 2000 will be based on the profits you make during the accounting period which ended during that tax year (the current year basis of taxation).

However, there are special rules if you are in the opening or closing years of the business or, have changed your accounting date.

STARTING OR CLOSING A BUSINESS

If you start a business, special rules say how you will be taxed in the first two or three years.

First tax year during which you're in business

You are taxed on your profits from the date your business started to the end of the tax year (that is the following 5 April). This is worked out by waiting until your first set of accounts is drawn up and then allocating a proportion of those profits to the period up to the end of the tax year. This is usually done on the basis of days. For example, suppose you started in business on 1 January 2000 and your first accounting period runs to 31 January 2001. Out of that first 397-day accounting period, 96 days fall between 1 January to 5 April, so your profits for the tax year ending 5 April 2000 are deemed to be $^{96}/_{397}$ths of the profit for the whole accounting period.

Second tax year during which you're in business

In most cases, the end of an accounting period (not necessarily your first) will fall sometime during this second tax year. Provided you have been trading for at least 12 months, your tax bill will be based on profits for the 12 months up to that date. In the example above, there is an end accounting date falling within the tax year ending 5 April 2001. This is 31 January 2001 and, at that date, the business has been running for more than a year. Therefore, tax will be based on profits for the 12 months up to 31 January 2000 – that is $^{366}/_{397}$ths of the profits for the whole accounting period.

If there is an accounting date within the tax year, but you have been trading for less than 12 months, your tax is based on the first 12 months of trading, with a proportion of the profits from your next accounting period being used to make up the full 12 months. For example, suppose you started in business on 1 March 1999 and draw up your accounts to 30 June 1999 and then to each subsequent 30 June. Tax in your second year, the year ending 5 April 2000, would be based on the whole of the profits for the period 1 March to 30 June 1999 (122 days) and and $^{244}/_{366}$ths of the profits for the accounting year from 1 July 1999 to 30 June 2000.

If there is no accounting date at all during your second tax year, tax is based on the profits for the tax year itself – that is from 6 April to 5 April. For example, if you started in business on 1 March 1999 but did not draw up your first accounts until 30 June 2000, an accounting period of 483 days, you would be taxed on $^{366}/_{483}$rds of the profits for that whole period.

Third tax year during which you're in business

If an accounting period at least 12 months after you started up finished during your second tax year, from the third year onwards, you are simply taxed on the profits for the accounting year ending during the tax year – that is normal current year basis.

Where the first accounting period to end at least 12 months after start-up comes to a close in your third tax year of trading, you are taxed on profits for the 12 months to the end of that period. From the fourth year onwards, you are taxed on the normal current year basis.

Overlap profits

As you can see, the opening year rules described above mean that some profits may be taxed twice. For example, for the business which started on 1 January 2000, the profits for the first two years were as follows:

Tax year	Profits on which your tax bill is based
Year ending 5 April 2000	$^{96}/_{397}$ths x profit for accounting period from 1 January 2000 to 31 January 2001
Year ending 5 April 2001	$^{366}/_{397}$ths x profit for the period from 1 January 2000 to 31 January 2001

This means that (96 + 366) – 397 = 65 days' worth of profit have been taxed twice. This is called 'overlap profit' and the period over which it arose is called the 'overlap period'. One of the principles of the current year basis tax

---

EXAMPLE

Jim Newall started working as a freelance computer consultant on 1 July 1997 and drew up his first accounts on 30 April 1998. 30 April is his normal accounting year end. His profit and tax position for the first few years of business was as follows:

Accounting period	Profit for the period
1 July 1997 – 30 April 1998	£ 4,000
1 May 1998 – 30 April 1999	£ 8,500
1 May 1999 – 30 April 2000	£18,500

Tax year	Tax basis	Profits on which tax based
1997-98	Profits for tax year	279 ÷ 304 x £4,000 = £3,671
1998-99	First 12 months of trading	£4,000 + (61 ÷ 365 x £8,500) = £5,420
1999-2000	Profits for 12 months to 30 April 1999	£8,500
2000-01	Profits for accounting year ending on 30 April 2000	£18,500

The profit for the period 1 July 1997 to 5 April 1998 is taxed twice, as is profit for the 61 days from 1 May to 30 June 1998. This gives Jim an overlap profit of £3,671 + (61 ÷ 365 x £8,500) = £3,671 + £1,420 = £5,091.

system is that, over the lifetime of your business, all your profits should be taxed, but only taxed once. Therefore, you are given overlap relief to compensate you for having paid tax on some profits twice in your opening year. But there is a snag: overlap relief is usually given only when you finally close the business down (see opposite) and inflation in the meantime will reduce its value.

Fiscal accounting

You can avoid all the problems of opening year rules and overlap relief, if you opt for fiscal accounting. This means using the tax year as your accounting year. By Inland Revenue concession, this includes having an accounting date of 31 March, rather than exactly on the tax year end of 5 April. For example, you might have started in business on 1 September 1999, drawing up your first accounts on 31 March 2000 and on each 31 March thereafter. Your tax for the tax year ending 5 April 2000 will be based on your profits from 1 September 1999 to 31 March 2000. Your tax for the next year will be based on profits for 1 April 2000 to 31 March 2001 and so on.

For further information see Help Sheet *IR222 How to calculate your taxable profits*.

TAX-SAVING IDEAS

Fiscal accounting makes accounting for tax very simple, especially in your opening years, but it has drawbacks too: you don't have long to make up your accounts and there's only a short delay between making your profits and paying tax on them (see left).

If you don't choose fiscal accounting, try to keep your profits as low as possible during the first year or two, so that your overlap profit is small.

Changing your accounting date

Changing your accounting date can bring tax benefits: special rules to determine the profits on which you are taxed can work to your advantage. If you change to a date later in the tax year, you can also use some of the overlap relief you may have acquired so far. But in order to count as a change of accounting date in the Inland Revenue's eyes, all of the following conditions must be satisfied: the first accounting period running up to the new date must not be more than 18 months; you must notify the Revenue in your tax return; and either you must not have made a change of accounting date (effective for tax purposes) in the previous five tax years or, if you have, the Revenue must be satisfied that the latest change is for bona fide commercial reasons.

If you have changed accounting date, you can satisfy the requirement to notify the Revenue by ticking box 3.8A. If you have changed accounting date in previous years, also tick 3.8B and explain your reasons for doing so in the Additional information box at the back of the basic tax return.

Closing your business

In the tax years up to the one before closure, you are taxed on the normal current year basis. For the tax year in which you close down, you're taxed on profits from your last accounting date up to the date on which you close down less any overlap profits which you have been carrying forward (see p. 229). The position for a business closing down in the tax year ending 5 April 2000 is summarised below.

Tax year ending	*Profits on which your tax bill is based*
5 April 1998	Profits for accounting year ending in 1997-98
5 April 1999	Profits for accounting year ending in 1998-99
5 April 2000	Profits from day after end of accounting year ending 1998-1999 up to date of closure less overlap profits

For how to claim relief on these overlap profits, see p. 246.

INCOME

If your turnover is less than £15,000 a year

Complete boxes 3.11 to 3.13. You can get guidance on what expenses are allowable by reading pp. 234 to 240.

You do not need to give full details of your accounts. This does not mean

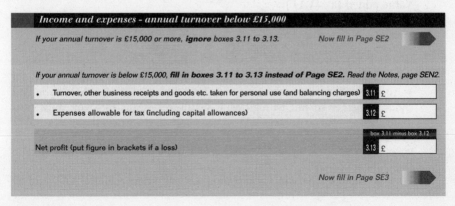

Income and expenses - annual turnover below £15,000

If your annual turnover is £15,000 or more, **ignore** boxes 3.11 to 3.13.   *Now fill in Page SE2*

If your annual turnover is below £15,000, **fill in boxes 3.11 to 3.13 instead of Page SE2.** *Read the Notes, page SEN2.*

| Turnover, other business receipts and goods etc. taken for personal use (and balancing charges) | 3.11 £ |
| Expenses allowable for tax (including capital allowances) | 3.12 £ |

box 3.11 minus box 3.12

| Net profit (put figure in brackets if a loss) | 3.13 £ |

Now fill in Page SE3

that you can get away without preparing proper accounts – you must have these ready, in case your tax inspector asks to see them, together with all the background paperwork (see p. 14). Note that £15,000 is the annual limit – if your accounts cover a period of under a year, it will be reduced proportionately, and increased if you have a longer accounting period.

Do not complete page 2 of the Self-employed supplement, but go straight to page 3. Turn to p. 241 for guidance on filling in boxes 3.61 and beyond.

If your turnover is £15,000 a year or more

You should complete the details asked for on page 2 of the Self-employed supplementary pages. You don't need to attach a copy of your accounts. If the headings do not tally with the headings you use in your own accounts, don't be tempted to leave any out. Instead, use your judgement to allocate them to boxes on page 2, but make sure that whatever method you adopt is the same as last year and next year's, that is it is consistent between years.

If the period over which you are being taxed is covered by two sets of accounts, you need to complete two Self-employment supplements (unless you have already given all the information in last year's tax return).

If you produce a balance sheet, there is space for the entries on page 4 of the supplement. Enter the amounts in boxes 3.93 to 3.109. If you don't have a balance sheet, leave these boxes blank.

Value added tax (VAT)

If your turnover is £51,000 a year or more from 1 April 1999 (£52,000 from 1 April 2000), you must register for VAT. Below that threshold, you can choose whether or not to register. Registration means that you must normally charge your customers VAT on the goods and services that you sell, but you can usually reclaim VAT on the things that you buy to sell, or use, in your business. You must regularly hand over to the Customs & Excise department of the government the net amount of VAT you have collected (or claim a refund if what you are claiming comes to more than the VAT paid by your customers). This VAT does not form part of your profits and needs to be stripped out before your tax bill is calculated. For this reason, the tax office needs to know whether the figures you report in your tax return include VAT or have already had the VAT element stripped out.

If you are registered for VAT, and have entered VAT-inclusive figures, you will need to enter the net amount of VAT paid over to Customs & Excise as other expenses in box 3.50 or the net refund you received over the year as other income/profits in box 3.37. You may have bought capital equipment on which you claim capital allowances (see p. 241) instead of deducting them as expenses. If you are entering VAT-inclusive figures, there won't be an obvious place to enter the VAT on these capital items. You deal with this by adding the VAT to the amount entered in box 3.50 or (if you received a net refund from Customs & Excise) deducting it from the figure entered in box 3.37. Also write in the amount of VAT on capital items in the Additional information box on page 4.

If you are not registered for VAT, you do not charge your customers VAT and the VAT you pay to your suppliers counts as a legitimate business expense. Your figures should include the VAT you have been charged. If you were registered for VAT for part of the year, but not for all, explain why, when the change occurred, and whether your figures are VAT-inclusive or not, in the Additional information box on page 4.

Gross profits

Your taxable profits are the income of your business less all the allowable expenses – that is the expenses you are allowed to deduct under the tax rules.

The starting point for working out your taxable profits is your gross profits. If you are in the business of selling something, this will be the income you get from sales less the cost of buying in the items you sell. If you sell your services, this will be the income you receive. For more information on how to take stock and work in progress into account, see Help Sheet *IR222 How to calculate your taxable profits.*

In your accounts, direct costs (for example, marketing, sales discounts) might include a figure for depreciation of equipment or machinery used in producing your goods. This is not an allowable expense (see Capital allowances on p. 241) and should be entered in box 3.19.

Other income or profits (box 3.37) includes things like income from renting out premises, interest on bank and building society accounts, discounts you get, and so on. If you receive any Business Start-up Allowance, put this in box 3.87, not here.

EXPENSES

You don't need to complete page 2 of the Self-employment supplement if your annual turnover is less than £15,000. If it is £15,000 or more, you need to allocate your costs and expenses to boxes 3.17 to 3.50. In the boxes in the right-hand column you should enter total expenses under each heading. In the left-hand column you should enter the amount of any expenses not allowed but which have been included in the right-hand column.

You total the amounts in boxes 3.17 to 3.32 and enter the total in box 3.53.

Deducting an expense from your business income has the effect of giving you tax relief at your top rate(s) of tax, so it is important to claim all the expenses you can. According to tax law, you get tax relief on an expense only if it is incurred wholly and exclusively for business. Strictly speaking, this means you can't get relief at all on expenditure which is partly for your private benefit. In practice, the Inland Revenue does allow you to claim a proportion of some costs where something – for example, your car or home – is used partly for business. However, your tax office may baulk at some expenses which arise because of a joint business and private purpose – for example, combining a trip abroad to see a client with a holiday.

It is hard to lay down hard and fast rules which apply to all businesses. Different types of businesses can claim different expenses and to a different extent. It is up to you to show that any claim is justified within the context of your own line of work.

You can claim expenses you incur before you open for business if they would have been allowable anyway. Treat them as expenditure incurred on the first day of business.

TAX-SAVING IDEAS

Claim all the allowable expenses you can. If you're not sure whether an expense is allowable, deduct it from your taxable profits but ask your tax office to confirm whether this is correct.

If you work from home, beware of allowing any part of it to be used exclusively for business. Although you might be able to claim more relief against income tax, you could become liable for business rates and, when you eventually come to sell the home, there could be capital gains tax to pay on part of the home (see p. 58).

Expenses which you incur after you close down can be set against any late income which comes into the closed business. However, if there is no income, tax relief on the expenditure is usually lost. With a few particular types of expense, you can get tax relief by setting the expenses against any other income or gains you have for up to seven years (in box 15.11 of the basic tax return, see p. 185).

Employee costs

| Employee costs | 3.20 £ | 3.38 £ |

Normally allowed
Salaries, bonuses, overtime, commissions etc paid to your employees, together with the add-on costs, such as National Insurance contributions, pension and insurance benefits. The costs of hiring locums to stand in for you or fees paid to people to whom you subcontract work. Training. Council tax paid on behalf of employees if a genuine part of the pay package, taxed as normal through PAYE. Include the cost of employing your wife, husband or other family member in the business, provided their pay is reasonable for the work done. Costs of entertaining staff – for example, a Christmas party.

Not allowed
Your own wages, National Insurance, income tax, pension costs (though you

can get personal tax relief for these), your drawings from the business. Wages to employees which remain unpaid nine months after the accounting date (although they can be deducted in the accounting period in which they are eventually paid). Payments to family members if excessive for the work done – be especially careful employing young children which might, in any case, be illegal.

Premises costs

Normally allowed
If you work from dedicated business premises, include any rent, business rates, water rates, cost of lighting, heating, power, insurance, cleaning, security, and so on. If you work from home, you can claim a proportion of your

---

E X A M P L E

Hannah Brown has converted the garage at her home into an office which is used exclusively for her computer software business. She can claim part of her household expenses as allowable expenses for business purposes and, because she uses part of the home exclusively for business, she can also claim part of her mortgage interest. She makes the following calculation:

add up total household expenses	£1,800
add up the number of rooms in the house, ignoring separate toilets, halls and landings (unless large enough to be used as rooms)	8 rooms
divide the expenses by the number of rooms to give a cost per room figure	£1,800 ÷ 8 = £225 per room
multiply the cost per room by the number of rooms used for business (or by the relevant fraction of a room, if a room is used only partly for business)	1 × £225 = £225

She also claims one-eighth of her mortgage interest as a business expense. This comes to $\frac{1}{8}$ × £3,600 = £450. However, Hannah may become liable for business rates and, when she sells her home, capital gains tax on the garage.

---

home related expenses – for example, heating, lighting, power, cleaning, maintenance. If part of the home is used exclusively for business, part of your mortgage interest. Also part of your council tax, though the tax rules are not clear on whether it's enough just to work from home or whether part of it must be dedicated exclusively to business use. The proportion you claim must relate to your business use of the home – for example, based on the number of rooms used or floor area. You should explain the basis used in the Additional information box on page 4 of the supplement.

Not allowed
Cost of buying premises (see Capital allowances on p. 241), costs relating to any part of the premises not used for business.

Repairs

| . Repairs | 3.22 £ | 3.40 £ |

Normally allowed
General maintenance and repairs to your business premises and machinery, cost of replacing small tools.

Not allowed
Costs of alterations and improvements (see Capital allowances on p. 241), costs relating to any part of the premises not used for business, general reserve for repairs.

General administrative expenses

| . General administrative expenses | 3.23 £ | 3.41 £ |

Normally allowed
Office expenses, such as postage, telephone, stationery, printing, subscriptions to trade journals, professional fees, accountancy and audit fees and regular expenses not included elsewhere. You can claim the cost of computer software where you pay a regular licence fee to use it or where the software has a limited lifetime (generally taken to be less than two years). In most other cases, software costs count as capital expenditure for which you can claim capital allowances (see p. 241).

Not allowed
Personal expenses, payments to political parties, most donations and fees to

clubs, charities and churches. Any non-business part of a cost.

Motor expenses

• Motor expenses	3.24 £	3.42 £

Normally allowed
Costs of running a vehicle used in your business – for example, insurance, servicing, repairs, road tax, breakdown insurance, parking charges, fuel, hiring or leasing charges. A proportion of those costs if you also use the vehicle privately.

Not allowed
Travel between your home and business premises. Cost of buying a vehicle (see Capital allowances on p. 241). Parking fines, other fines.

Travel and subsistence

• Travel and subsistence	3.25 £	3.43 £

Normally allowed
Rail, air and taxi fares, hotel accommodation.

Not allowed
Cost of lunches.

Advertising, promotion and entertainment

• Advertising, promotion and entertainment	3.26 £	3.44 £

Normally allowed
Advertising, mail-shots, free samples, gifts up to £10 a year to clients provided they promote your firm or its products or services and are not food or drink.

Not allowed
Entertaining clients, business associates etc (only entertaining staff within certain limits is allowed), gifts except those specifically allowed (see above).

Legal and professional costs

• Legal and professional costs	3.27 £	3.45 £

Normally allowed
Fees charged by accountants, auditors, solicitors, surveyors, stocktakers and so on, professional indemnity premiums.

Not allowed
Legal costs of buying premises, equipment etc (treated as part of their cost – see Capital allowances on p. 241), legal expenses on forming a company, cost of settling tax disputes, fines etc as a result of acting illegally.

Bad debts

• Bad debts	3.28 £	3.46 £

Normally allowed
Items you have sold or amounts you have invoiced but for which you no longer expect to be paid. A proportion of a bad debt given up under a voluntary arrangement. If in a later tax year you are paid, include the amount recovered in box 3.37 (other income/profits).

Not allowed
General pool for bad debts.

Interest

• Interest	3.29 £	3.47 £

Normally allowed
Interest and arrangement fees for a business loan or overdraft.

Not allowed
The part of loan payments which represents capital repayments.

Other finance charges

Normally allowed
Charges on your business current account, credit card interest and fees, the interest element of hire purchase charges, leasing payments.

Not allowed
The part of any payment which represents capital repayment.

Depreciation and loss/(profit) on sale

Not allowed
None of these costs are allowable – instead you claim capital allowances (see opposite). The figure you enter at 3.49 should exactly match the amount you put in box 3.31 – unless some of the costs relate to finance leases, in which case ask your tax office what you can deduct.

Other expenses

Normally allowed
Any expenses which you haven't found a place for in boxes 3.33 to 3.49. For example, any insurance premiums not included elsewhere, contributions (up to 30 March 2000) to Business Links, trade and part or all of professional subscriptions which secure some benefit for your business or to societies which have an arrangement with the Inland Revenue.

Not allowed
The non-business element of any expenses included in box 3.50. This includes, for example, ordinary clothing even if you bought it specially for business and would not normally wear it otherwise, buying a patent (see Capital allowances opposite), cost of computer hardware and any software costs not claimed in box 3.41 (see Capital allowances opposite).

Tax adjustments to net profit or loss

Tax adjustments to net profit or loss

		total of boxes 3.17 to 3.32	
•	Disallowable expenses	3.53 £	
•	Goods etc. taken for personal use and other adjustments (apart from disallowable expenses) that increase profits	3.54 £	
•	Balancing charges	3.55 £	boxes 3.53 + 3.54 + 3.55
	Total additions to net profit (deduct from net loss)		3.56 £
•	Capital allowances	3.57 £	boxes 3.57 + 3.58
•	Deductions from net profit (add to net loss)	3.58 £	3.59 £
	Net business profit for tax purposes (put figure in brackets if a loss)	boxes 3.52 + 3.56 minus box 3.59	3.60 £

All the expenses which are not allowable are added together and the total entered in box 3.53. In the next box, you must enter the profit attributable to any goods which you took for personal use. These are added to your profits.

CAPITAL ALLOWANCES

		Capital allowances	Balancing charge
•	**Motor cars** (Separate calculations must be made for each motor car costing more than £12,000 and for cars used partly for private motoring.)	3.61 £	3.62 £
•	Other business plant and machinery	3.63 £	3.64 £
•	**Agricultural or Industrial Buildings Allowance** (A separate calculation must be made for each block of expenditure.)	3.65 £	3.66 £
•	Other capital allowances claimed (Separate calculations must be made.)	3.67 £	3.68 £
		total of column above	total of column above
	Total capital allowances/balancing charges	3.69 £	3.70 £

When you buy capital items for your business – that is things which will be in use for many years – you are not allowed to set the full cost against your business income in the year you buy the item. In your ordinary business accounts, you'll deduct depreciation each year which varies from business to business and is not allowed as an expense. Instead you deduct capital allowances calculated according to standard rules.

To be eligible for capital allowances, the item you have bought must generally be wholly and exclusively for business use. But, as with allowable expenses (see p. 234), in some cases, you can claim a proportion of the allowance if the item is used partly for business and, in part, privately.

How much you can claim

The basic capital allowance is called a writing-down allowance and it is available for plant and machinery (which covers most of your ordinary business equipment), cars and vans, patents and know-how. In general, capital allowances are not given for what you spend on buying business premises (for example a shop or office), but industrial and agricultural buildings and some hotels with ten or more bedrooms are exceptions. Expenditure which qualifies for allowances is lumped together in one or more pools and you can claim a certain proportion of the pool at the end of each tax year as a writing down allowance.

The maximum you can claim is:

- 25 per cent a year for machinery, plant, vans, patents, know-how (for small and medium-size businesses there is an initial allowance of 50 per cent for expenditure incurred between 2 July 1997 and 1 July 1998, inclusive, and 40 per cent after that date up to 1 July 2000)
- 25 per cent a year for cars but, for any car costing over £12,000, there is also a cash limit of £3,000 a year
- 4 per cent a year for industrial and agricultural buildings and qualifying hotels, and an initial allowance in the first year of 100

> **TAX-SAVING IDEA**
> An initial allowance of 40 per cent is available to small and medium-sized businesses buying machinery or plant (excluding cars) for expenditure before 2 July 2000.

per cent for industrial buildings in an enterprise zone. If part of this is not claimed, you can claim 25 per cent a year of the remaining cost.

You can claim less than the maximum. It would be worth restricting your claim if your taxable profits or income were so low that some of the maximum allowance would be wasted. The allowance is not lost. The effect is to carry forward a higher value of assets in your pool of expenditure. This increases the value of the maximum writing-down allowances you can claim in future years. For example, suppose your pool of expenditure is valued at £10,000. If you claimed the full writing-down allowance of 25 per cent, the allowance would be £2,500 and the value of the pool carried forward would be £7,500, so next year you could claim up to 25 per cent x £7,500 = £1,875. If instead, you claimed only a 10 per cent allowance in the first year, the pool carried forward would be £9,000 and the maximum allowance in the second year would be 25 per cent x £9,000 = £2,250.

Various categories of capital expenditure have to be allocated to their own separate pools. These are:

- any car costing more than £12,000 must be hived off to its own pool and the writing-down allowance is limited to the smaller of 25 per cent or £3,000 in each year. Cars costing £12,000 or less are in another pool. Vans, lorries and so on do not count as cars
- industrial and agricultural buildings
- an asset used partly for private use must have its own pool and you can claim only a proportion of the allowance reflecting the proportion of business use
- short-life assets. Capital equipment (other than cars) which you expect to have a useful life of no more than five years can be put in a separate pool. The advantage of doing this is that you get tax relief on the full cost of the item more rapidly than if it were in the general pool of expenditure (see Buying and selling capital items below).

You do not get capital allowances on items you lease rather than buy. Instead the leasing charge counts as an allowable expense (see p. 240). If you buy something on hire purchase, the capital element of the charges can qualify for capital allowances but the interest element is treated as an allowable expense (see p. 240).

Buying and selling capital items

When you buy an item of capital, its cost is added to the appropriate pool of expenditure. This increases the year-end value of the pool on which the writing-down allowance is worked out.

When you first start in business, you might take into the business capital equipment you already own – for example a desk, shelving, a computer. Although no money changes hands, you are treated as having sold the item to your business and you can claim capital allowances in the normal way. Value each item at its second-hand market value given its age, state of repair and so on.

When you sell a capital item, the amount you get for it (up to its original cost) is deducted from the expenditure pool. Occasionally, this may be more than the total value of the pool, in which case, the excess (called a balancing charge) is added to your profits or (taxable income) for the year, increasing your tax bill. These are entered in boxes 3.62, 3.64, 3.66 and 3.68 and the total is added to your profits at box 3.55.

If you sell the item for less than its written-down value – at the extreme, you might scrap it for nothing – the shortfall remains in your pool of expenditure and continues to be written down. So you could be claiming allowances on an item for many years after you have sold it. Only when you finally close down the business can you claim a balancing allowance for any remaining value of the pool. This is where short-life assets come into their own.

If you scrap a short-life asset within five years, you can claim tax relief on the difference between what you get (if anything) for the asset and its written-down value. The relief is given in the tax year in which you scrap it – you don't have to wait until the business closes down. If, having declared an asset as short life, you actually go on using it beyond five years, it is transferred into your general pool of expenditure and treated like any other capital item.

If you are registered for VAT, the amount you put in your expenditure pools should not include VAT. If you are not registered for VAT, you claim capital allowances on the cost including VAT.

Claiming capital allowances
Capital allowances are given as a deduction in working out your taxable profits for the year. Enter the capital allowances you are claiming in boxes 3.61, 3.63, 3.65 and 3.67 and the total is deducted from your profits at box 3.57.

ADJUSTMENTS

So far, in completing the Self-employment supplement, you have entered figures for one particular accounting period. As explained on p. 227 this may not be the same as the period over which you are actually taxed. This period is known to the Inland Revenue as your basis period. After the first two or three years in business, your basis period (and the dates you enter in 3.71 and 3.72) will normally be the same as your accounting period. But in the early years of the business, or if you change your accounting date, you may have to enter different dates.

If your basis period does differ from your accounting period, you have to make an adjustment in box 3.74 by allocating a proportion of the profits made in your first accounting period to the tax year. This is explained on p. 227 and in Help Sheet *IR222 How to calculate your taxable profits*. Remember to enter the adjustment in brackets if it is a deduction.

Example

Joe Morris has been running a dairy since 1978. He makes up his accounts to 31 December each year. For the year to 31 December 1999, he made the following purchases and sales of capital items:

Date	Capital item	Purchase/sale price
10 March 1999	New van bought	£17,000
5 May 1999	Old van sold (cost £12,000 when new)	£ 5,000
2 November 1999	Second-hand cream separator bought	£38,000

On 31 December 1998, after claiming writing-down allowances, Joe's general pool of capital expenditure stood at £158,000. Because the cream separator was bought between 2 July 1998 and 1 July 2000, Joe can claim an initial allowance of 40 per cent x £38,000 = £15,200. The van also qualifies for 40 per cent initial allowance, so he can claim £17,000 x 40 per cent = £6,800. Joe deducts the £5,000 from selling the old van to give a general pool expenditure at 31 December 1999 of £158,000 − £5,000 = £153,000. Joe can claim a maximum writing-down allowance of 25 per cent x £153,000 = £38,250. This gives allowances of £15,200 + £6,800 + £38,250 = £60,250 to set against his taxable income for the year. In fact, he has only enough profits and other income to use up £37,000 of the allowances. His capital pool at 1 January 2000 (including the balance of the expenditure on the van and the cream separator) becomes £158,000 − £5,000 (sale of van) + £17,000 (for van) + £38,000 (for cream separator) − £37,000 of allowances = £171,000.

If you are a foster carer or adult carer, or you run a business overseas, you may not need to complete the whole of the Self-employment pages. Tick box 3.72B if this applies.

Example

Sam started his business as a self-employed landscape gardener on 6 July 1999. His basis period for the tax year ending 5 April 2000 is the period between 6 July 1999 and 5 April 2000. He draws up his first set of accounts on 5 June 2000. In all the boxes up to 3.73 he enters the figures for his first accounting period, running to 5 June 2000. His profit in this accounting period was £8,000. Because he was only in business for 275 of the 366 days in the year to 5 April 2000, his profits for the tax year were 275/366 x £8,000 = £6,010. At box 3.74 he enters an adjustment (in brackets) of £8,000 − £6,010 = £1,990.

Overlap relief

You may pay tax on the same lot of profits twice. These profits are called 'overlap profits' and they arise if your basis period for one year has over-lapped with that for another year. This can happen if your accounting date is not 5 April, either because of the special rules for new businesses (see p. 227) or because of the transition to the current year basis of taxing prof-its which happened in the tax year ending 5 April 1997. You can use your overlap profits to reduce your profits if you closed your business in the year to 5 April 2000, or if you changed your accounting date.

Enter your total overlap profits in box 3.75, and the amount you want to set against your profits in box 3.76.

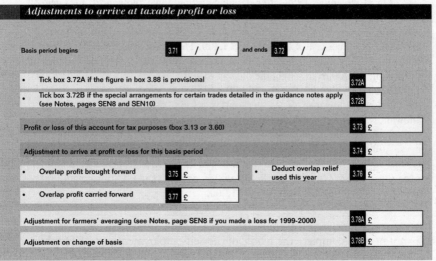

You can carry forward any unused overlap profits to set against the profits from the same business in future years, but you cannot set them against other types of income. If you are continuing your business, enter any unused amount in box 3.77. If you are closing down or selling your business, deduct all the overlap profits and you will end up with a loss on which you may qualify for tax relief.

LOSSES

If you make a loss, there are several ways you can get tax relief on it.

Other income or gains for this year

Net profit for 1999-2000 (if loss, enter '0')	3.79 £
Allowable loss for 1999-2000 (if you make a profit, enter '0')	3.80 £
• Loss offset against other income for 1999-2000	3.81 £

Complete box 3.81 to set the loss against other income you have during the tax year ending 5 April 2000 – for example, from working for an employer or from your savings. If this does not use up all the loss, you can ask for the rest to be set against any taxable capital gains for tax year ending 5 April 2000. If any loss still remains, you can ask for relief on it to be given in some other way. The time limit for making this choice with respect to losses made in the accounting period being declared for the tax year ending 5 April 2000 is 31 January 2002.

Other income and gains for the previous year

• Loss to carry back	0.00 £

Complete box 3.82 to carry back the loss to the tax year ending 5 April 1999 to set against your income from any source for that year. If this does not use up the full loss, you can ask for the rest to be set against any capital gains for the tax year ending 5 April 1999. If some loss still remains, you can ask for relief on it to be given in some other way. The time limit for making this choice is 31 January 2002.

> ### TAX-SAVING IDEAS
> You do not have to make up your mind about how to get tax relief for your losses straightaway. You have a while to wait and see how your business affairs turn out. But the time limits for each option are strict, so don't delay so long that you miss them.

Other income for earlier years
You can ask for a loss made in the first four years of the business to be carried back and set against income (but not gains) for the previous three tax years – that is, those ending 5 April 1997, 1998 and 1999. The loss is set against the earliest year first. The time limit for this choice is also 31 January 2002.

Future profits
Complete box 3.83 to carry the loss forward to set against your future profits

Loss to carry forward (that is allowable loss not claimed in any other way)	3.83 £

from the same business. It will be set against the next profits you make with any remaining loss being rolled forward to set against the next profits and so on until the loss is completely used up. You have until 31 January 2006 to make this choice.

EXAMPLE

Sonja Frisk has been an antiques dealer for the last ten years. Normally, she makes a reasonable living but, in 1999, the sale of some expensive artifacts fell through and Sonja made a £7,000 loss for the tax year.

Sonja could set the remaining loss against other income which she had in the tax year ending 5 April 2000 from a part-time job lecturing in art history at the local university. Alternatively, she can carry back her loss to the tax year ending 5 April 1999, or carry it forward to set against future profits from her antiques business. She doesn't want to use her loss this year, because she will pay only 10 per cent tax on her lecturing income, compared with the 23 per cent top rate of tax she paid last year; nor is she keen to carry forward her loss because she does not expect to pay a higher rate of tax in future. She claims to carry back her loss to the year ending 5 April 1999, qualifying for tax relief of 23 per cent x £7,000 = £1,610.

Closing down

If your business closed down during the tax year ending 5 April 2000, you have a further option. A loss you made during your last 12 months of trading can be set against your profits for the three previous tax years – that is you can go back to the tax year ending 5 April 1997. The time limit for this choice is also 31 January 2006.

For more information see Help Sheet *IR227 Losses*.

NATIONAL INSURANCE

Running your own business, you will usually have to pay National Insurance contributions (NICs) both for yourself and for any people you employ. You will have to pay: Class 2 contributions at a flat-rate of £6.55 a week in the tax year ending 5 April 2000 and £2 a week in the tax year ending 5 April 2001. If your profits are less than £3,770 in the tax year ending 5 April 2000, you can opt not to pay. The reduction in Class 2 contributions from 6 April 2000 is combined with an increase in Class 4 contributions – see below.

Class 4 National Insurance Contributions		
• Tick this box if exception or deferment applies	3.89	
• Adjustments to profit chargeable to Class 4 National Insurance Contributions	3.90	£
Class 4 National Insurance Contributions due	3.91	£

Class 2 NICs help you to qualify for certain state benefits, such as jobseeker's allowance and incapacity benefit, so it might be better to carry on paying even if your profits are low. Class 2 contributions are paid direct to the Inland Revenue, usually by direct debit.

You may also have to pay Class 4 contributions. Unlike other types of National Insurance, Class 4 contributions do not entitle you to any state benefits – they are simply a tax on profits which is collected along with your income tax. In the tax year ending 5 April 2000, Class 4 NICs were payable at a rate of 6 per cent on profits over £7,530 up to £26,000. For the tax year ending 5 April 2001, the rate increases to 7 per cent. The lower limit falls to £4,385 and the upper limit rises to £27,820, bringing more profits within the scope of this tax. There are no Class 4 NICs to pay on profits below the lower limit and above the upper limit. If your profits are less than the lower limit, you do not pay any Class 4 NICs at all.

A few groups of people are excluded from having to pay Class 4 NICs. They include people over state pension age (currently 60 for women and 65 for men), people under age 16 if they have been granted an exemption by the Inland Revenue (ask for leaflet CA03 at your local tax office) and people who are not resident in the UK.

In some circumstances, you might have earnings which count as profits of your business and on which Class 4 NICs might be payable, but which have already had Class 1 NICs deducted – for example, where part of your income derives from fees for teaching in a school. There is a cap on the overall amount you have to pay in National Insurance, so it may be that Class 4 NICs won't be payable after all. However, you usually don't know whether this is the case until after part of the Class 4 NICs would have become payable, so you can ask to have payment deferred until the position is known.

If you are either excluded from paying Class 4 NICs or your tax office has agreed that you can defer paying them, you should tick the box at 3.89 and put 0 in boxes 3.90 and 3.91. In all other cases, leave box 3.89 blank. If you have any losses which have been carried forward to set against your profits for the tax year ending 5 April 2000, enter them in box 3.90 because they can also reduce your profits used for working out Class 4 NICs. If you have paid interest for business purposes but it has not been deducted in working out your profits for income tax purposes, you might be able to deduct it for Class 4 NICs purposes. If this applies enter the amount of interest also in box 3.90.

Box 3.91 invites you to write down the amount you owe in Class 4 NICs. You don't have to do this sum yourself. Provided you send in your tax return by the 30 September deadline, you can leave the box blank and let your tax office do the sums. If you prefer to work out your Class 4 NICs yourself, there is a calculator included in the notes accompanying your Self-employment supplement. (The calculator is not suitable if you run more than one business, see Help Sheet *IR220 More than one business*.)

TAX-SAVING IDEAS

Losses can be used to reduce your Class 4 National Insurance contributions as well as your income tax bill.

If you're paying both Class 1 and Class 4 National Insurance on some of your income, ask to have the Class 4 liability deferred until you know precisely how much is due. Otherwise, you could end up paying too much in contributions.

EXAMPLE

Jim Newall has profits for income tax purposes of £8,500 for the tax year ending 5 April 2000. These are also the profits on which his Class 4 NICs are based. They are calculated as follows:

Profit for Class 4 NICs purposes	= £8,500
Less lower profit limit	= £7,530
Amount chargeable (£8,500 – £7,530)	= £970
Class 4 NICs at 6 per cent x £970	= £58.20

Class 2 and Class 4 contributions are not allowable expenses and can't be deducted when working out your profits for income tax purposes. If you have employees, you have to pay employer's Class 1 NICs for them if they earn more than the lower earnings limit (£83 a week for the tax year ending 5 April 2000 and £84 a week for the tax year ending 5 April 2001). In this case, the amount you pay counts as an allowable expense (see p. 235).

PARTNERSHIP

If you are in business with one or more partners, you should answer YES to Q4 in the basic tax return and fill in the Partnership supplement. There are two versions:

- short version. Use this if the partnership income is from trading profits or interest from bank or building society accounts which has already been taxed at the savings rate. This version will be adequate for most partners

- full version. If your partnership earnings are more complex because you have untaxed investment income, foreign income or income from land and property, for example, you'll need to complete this longer supplement.

The partnership should already have provided you with a Partnership Statement summarising your share of the profits, losses and other income. If you received the full statement, you need the full version of the supplementary pages; if you received a short statement, you need only the short supplement. If you haven't received a Partnership supplement or you need the full version, phone the Inland Revenue Orderline (see p. 139).

You and your fellow partners are jointly responsible for the partnership tax return, although one partner may be nominated to deal with it. This is a separate document from the partnership supplement. Profits are calculated on the return as if the partnership were a single person using largely the same rules as for a self-employed person (see Chapter 18). How profits are shared between partners depends on your partnership agreement.

Once the partner dealing with the tax return has worked out the taxable profits for the partnership as a whole, he or she must show each partner's share of the profits, losses and tax paid on the Partnership statement at the end of the Partnership return. The Partnership statement gives each individual partner the information needed to complete their own Partnership supplement. Each partner is then responsible for the tax on their own share of the profits.

Each partner is treated as if they were carrying on a business on their own, and the short version of the Partnership supplement is very similar to the Adjustments to arrive at taxable profit and loss and Class 4 National Insurance sections of the Self-employment supplement (see pp. 244-50). The other sections of the supplement simply summarise your share of any tax that the partnership has already paid. For this reason, we have not gone through the Partnership supplement in detail.

Becoming a partner

Partnership details	
Partnership reference number	**Partnership trade or profession**
4.1	4.2
• Date you started being a partner (if during 1999-2000) 4.3 / /	• Date you stopped being a partner (if during 1999-2000) 4.4 / /

When you join a partnership, the normal opening rules described on pp. 227-8 apply. The period on which your tax is based is likely to be different from the accounting year for the partnership. The dates you put in boxes 4.5 and 4.6 should reflect how the opening year rules apply to you. The opening year rules may result in overlap profits (see p. 229) on which you can eventually claim tax relief either when you leave the partnership or, possibly, if the partnership accounting date is changed. Once the special opening year rules have worked through, you are taxed on the normal current year basis. The period on which your tax is based will then be the same as the accounting year of the partnership, so you put the start date of the partnership year in box 4.5 and the end date in box 4.6.

Ceasing to be a partner
If you leave a partnership you are treated as if you are closing down your own business. The normal closing rules apply (see p. 231), including the claiming of tax relief on any overlap profits carried forward from the opening years.

LAND AND PROPERTY

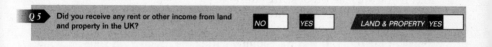

Q5 Did you receive any rent or other income from land and property in the UK? NO ☐ YES ☐ LAND & PROPERTY YES ☐

If you ticked the YES box against Q5 on page 2 of the tax return, you will need the Land and property supplementary pages. Many people renting out the odd room in their home may have to do little more than tick one box on the first page. But there is also space for details of more substantial lettings businesses and for income from holiday homes.

If you take in lodgers in your home, providing meals and other services, this may amount to a form of business and details should be entered on the Self-employment supplementary pages (see Chapter 18). Income from property abroad is entered on the Foreign pages (see Chapter 21).

The documents you need
You will need details of the rents you have received and any receipts or invoices for expenses. With furnished holiday lettings, you will also need records of the periods the properties were available for letting out.

If any of these properties is jointly owned, remember to enter only your share from these documents when filling in the tax return.

THE RENT A ROOM SCHEME

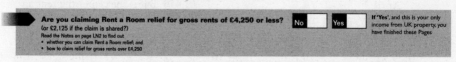

Are you claiming Rent a Room relief for gross rents of £4,250 or less? (or £2,125 if the claim is shared?) No ☐ Yes ☐ If 'Yes', and this is your only income from UK property, you have finished these Pages
Read the Notes on page LN2 to find out
• whether you can claim Rent a Room relief; and
• how to claim relief for gross rents over £4,250

The rent a room scheme means that a modest rent from letting out furnished accommodation in your home is tax-free. The scheme applies whether you own your home or are yourself a tenant. But it must be your only or main home (see p. 51) and in the UK. And you cannot claim rent a room relief if you have gone abroad or moved into job-related accommodation (see p. 55).

For the tax year ending 5 April 2000, you could have rent before deduction of any expenses of up to £4,250 tax-free. If you are married or share your home, the income is treated as belonging to the person who actually rents out the room. If you were jointly letting the rooms with your husband, wife or partner you can each have rent before deduction of any expenses of up to £2,125 tax-free.

If your gross rent is below these levels, tick the YES box. If this is your only letting income, there is nothing more to enter – you don't even need to bother claiming expenses.

For the tax year beginning 6 April 2000, the amount of rent before deduction of any expenses you can have tax-free remains at £4,250 – or £2,125 if you are jointly letting the rooms.

Rent just above the rent a room scheme level?

If your gross letting income – that is rent before deduction of expenses – is higher than the maximum for the rent a room scheme, you have two options:

- you can choose to pay tax on the amount by which the gross rent exceeds the maximum (that is, £4,250 for the tax year ending 5 April 2000)
- you pay tax on the letting income in the same way as any other property income – you pay tax on the net income (the rent after deduction of various expenses and allowances).

EXAMPLE

Natalie Lean lets out three rooms in her house, bringing in a total of £150 a week in rent. This means her gross rental income for the tax year beginning 6 April 2000 will be £7,800, on which she could claim expenses and allowances of £2,350.

If the rental income is taxed as normal property income, she will pay tax on £7,800 – £2,350 = £5,450. But if she claims the rent a room relief, she will pay tax on the excess of the gross rental income of £7,800 over £4,250 – that is, on £3,550.

Rent a room relief means Natalie will pay tax on £1,900 less income.

If your gross letting income is just over the rent a room maximum, you will almost certainly be better off with the first option. For example, if your gross letting income was £4,500 in the tax year ending 5 April 2000, you could choose to pay tax on £4,500 – £4,250 = £250.

If you want to choose the first option, tick the NO Box and put the rent before deduction of expenses in box 5.20 on the second page. Don't enter any expenses in boxes 5.24 to 5.30, or claim any capital allowances in box 5.36 (or wear and tear allowance in box 5.37). Enter the tax-free amount you are claiming under the rent a room scheme in box 5.35 (either £4,250 or £2,125) and don't enter any claim for losses.

If you want to choose the second option (that is the income taxed as other property income), tick the NO box and follow the instructions for Other property income (see p. 260).

FURNISHED HOLIDAY LETTINGS

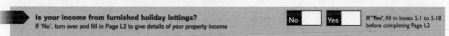

Is your income from furnished holiday lettings?
If 'No', turn over and fill in Page L2 to give details of your property income

No ☐ Yes ☐

If 'Yes', fill in boxes 5.1 to 5.18 before completing Page L2

If you have no income from short-term furnished lettings, tick the NO box and turn over to page L2 and to p. 260.

Tax benefits of furnished holiday lettings
Income from furnished holiday lettings is treated differently from other forms of property income, to reflect the fact that it is a form of business for many owners. This offers several tax benefits:

- you can claim capital allowances on plant and equipment (see p. 241)
- losses can be set off against other income for the same or next tax year and losses in the first four years of the business can be deducted from other income from the previous three years (see p. 246)
- it counts as relevant earnings for tax relief on pension contributions (p. 72)
- you can claim the special business reliefs for capital gains tax (p. 124).

To count as furnished holiday lettings, the property must meet all the following conditions for the tax year ending 5 April 2000:

- be available for letting to the general public on a commercial basis (that is, with a view to a profit) for at least 140 days
- actually let for at least 70 of those days
- not let for more than 31 days in a row to the same person in a period of at least seven months.

WHAT INCOME IS TAXED?

Income from land and property is now taxed in the same way – irrespective of its type. All income from land and property in the UK is added together. You pay tax on the total after deduction of allowable expenses, interest paid on loans to buy or improve the properties and losses from letting out property in the past. You can also claim allowances for some equipment you buy.

The tax you pay in a tax year is based on the property income and expenditure during that year. If you make up accounts for your property business for the year ending 5 April, the figures in your accounts will be the ones to use in filling in your tax return.

But if your accounting year runs to different dates, you will have to use two sets of accounts to work out what your property income and expenditure was for the tax year (see p. 226).

If you first started letting the property during the tax year ending 5 April 2000, these conditions must be satisfied for the first 12 months of letting. If you finished letting the property during that tax year, the conditions must have been met for the 12 months ending with the last letting. If you own more than one furnished holiday letting, you can average out the letting and occupancy periods between all of them.

Income

Furnished holiday lettings		
• **Income from furnished holiday lettings**	5.1	£

Enter the total income from all your furnished holiday lettings in the UK for the tax year ending 5 April 2000 – before any deductions such as agents' commission. Include any income for services provided to tenants, such as cleaning, linen hire and use of additional facilities. Also include any money received from insurance policies for loss of rent.

Expenses

■ *Expenses* (furnished holiday lettings only)

If your total property income is less than £15,000, enter your total expenses in box 5.7, as Other expenses – you don't need to give details of individual expenses. If your total property income is over this limit, you need to list expenses separately:

Rent, rates, insurance, ground rents etc

Enter the amount of rent, business rates, council tax, water rates, ground rent and insurance premiums on the furnished holiday lettings (including for insurance against loss of rents) in box 5.2.

Repairs, maintenance and renewals

Claim in box 5.3. Any work that prevents the property deteriorating is a repair – such as painting and damp treatment. You can't claim here the cost of improvements, additions or extensive alterations, but if the work makes repairs unnecessary you can claim part of the outlay equal to what the repairs would have cost.

If you aren't claiming capital allowances for the furniture, fixtures and fittings, you can claim a renewals deduction for the cost of replacing them. If the new items are better, you cannot claim the full cost. And if any of the old items are sold, the proceeds should be deducted from the amount you claim.

Finance charges

Enter in box 5.4 the cost of any loan you took out to buy the property – including interest paid and charges for setting up the loan.

Legal and professional costs

You can claim legal and professional expenses for a letting of less than a year, including fees for agents, surveyors and accountants and commission. You can also claim such costs when renewing the lease for a longer letting provided it is for less than 50 years. But you cannot claim expenses incurred in the first letting of a property for more than a year. Nor can you claim costs of registering title to land, getting planning permission or in connection with the payment of a premium on renewal of a lease. Enter the total in box 5.5.

Cost of services provided

You can claim as an expense the cost of services such as gardening, cleaning and porterage. You can't claim the cost of your own time, but you can claim the cost of paying other people such as a member of your family.

Enter the total in box 5.6. If you are paid for any services you provide, this should be included as part of the income in box 5.1.

Other expenses

Other expenses include advertising costs, stationery, telephone calls, rent collection and travel to the property when solely for the letting.

Add together the figures in boxes 5.2 to 5.7 and enter the total in box 5.8.

Net profit

Net profit is income minus expenses. Deduct the figure in box 5.8 from that in box 5.1 and put the amount in box 5.9, in brackets if it is a loss.

Tax adjustments

■ *Tax adjustments*	
• Private use	5.10 £

Private use
If a furnished holiday letting is partly used for your own enjoyment or that of friends staying rent-free, this counts as private use. Part of the costs must be apportioned to this private use, and cannot be claimed as an expense. If it was available for letting for nine months of the year and used by you for the rest of the time, you can claim only three-quarters of the costs of owning it. (You can still claim the full costs of letting it out as expenses.)

There are two ways to make an adjustment to reflect private use. You can enter the appropriate share of the costs in boxes 5.2 to 5.7, but let your tax inspector know what you've done. Or, better, you enter the costs in full in these boxes and enter in box 5.10 a figure for private use which is deducted from the total.

Capital allowances and balancing charges

You can claim capital allowances for the cost of buying furniture, machinery such as a lawnmower or equipment such as a water pump. If you get rid of an item you have claimed capital allowances on, a balancing charge may be added to your profits to reflect its second-hand value. There's more on p. 240 about capital allowances and balancing charges. You might also find it useful to get Help Sheet *IR250 Capital allowances and balancing charges in a rental business* from the Orderline.

Enter the amount of any capital allowances you are claiming for the tax year ending 5 April 2000 in box 5.13 and the amount of any balancing charge in box 5.11. Add the figures in boxes 5.10 and 5.11 together and enter the total in box 5.12.

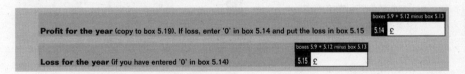

Total boxes 5.9 and 5.12 and subtract the amount in box 5.13. If the answer is a negative number, you have made a tax loss on your furnished holiday lettings. Enter 0 in box 5.14 and put the amount of the loss in box 5.15. If you have made a profit, enter it in box 5.14.

Losses for the year
Any loss in box 5.15 can be used to reduce the amount of tax you pay on other income or capital gains in the tax year ending 5 April 2000 or earlier tax years:

- other income for the tax year ending 5 April 2000 (enter the amount you wish to claim in box 5.16)
- capital gains for the same tax year – include the amount you wish to

• Loss offset against 1999-2000 total income	5.16 £
• Loss carried back	see Notes, page LN4 5.17 £
• Loss offset against other income from property (copy to box 5.38)	see Notes, page LN4 5.18 £

claim in the total you enter in box 8.5 of the Capital gains supplementary pages (see p. 283)
- income and gains for earlier tax years – enter the amount you wish to claim in box 5.17.

If you haven't used all the loss in box 5.15, you can set off what remains against other property income for the tax year ending 5 April 2000. Enter what is left in box 5.18 and copy it into box 5.38 on page L2 of the Land and property supplementary pages.

OTHER PROPERTY INCOME

Income

Other property income	
■ *Income*	
• Furnished holiday lettings profits	copy from box 5.14 5.19 £

Copy the figure for profits on furnished holiday lettings from box 5.14 to box 5.19.

Rents and other income from land and property

		Tax deducted	
• Rents and other income from land and property	5.20 £	5.21 £	

Enter in box 5.20 the total income from all your lettings in the UK except furnished holiday lettings for the tax year ending 5 April 2000 – before any deductions such as agents' commission. Include the following:

- rent you will receive after 5 April 2000 which is payment in arrears for the tax year ending 5 April 2000 (equally, leave out any rent received on or before 5 April 2000 which is payment in advance for rent for periods after 5 April 2000)
- any income for services provided to tenants, such as cleaning, gardening

or porterage
- any money received from insurance policies for loss of rent
- ground rent and feu duties
- grants from local authorities for repairs (you can claim the cost of repairs as an expense)
- payments for using your land – for example, to shoot or graze.

If any tax has been deducted from the income before you get it, enter the total in box 5.21. The figure you enter in box 5.20 should be the before-tax amounts – so should include the amount in box 5.21.

If you own and let the property jointly with someone else, enter only your share of the income in box 5.20, and your share of the expenses lower down. If you only know your share of the profit after expenses, enter this in box 5.20 or any loss in box 5.29.

Chargeable premiums, reverse premiums

•	Chargeable premiums	5.22 £		
			boxes 5.19 + 5.20 + 5.22 + 5.22A	
•	Reverse premiums	5.22A £	5.23 £	

If you receive a premium from a tenant in return for granting a lease, you will have to pay income tax on part of it if the lease lasts less than 50 years (and capital gains tax on the rest). Any work the tenant agrees to do for you on being granted a lease counts as a premium.

If you are paid the premium in instalments, the total premium is still taxable in the year the lease is granted. But if paying in one go would cause you hardship, you can ask your tax inspector to allow you to pay by yearly instalments. The maximum number of instalments is eight (or the number of years you are getting the premium over, if less).

The proportion on which you will have to pay income tax is calculated as follows:

$$\frac{51 - \text{number of years of the lease}}{50}$$

So if the lease is a 20-year one, the proportion of the premium which is taxable is:

$$\frac{51 - 20}{50} = \frac{31}{50}$$

Enter the taxable amount in box 5.22.

If the property you let out is one you are yourself letting and you received a payment or other benefit such as a contribution towards fitting out the property to persuade you to take it on, this is a reverse premium. If actual money has been laid out by the landlord, it is taxed as income. Give the amount in box 5.22A – if you are not sure whether you have received a reverse premium, ask your tax inspector or your business adviser.

Add the figures in boxes 5.19, 5.20, 5.22 and 5.22A together and enter the total in box 5.23.

Expenses

■ *Expenses* (do not include figures you have already put in boxes 5.2 to 5.7 on page L1)

• Rent, rates, insurance, ground rents etc	5.24	£
• Repairs, maintenance and renewals	5.25	£
• Finance charges, including interest	5.26	£
• Legal and professional costs	5.27	£
• Costs of services provided, including wages	5.28	£
• Other expenses	5.29	£

total of boxes 5.24 to 5.29

5.30	£

If your total property income for the tax year ending 5 April 2000 is less than £15,000, go straight to box 5.29 and enter your total expenses in it. If your total property income is over this limit, you need to list the expenses incurred in the tax year ending 5 April 2000 separately.

The details of what expenses you can claim in boxes 5.24 to 5.29 are given under Furnished holiday lettings on pp. 255-8. Note that with furnished property, you can claim a renewals deduction in box 5.25 for the cost of replacing furniture, fixtures and fittings, but not if you are already claiming a wear and tear allowance on the property (see p. 264).

Don't include any expenses you have already claimed in boxes 5.2 to 5.7.

Add together the figures in boxes 5.24 to 5.29 and enter the total in box 5.30.

box 5.23 *minus* box 5.30

Net profit (put figures in brackets if a loss) | 5.31 | £

> ## EXAMPLE
>
> Miriam Patel has divided most of her house into furnished rooms which she lets out, providing cleaning. The total yearly income is £9,640 but she can deduct these expenses:
>
> - a proportion of the outgoings on the house (council tax, water rates, gas, electricity and insurance) which add up to £2,400 a year. Miriam is letting out three-quarters of the house and claims this proportion
> - the cost of cleaning (cleaner's wages plus materials) – £1,300 a year
> - an allowance for wear and tear of the furniture and furnishings – Miriam claims the actual cost of replacement (£300 for this year).
>
> Thus Miriam's tax bill would be calculated as follows:
>
> | | | |
> |---|---|---|
> | Total rent received | | £9,640 |
> | *Less expenses* | | |
> | Three-quarters of the outgoings of £2,400 a year | £1,800 | |
> | Cost of cleaning | £1,300 | |
> | Cost of replacing furniture and furnishings | £300 | |
> | Total allowable expenses | | £3,400 |
> | Taxable rental income | | £6,240 |
>
> If Miriam does the cleaning, no allowance can be made for her time. But if she pays someone else to do the work (her mum, say), she can claim this cost as an allowable expense.

Subtract the figure in box 5.30 from that in box 5.23 to find the net profit or loss on the letting. Enter the figure in box 5.31, in brackets if it is a loss.

Tax adjustments

Box 5.32 is where you enter a figure for any private use of the property, in the same way as for furnished holiday lettings (see p. 258).

Any balancing charges (see p. 259) should be put in box 5.33. Add together the amounts in boxes 5.32 and 5.33 and put the total in box 5.34.

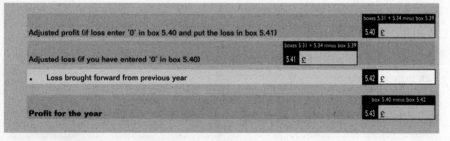

				total of boxes 5.35 to 5.38
• Rent a Room exempt amount	5.35 £			
• Capital allowances	5.36 £			
• 10% wear and tear	5.37 £			
• Furnished holiday lettings losses (from box 5.18)	5.38 £			5.39 £

Enter in box 5.35 any tax-free amount you are claiming under the rent a room scheme (see p. 254). Otherwise leave it empty.

If you want to claim capital allowances (see p. 259), enter the amount in box 5.36. You can't claim capital allowances if you let a furnished home (other than as furnished holiday lettings). You can instead claim a renewals deduction for the cost of replacing such items (in box 5.25 above). Or you can claim a wear and tear allowance in box 5.37 of 10 per cent of the rent less service charges and local taxes. Once you have chosen a method, you can't switch. And if you have been using a different method of allowing for wear and tear agreed with your tax inspector before 6 April 1976, you can carry on using it.

You should already have filled in box 5.38 if you wish to set off a loss on furnished holiday lettings against other property income (see box 5.18).

In box 5.39 enter the total of boxes 5.35, 5.36, 5.37 and 5.38.

		boxes 5.31 + 5.34 minus box 5.39
Adjusted profit (if loss enter '0' in box 5.40 and put the loss in box 5.41)		5.40 £
	boxes 5.31 + 5.34 minus box 5.39	
Adjusted loss (if you have entered '0' in box 5.40)	5.41 £	
• Loss brought forward from previous year		5.42 £
		box 5.40 minus box 5.42
Profit for the year		5.43 £

Add the figures in boxes 5.31 and 5.34 together and subtract the figure in box 5.39. If the answer is a negative number, you have made a tax loss on your property interests. Enter 0 in box 5.40 and put the amount of the loss in box 5.41. There are several ways that a tax loss on property income can be used to reduce your tax bill (see boxes 5.44 to 5.46, below).

If you have made a profit, enter it in box 5.40. You can reduce this – and the amount of tax you pay on your property income – if you made a loss on property income from the tax year ending 5 April 1999. Enter the total loss from that year in box 5.42, and subtract it from the figure in box 5.40.

If the answer is a negative number, enter 0 in box 5.43 and put the balance in box 5.45. If the answer is more than zero, you have made a taxable profit on your property income for the tax year ending 5 April 2000.

Losses

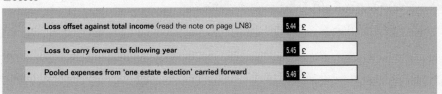

You can deduct a property income loss from other forms of income for the tax year ending 5 April 2000. However, you can set off some of the loss in box 5.41 against other income only if you have claimed capital allowances in box 5.36. Even then, the maximum loss you can set off in this way is the amount of capital allowances minus any balancing charge – box 5.36 minus box 5.33.

If this is what you want to do, enter the amount you wish to deduct in this way in box 5.44. Alternatively, a loss which reflects an excess of capital allowances over balancing charges can be carried over to next year and set against your income for the tax year ending 5 April 2001. If this is what you would like to do, make a note of the figure to enter in the 2001 tax return.

Finally, any other unused losses can be carried over to deduct from future profits from property – enter these in box 5.45. If the figure in box 5.43 is 0 you will have already entered the right figure in box 5.45. If the figure in box 5.40 is 0, you find the figure to enter in box 5.45 by adding together the figures in boxes 5.41 and 5.42 and subtracting the figure in box 5.44.

Ignore box 5.46 unless you own agricultural land. If you think it might apply to you, ask for Help Sheet *IR251 Agricultural land and land managed as one estate* to see what you should enter.

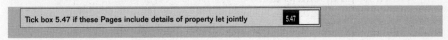

Tick box 5.47 if you own and let property jointly with someone else – and give the name and address of the person who keeps the records in the Additional information box on page 8 of the basic tax return.

FOREIGN

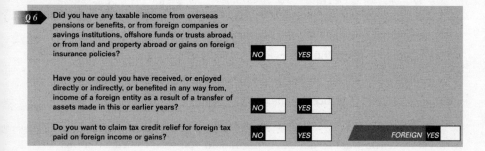

Q6 — Did you have any taxable income from overseas pensions or benefits, or from foreign companies or savings institutions, offshore funds or trusts abroad, or from land and property abroad or gains on foreign insurance policies?　NO ☐　YES ☐

Have you or could you have received, or enjoyed directly or indirectly, or benefited in any way from, income of a foreign entity as a result of a transfer of assets made in this or earlier years?　NO ☐　YES ☐

Do you want to claim tax credit relief for foreign tax paid on foreign income or gains?　NO ☐　YES ☐　　FOREIGN YES ☐

If you ticked any of the three YES boxes at Q6 on page 2 of the basic tax return, you will need the supplementary pages called Foreign. These have space to give details about your foreign savings, pensions and benefits, property income and other investment income from abroad. Earnings from work abroad should be entered in the Employment, Self-Employment or Partnership pages of the tax return as appropriate. Similarly, details of capital gains on overseas transactions should be entered in that supplement.

This chapter tells you how to fill in the Foreign pages, and about the expenses and allowances you can claim. But the tax treatment of people who live abroad is beyond the scope of this guide. If this applies to you, seek professional advice from your bank or accountant.

How foreign income is taxed
Income from abroad is taxable in the UK, even if you have already paid foreign tax on it. You can deduct any foreign tax paid from the income before working out your UK tax bill – so you pay UK tax only on what you get after paying foreign tax.

But in most cases, you can instead claim a deduction from your UK tax bill to reflect the foreign tax paid, known as tax credit relief. This is likely to mean paying less in UK tax than if you simply deduct the foreign tax from the gross income before working out the tax bill.

However, working out the amount of tax credit relief can be complicated and this guide assumes you are leaving the calculations to your tax inspector. If you feel up to the calculations, you can use the guidance notes sent out by the Inland Revenue to calculate your tax credit relief and thus your UK tax bill on such income.

Note that if the amount of foreign tax is adjusted, you must notify your tax inspector if it means any deduction for that tax was bigger than it should have been.

> ## EXAMPLE
> Bill Livingstone made £2,500 after expenses last year letting out his villa in Freedonia. He paid the equivalent of £400 tax on this to the Freedonian tax authorities.
>
> In calculating his UK tax, he could have simply deducted the £400 of Freedonian tax from the £2,500 and paid tax on £2,100. Since he paid tax on the income at the basic rate of 23 per cent, the tax bill would have been £483.
>
> But he claimed tax credit relief, so the full £2,500 was taxable at 23 per cent – £575 in tax. He could then deduct the £400 of Freedonian tax, making his UK tax bill just £175.

What income is taxed
The instructions below are for people who are domiciled in the UK and ordinarily resident here. Their foreign income is taxed on an arising basis – when they get it or it is credited to them, not when it is brought back to the UK. You should enter the amounts you got in sterling, using the exchange rate at the time the income arose.

There are different rules for people who are not domiciled or ordinarily resident in the UK. The latter is likely to apply to you only if you don't visit the UK regularly and either have no home here or spend less than 91 days on average here in a tax year. If it does apply, you will need to fill in the Non-residence supplementary pages (see p. 295). And your foreign income will be taxed on a remittance basis – enter the amounts of income received in the UK and the equivalent share of any foreign tax deducted from it.

Tax-free foreign income
The following types of foreign income are tax-free in the UK:

- pensions paid by Germany or Austria to the victims of Nazi persecution and to pensioners who have fled from persecution
- the extra foreign pension paid to you if you have been retired because you were disabled by injury on duty or by a work-related illness
- any part of a pension from overseas that reduces the amount of tax-free UK war widows' and dependants' pensions

- social security benefits which are similar to UK benefits that are tax-free – child benefit, maternity allowance, guardian's allowance, child's special allowance, widow's payments, incapacity benefit (only for the first six months if it began on or after 13 April 1995), attendance allowance, disability living allowance and severe disablement allowance.

A tenth of overseas pensions funded by an overseas employer or pension fund is tax-free in the UK unless it is taxed on a remittance basis (see p. 267).

Income stuck in a foreign country
In some cases, you will be unable to remit foreign income to the UK because it arises in a country which has exchange controls or is short of foreign exchange. If income is unremittable, give details of the amount of income and foreign tax in the currency of the country concerned – you will be unable to give other information asked for.

The documents you need
You will need to gather together dividend vouchers for overseas shares, bank statements for overseas bank accounts, pension advice notes, foreign property bills – as well as details of any foreign tax paid.

FOREIGN SAVINGS

Foreign savings

Fill in columns A to E, and tick the box in column E if you want to claim tax credit relief.

Country A tick box if income is unremittable ▼	Amount before tax B	UK tax C	Foreign tax D	Amount chargeable tick box to claim tax credit relief E ▼	
■ Interest and other income from overseas savings - see Notes, page FN4	£	£	£	£	
	£	£	£	£	
	£	£	£	£	

On page F1 give details of foreign interest and other savings income for the tax year ending 5 April 2000 unless you are taxed on a remittance basis (see p. 267).

Enter each source of income on a separate line. If any of these types of income is from joint holdings, enter your share only. In column A give the name of the country where the income arose and tick the box if the income cannot be remitted to the UK. In columns B, C, D give the amount of income before tax, the amount of any UK income tax deducted and the amount of foreign tax paid.

Under double taxation agreements signed between the UK and more than 100 countries, tax should be deducted from investment income by the foreign country at a reduced rate which is then taken into account in calculating your UK tax bill. If the figure in column D is more than you should have paid under such an agreement, ask the foreign tax authority for a refund.

The amount you enter in column E depends on whether you wish to claim tax credit relief:

- if you intend to claim it, enter the amount in column B and tick the box
- if you are not claiming tax credit relief, enter the figure in column B less any foreign tax in column D.

Add the figures in column C and enter the total in box 6.1. Put the total for column E in box 6.2.

Enter the same information for dividends received for the tax year ending 5 April 2000 unless you are taxed on a remittance basis (see p. 267). The following should not be included:

- distributions by a foreign company in the form of shares (but enter any cash alternative you took instead)
- stock dividends from foreign companies
- bonus shares from a scrip issue by a foreign company
- capital distributions – for example, the return of your capital or distributions in the course of a liquidation.

Add the figures for dividends in column C and enter the total in box 6.1A. Put the total for dividends in column E in box 6.2A.

On page F2, give the same information for foreign pensions, social security benefits and property income. And if you are taxed on your foreign income on a remittance basis (see p. 267), this is where you give details of foreign interest, dividends and other savings income.

Pensions and social security benefits
Exclude pensions and benefits which are free of UK tax – see p. 267. If only part of a payment is free of UK tax, give the amount which is not exempt in column E.

INCOME FROM FOREIGN LAND AND PROPERTY

Income from overseas property is taxed in much the same way as that from UK property (see p. 253). You can deduct expenses including the cost of managing the property and collecting the income (for example, paying an agent). If you buy equipment, you may be able to claim a capital allowance or some other form of deduction (see p. 259). And you can deduct loan interest on the property.

As for UK property, there are certain expenses you cannot claim. These include personal expenses – such as the costs incurred while the property is not let. Nor can you claim any loss you make when you sell the property.

There is space on page F2 of the Foreign supplement for details of the income and tax paid on overseas property and land. But before you fill this in, you must turn to page F4 and complete a copy of it for each property, giving details of the income, expenses and other deductions for the tax year ending 5 April 2000. If your foreign income is taxed on a remittance basis (see p. 267), you do not need to complete page F4.

OTHER OVERSEAS INCOME

This is where you give details of miscellaneous other types of overseas income. If you have these complex investments, you should take specialised tax advice.

• Disposals of holdings in offshore funds, income from non-resident trusts and benefits received from overseas trusts, companies and other entities – see Notes, page FN10

The income from an offshore fund should be entered as savings income on page F1 of the foreign pages. Here you must give details of any gain made on cashing in part or all of your investment unless the fund qualifies as a distributor fund – one which distributes most of its income as dividends. This is to stop investors rolling up income in offshore funds to create capital gains and reduce their income tax bills.

If the fund does not count as a distributor fund, enter the gain in box 6.5. If you have received an equalisation payment from a distributor fund, you should enter the part of the gain taxable as income in box 6.5. The taxable amount will be shown on the voucher given to you by the fund manager.

Income from non-resident trusts
If you are entitled to the income from a trust that is not resident in the UK, enter the amount from foreign sources in box 6.5. Any of the trust's income from UK sources should have been entered in the appropriate boxes of the Income part of the tax return as if it had been paid direct to you.

Any income paid to you from a non-resident trust at the discretion of the trustees should be entered in box 6.5.

Income received by trusts or companies abroad
If you have transferred assets so the income is paid to anybody abroad – such as a company or trust – and you get a benefit from it, enter the income or capital sum received in box 6.5.

Also enter the value of any payment or benefit such as a loan received from other sorts of offshore funds such as offshore bonds. You must include the amount of any unexpended income from such sources – income held in trust or by a company on your behalf. Give the full name of the trust in the Additional information box at the foot of page F3, or the name and address of the company receiving the income. If you have these complex types of investments, you should take specialised tax advice.

If the purpose of the transfer of assets was not to avoid tax, you won't need to give details here. Tick box 6.5A.

Foreign life insurance policies

	Number of years	Tax treated as paid	Gain(s)
Gains on foreign life insurance policies etc.	6.6	6.7 £	6.8 £

Give details here of any gains you have made on foreign life insurance policies – whether because the policy has come to an end or because you have drawn some benefit from it. Enter the number of years you have held the policy in box 6.6 and the gain in box 6.8.

Most such gains are simply added to your taxable income because no foreign tax has been paid on them. If foreign tax has been deducted, you may be able to get a 'credit for notional basic rate tax' which means the gain will be taxed only at the difference between the basic and higher rate in the same way as a UK life insurance policy gain (see p. 164). Enter the amount of any notional income tax credit in box 6.7.

TAX CREDIT RELIEF

Tax credit relief for foreign tax paid on employment, self-employment and other income

See Notes, page FN13

Enter in this column the Page number in your Tax Return from which information is taken. Do this for each item for which you are claiming tax credit relief ▼	Country A	Foreign tax D	Amount chargeable E tick box to claim tax credit relief ▼
		£	£
		£	£
		£	£

With all types of foreign income, you can simply deduct any foreign tax already paid from the income before working out the UK tax bill. But you are likely to pay less UK tax if you claim tax credit relief which reduces the UK tax bill to reflect the foreign tax already paid.

This section is for calculating tax credit relief on all your foreign income, including that from investments, pensions, benefits and property already entered above. But you can also claim the relief on foreign income from employment, self-employment and partnerships which you will have entered elsewhere on the tax return.

First you must enter details of these other forms of foreign income. Give the country the income arose in, the amount of foreign tax paid on it and the gross amount of the income before deduction of foreign tax. In the first column, give the page number of the tax return where the income is fully reported.

Next, there is room to enter the amount of tax credit relief you wish to claim on all of your foreign income. This is only for people who want to do the sums themselves – if you don't want to get involved in the calculations, go on to the next section.

If you want to work out your tax credit relief, you need to use the Tax Credit Relief Working Sheet on page FN16 of the Tax Return Guide. There are full instructions beginning on page FN15, and all the data you need to complete it on the following pages. You won't be able to complete the working sheet until you have completed most of the rest of the tax return. Some of the figures you have to enter on it are drawn from the Tax Calculation Guide which you use to work out your overall tax bill.

• If you are calculating your tax, enter the total tax credit relief on your income in box 6.9	6.9 £

Fill in a separate working sheet for each item of foreign income you wish to claim relief for. Enter the total amount you wish to claim in box 6.9.

Tax credit relief for foreign tax paid on chargeable gains reported on your Capital Gains Pages

See Notes, page FN14

Amount of gain under UK rules	Period over which UK gain accrued	Amount of gain under foreign tax rules	Period over which foreign gain accrued	Foreign tax paid D	tick box to claim tax credit relief ▼
£	days	£	days	£	
£	days	£	days	£	
£	days	£	days	£	

The bottom half of the page is for details of capital gains you wish to claim tax credit relief on. Help Sheet *IR261 Tax Credit Relief: Capital Gains* tells you what to enter and how to do the sums if you wish to calculate the tax credit relief on your foreign gains.

• If you are calculating your tax, enter the total tax credit relief on your gains in box 6.10	6.10 £

If you have calculated the tax credit relief on your capital gains, enter the total in box 6.10.

TRUSTS

Q7 Did you receive, or are you deemed to have, income from a trust, settlement or deceased person's estate? NO [ ] YES [ ] TRUSTS ETC YES [ ]

If you ticked the YES box at Q7 on page 2 of the basic tax return, you will need the supplementary page called Trusts etc. You should give details about taxable income from trusts and other forms of settlement such as a transfer of assets, and from the estates of people who have died. In some cases, you may have to give details of income from trusts you have set up. Even though the money has been paid to someone else, it may be treated as yours.

The documents you need
You require details of any income received. With a payment from a discretionary trust, the trustees should have given you a certificate R185 setting out the details; personal representatives handling the estates of people who have died should give similar statements when handing over income.

If you have directly or indirectly provided funds for a settlement and are not sure whether the income will be treated as yours, Help Sheet *IR270 Trusts and settlements – income treated as the settlor's* should help. Ask the Orderline (p. 139).

INCOME FROM TRUSTS AND SETTLEMENTS

Income paid out by trusts and other forms of settlement in the tax year ending 5 April 2000 comes with a tax credit which reflects the amount of tax already deducted from it or deemed to have been paid on it. What you receive is the net (after-tax) amount of income. To find the gross (before-tax) amount, you need to add back the tax credit. You can find out the amount of the tax credit from certificate R185 or similar statement the trustees should give you.

How trust income is taxed
The amount of the tax credit depends on the type of trust:

- trust with an interest in possession where you have the 'absolute right' to the income from the trust. The tax credit will be at the rate of 20 per cent of the grossed-up amount of interest; 10 per cent of the grossed-up amount of share dividends and unit trust distributions; and for other sorts of income, such as rents or royalties, it will be at the basic rate of tax – 23 per cent for the tax year ending 5 April 2000
- a discretionary trust where the trustees have discretion about paying out the income. The tax credit will be 34 per cent of the grossed-up income, except for share dividends and distributions where it will be 25 per cent
- accumulation and maintenance trusts – the income also comes with a tax credit of 34 per cent, except for share dividends and distributions where it will be 25 per cent.

If the tax credit is more than the amount of tax you would have paid if the grossed-up income had come direct to you, you can claim a rebate. For example, if you get interest from a trust and your income – including the grossed-up trust income – is too low to pay tax, you could reclaim all the tax credit which comes with it. With a discretionary trust, anyone not liable to higher rate tax can reclaim part of the tax credits.

Higher rate taxpayers will have to pay extra tax on income from either sort of trust. With a discretionary trust, this would be an extra 6 per cent of the grossed-up amount (the difference between the 40 per cent higher rate and the 34 per cent tax credit that comes from the trust).

Trust income that might be treated as yours
If you have directly or indirectly provided funds for a settlement, the income from those funds may be treated as yours – even though you haven't received it.

The sorts of trust which might produce an income that would be treated as yours include:

- a trust you set up for your husband or wife or children
- a trust that has lent money to you or your spouse
- a trust where the capital would come back to you if the beneficiaries died before becoming entitled to it.

This treatment might also apply if you make some investments on

> **TAX-SAVING IDEA**
> Reclaim some or all of the tax credit that comes with income from trusts if it is more than you would have paid if the income had come straight to you. Unless you pay tax at the higher rate, you will always be entitled to a rebate on income from a discretionary trust.

EXAMPLE
Gerry Hall received £250 from a discretionary trust in the tax year ending 5 April 2000, which comes with a tax credit of £128.79. He pays tax at no more than the basic rate (even when the grossed-up trust payment of £378.79 is added to his income). So he should have paid tax on the payment at the basic rate of 23 per cent only – a tax bill of 23 per cent of £378.79, or £87.12. He is thus entitled to a rebate of:

£128.79 – £87.12 = £41.67

behalf of your children unless they are over 18 or married – for example, opening a savings account in their names. Any income from such investments is treated as yours unless it is £100 a year or less before tax. This exception applies to gifts from each parent, so a child can have up to £200 a year before tax in income from gifts from both parents without a problem.

You can't get round this by giving the funds to someone else who passes them on to your child. You would still have indirectly provided the funds and the income would be yours. The same would be true if you settled some money on a friend's child in return for him doing the same for you.

This income should be included as your own in Q10 in the basic tax return and not entered on the Trusts etc pages unless you create a proper trust.

Income from trusts and settlements

■ Income taxed at:

	Income receivable	Tax paid	Taxable amount
'rate applicable to trusts'	7.1 £	7.2 £	7.3 £
basic rate	7.1A £	7.2A £	7.3A £
the savings rate	7.4 £	7.5 £	7.6 £
the dividend rate	7.4A £	7.5A £	7.6A £

Enter the income from trusts in the tax year ending 5 April 2000 in these boxes. Also include here any income from trusts or settlements which is treated as yours even though you haven't received it. For discretionary trusts, put the actual amount received in box 7.1, the tax credit in box 7.2 and the gross income in box 7.3 (this should be the sum of boxes 7.1 and 7.2). For income from a trust with an interest in possession on which the tax credit is at the 23 per cent basic rate, give the same details in boxes 7.1A, 7.2A and 7.3A. For savings income on which the tax credit is 20 per cent, enter the details in boxes 7.4, 7.5 and 7.6. For dividends and distributions where the tax credit is 10 per cent, enter the details in boxes 7.4A, 7.5A and 7.6A.

You don't need to enter the following here:

- scrip dividends or foreign income dividends received from a trust with an interest in possession and paid by UK companies, authorised unit trusts or open-ended investment companies – give details of these on page 3 of the basic tax return (see p. 155)
- income from foreign sources paid to you by a trust with an interest in possession – give details on the Foreign supplementary pages (see p. 268)
- income from a discretionary trust where the trustees are not resident in the UK – this should also go on the Foreign pages.

INCOME FROM ESTATES

You do not pay income tax on anything you inherit from a dead person. And if you inherit something that produces an income, such as money in a bank savings account, you should enter the interest in the appropriate part of the main tax return.

However, you should give details in this section of the tax return of income you receive from the estate while it is being wound up by the personal representatives – the executors or administrators. You would be entitled to this income if you were a residuary beneficiary – the person or one of the people

Income from the estates of deceased persons			
Income bearing:			
	Income receivable	Tax paid	Taxable amount
basic rate tax	7.7 £	7.8 £	7.9 £
savings rate tax	7.10 £	7.11 £	7.12 £
repayable dividend tax	7.13 £	7.14 £	7.15 £
non-repayable basic rate tax	7.16 £	7.17 £	7.18 £
non-repayable savings rate tax	7.19 £	7.20 £	7.21 £
non-repayable dividend rate	7.22 £	7.23 £	7.24 £

who gets what is left after all the specific bequests and legacies have been made.

Such income will come with a tax credit in the same way as a trust with an interest in possession. For most types of income, this tax will be repayable if it is more than you would have paid; but the tax is not repayable for some types of income such as gains on life insurance policies and UK stock dividends.

The statement supplied by the personal representatives – tax certificate R185E – will show you the rate the income has been taxed at and whether it is repayable. Enter the details for the tax year ending 5 April 2000 in boxes 7.7 to 7.24. Give the name of the estate and the total amount paid to you in the Additional information box at the bottom of the page.

In some cases, income accrued during the life of the dead person and paid into the estate after their death will come to you after being taken into account in calculating the inheritance tax bill on the estate. There is a special tax relief that stops you having to pay higher rate tax on such income – ask your tax inspector for details.

Income from foreign estates
If you get income from a foreign estate, it will not have borne full UK tax – either because the personal representatives are outside the UK tax net or because the estate is that of someone who died while domiciled outside the UK and has income from non-UK sources. In this case, enter the full amount of such income in boxes 7.7 and 7.9. Don't enter anything in box 7.8, even if some foreign tax has been deducted.

If the foreign estate has some income from UK sources, it will have paid some UK tax. In this case, you can reduce the amount entered in boxes 7.7 and 7.9 by the following amount:

$$\frac{\text{net amount of income subject to UK tax}}{\text{total estate income less UK tax}} \times \text{total estate income before UK tax}$$

Foreign tax paid

• total foreign tax for which tax credit relief not claimed   7.25 £

If you have been paid income from an estate which has already been taxed in a foreign country, you may end up paying two lots of tax on it: tax in the foreign country and tax in the UK. You may be able to reduce the amount of UK tax you pay on the income to reflect the foreign tax paid – this is known as tax credit relief. You claim this on the Foreign supplementary pages (see p. 271).

If you don't want to claim tax credit relief – which can be quite complicated – you can instead deduct the foreign tax you have paid from the income. Enter the amount in box 7.25.

Leave box 7.25 blank if you are claiming tax credit relief.

CAPITAL GAINS

Q8 Capital gains

- Have you disposed of your exempt only or main residence? If 'Yes', read page 7 of your Tax Return Guide to see if you need the Capital Gains Pages.   NO ☐   YES ☐

- Did you dispose of other chargeable assets worth more than £14,200 in total?   NO ☐   YES ☐

- Were your total chargeable gains more than £7,100?   NO ☐   YES ☐   CAPITAL GAINS YES ☐

Please see page 7 of the Tax Return Guide if you wish to claim a capital loss.

If you have ticked any of the three YES boxes in Q8 on page 2 of the basic tax return, you will need the supplementary pages called Capital gains. These ask for details of taxable gains you have made on buying and selling assets such as shares, unit trusts and property. You may also have to report a taxable gain even though you haven't sold something – if you give it away, for example. And if you have made a loss on such assets, you should give details here also, since it might reduce your overall tax bill now or in the future.

This chapter tells you how to fill in the Capital gains supplementary pages. Chapter 10 explains how the tax works in detail with examples of the sometimes complicated calculations needed to fill in these pages. It also explains how to claim all the reliefs and allowances to minimise your capital gains tax bill.

The documents you need
You will need details of anything you have spent on buying or selling or maintaining the value of assets. With shares and unit trusts, you need any paperwork relating to share issues while you owned them or company reorganisations.

For assets owned on 31 March 1982, you may also need details of their value on that date (see p. 109). Use catalogues, press advertisements or stock market share price records to value them.

With assets that are jointly owned, you need enter only your share of any gains. With a husband and wife, the gain or loss is split 50:50 between them unless they have told their tax inspectors that the asset is not owned equally (see p. 102).

CHARGEABLE GAINS AND ALLOWABLE LOSSES

The first page of the Capital gains pages has space at the top for you to write your name and the tax reference you will find on the front of your basic tax return. What you do next depends on what transactions you carried out in the year ending 5 April 2000.

If you have only made relatively straightforward transactions in quoted shares or securities, you can use the simple grid on page CG1 (see overleaf). But you cannot use this page if you are able to claim taper relief on any of the gains made or you want to claim any other tax relief that would reduce your gains other than indexation allowance.

If your transactions are more than just quoted shares, or you can claim taper relief, or you want to claim reliefs such as reinvestment relief, you must fill in pages CG2 to CG6 instead (see p. 284).

In some circumstances, you may need to give details of capital gains or losses even though you haven't disposed of the assets they relate to in the tax year ending 5 April 2000. For example, if you have been given something and agreed to take over the gain from its previous owner (hold-over relief), you have to pay tax on that gain if you become non-resident within six years of the end of the tax year in which the gift was made (see p. 106).

Include anything you have been given as a result of the reconstruction or takeover of a company, building society or mutual insurance company (see p. 120). But you don't need to enter any details of disposals of assets on which gains are tax-free. Thus you should leave out possessions which are worth £6,000 or less when you disposed of them – these are known as chattels (see p. 111). However, if you made a loss on the disposal of a chattel, you should give details since it can be used to reduce your tax bill.

PAGE CG1: QUOTED SHARES AND SECURITIES ONLY

A Enter details of quoted shares or securities disposed of	B Tick box if estimate or valuation used	C Tick box if asset held at 31 March 1982	D Enter the date of disposal	E Disposal proceeds	F Gain or loss after indexation allowance, if due (enter loss in brackets)	G Further information, including any elections made
1			/ /	£	£	
2			/ /	£	£	

This page is for giving details of each taxable disposal made during the tax year ending 5 April 2000. If you are likely to run out of space on page CG1, make photocopies before filling it in. Put your name and tax reference on each sheet.

Column A: Give details to identify the shares or unit trusts – the name of the company or unit trust fund manager, types of shares or units and the number disposed of.

Column B: Tick this box if your figures include any estimates or valuations. This would be the case if you owned the asset on 31 March 1982 when you need to estimate its value on that date (p. 109). Transactions with connected people also involve market valuations (see pp. 105 and 116). Give details of why you have used an estimate in column G, or on page CG7 if there is not enough space.

Column C: Tick if you owned the asset on 31 March 1982 – there are special rules for calculating the gains and losses on such assets (see p. 109). Also tick if you are treated as having owned it then – for example if your spouse did and has since given it to you.

Column D: Enter the date you disposed of the shares or securities, in numerical form (so 24 August 1999 would be 24/08/99).

Column E: Enter the total disposal proceeds, including any cash or other asset to be received in the future. But if the disposal was a gift or a sale to a connected person you should enter the market value of the asset (see p. 105).

Column F: Enter the net gain or loss after any indexation allowance you are claiming. Put losses in brackets. See Chapter 10, p. 102, for how to work out the gain or loss.

Column G: Give any other relevant details on the disposal, including if it is a disposal of part of a larger holding of shares (p. 115) or if you are making a rebasing election (p. 110).

You don't have to submit the calculations done to reach any of these figures – but you can if you want to. There's space on page CG7 to give details.

Total gains	**F1** £	*Total your gains in column F and enter the amount in box F1*
Total losses	**F2** £	*Total your losses in column F and enter the amount in box F2*

Add all your gains in column F and enter the total in box F1. Add all your losses and enter the total in box F2.

	box F1 *minus* box F2	*If your net gains exceed £7,100, carry on. If they are below £7,100 there is no liability. If you have a net loss, please fill in the losses summary on Page CG8*
Net gain or loss	**F3** £	

Subtract your total losses in box F2 from your total gains in box F1 and enter the answer in box F3. If the amount in box F3 is more than £7,100, continue to box F4.

If the amount in box F3 is £7,100 or less, there is no capital gains tax to pay – enter the amount in box F7 and box 8.7 on page CG8. Also enter '0' in box 8.8 on page CG8. If the amount in box F3 is a net loss, go to p. 000 and fill in the Capital losses summary on page CG8.

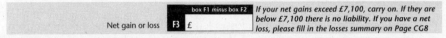

There are losses on several types of income you can deduct from a net chargeable gain if you haven't enough income to set them off against:

- any trading losses from self-employment (p. 247) or a partnership
- losses from furnished holiday lettings (p. 259)
- certain expenses incurred in the seven years after you have closed a business which would have been allowable against business income (post-cessation expenditure) – for example bad debts, costs of rectifying faulty work (p. 185)
- certain expenses incurred by employees up to six years after they have left their jobs (post-employment deductions) – for example, insurance premiums for policies that pay out against claims of faulty work.

If you have such losses, you can enter them in box F4 up to the amount in box F3.

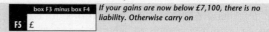

box F3 *minus* box F4 — If your gains are now below £7,100, there is no liability. Otherwise carry on

F5 £

Subtract the amount in box F4 from the amount in box F3 and enter the result in box F5. If the amount in box F5 is more than £7,100, continue to box F6.

If the amount in box F5 is £7,100 or less, there is no capital gains tax to pay – enter the amount in box F7 and box 8.7 on page CG8. Also enter '0' in box 8.8 on page CG8.

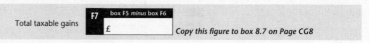

minus losses brought forward — **F6** £ — Enter losses brought forward up to the **smaller** of either the total losses brought forward or the figure in box F5 **minus** £7,100

You can deduct any allowable losses left over from previous tax years from the amount in box F5 (see p. 112). If you have enough losses held over, you can reduce your total taxable gains to £7,100, the amount that is tax-free for the tax year ending 5 April 2000.

If your losses from previous years are not big enough to reduce the amount in box F5 to £7,100, enter the full amount carried over in box F6. If your losses from previous years are more than enough to reduce the amount in box F5 to £7,100 enter in Box F6 the amount that subtracted from the amount in box F5 will leave exactly £7,100.

Total taxable gains — **F7** box F5 *minus* box F6

£ — Copy this figure to box 8.7 on Page CG8

Subtract the amount in box F6 from the amount in box F5 and enter the result in box F7. This is your total taxable gains for the year ending 5 April 2000. Copy this figure to box 8.7 on page CG8 and fill in the rest of that page. If there is any additional information you need to give, there is space on page CG7.

PAGES CG2 AND CG3: DISPOSALS OF MORE THAN QUOTED SHARES

Complete these pages if you have made disposals which include not only quoted shares and securities but also land, homes or unquoted shares. Also fill in these pages if you are claiming taper relief on disposals of shares or securities, or any other tax relief other than indexation allowance.

A Brief description of asset	AA* Type of disposal. Enter Q, U, L or O	B Tick box if estimate or valuation used	C Tick box if asset held at 31March 1982	D Enter the later of date of acquisition and 16 March 1998	E Enter the date of disposal	F Disposal proceeds	G Enter details of any elections made, reliefs claimed or due and state amount (£)
Gains on assets without mixed (business and non-business) use							
1				/ /	/ /	£	

Losses Description of asset	Type of * disposal. Enter Q, U, L or O	Tick box if estimate or valuation used	Tick box if asset held at 31March 1982	Enter the later of date of acquisition and 16 March 1998	Enter the date of disposal	Disposal proceeds	Enter details of any elections made, reliefs claimed or due and state amount (£)
13				/ /	/ /	£	

You will see there is space to give details of ten disposals that resulted in gains (two where the asset was used for both business and non-business purposes) and four that produced allowable losses. If you are likely to run out of space, make photocopies of pages CG2 and CG3 before filling them in. Put your name and tax reference on each extra sheet you submit.

Column A: Give details to identify the asset – the address of the property, for example, or the name of the company with shares, the type of share and the number disposed of.

Column AA: Enter one of the following letters in this column:

- Q for quoted shares or securities
- U for unquoted shares or securities
- L for land or property
- O for other assets (for example, goodwill).

Column B: Tick this box if your figures include any estimates or valuations. This would be the case if you owned the asset on 31 March 1982 when you need to estimate its value on that date (p. 109). Transactions with connected people also involve market valuations (see pp. 105 and 116). Give details of why you have used an estimate in column G, or on page CG7 if there is not enough space.

Column C: Tick if you owned the asset on 31 March 1982 – there are special rules for calculating the gains and losses on such assets (see p. 109). Also tick if you are treated as having owned it then – for example, if your spouse did and has since given it to you.

Column D: Enter the date you acquired the asset if it was after 16 March 1998. If it was on or before 16 March 1998, enter that date. Give the date in numerical form (so 24 August 1999 would be 24/08/99).

Column E: Enter the date you disposed of the asset, in numerical form.

Column F: Enter the total disposal proceeds, including any cash or other asset to be received in the future. But if the disposal was a gift or a sale to a connected person you should enter the market value of the asset (see p. 105).

If you have been given the right to something in the future in return for the disposal, this should also be included unless it would be taxed as income (for example, dividends or royalties). If it is not clear what you will get in the future – as with a share of any profits – include an estimate in the disposal proceeds. When that uncertain part is finally paid, this will count as another disposal – the right to the share of the profits will have been exchanged for real cash. There will then be another capital gain or loss to report at that time.

Column G: If you wish to claim any tax relief on the gain other than indexation allowance, give details here plus the amount claimed. These include private residence relief on your only or main home (p. 56), retirement relief when you retire from a business (p. 125) and rebasing relief (p. 110). Also say here if you are making any claim that defers the tax such as hold-over relief (p. 123), reinvestment relief (p. 123) or roll-over relief (p. 126). Special claim forms may be needed in addition to the tax return.

H	I	J	K			L	M
Chargeable Gains after reliefs but before losses and taper	Enter 'Bus' if business asset	Taper rate	Losses deducted			Gains after losses	Tapered gains (gains from column L x % in column J)
			K1 Allowable losses of the year	K2 Income losses of 1999-2000 set against gains	K3 Unused losses b/f from earlier years		
£	%	£	£	£	£	£	£
£	%	£	£	£	£	£	£

Column H: Enter in the *Gains* section the net gain after any indexation allowance or other relief, but before losses and taper relief. Enter any losses in the *Losses* section. If the assets are in rows nine or ten for mixed business and non-business use, split the gains and losses appropriately.

Add all your gains in column H and enter the total in box 8.1. Add all your losses and enter the total in box 8.2. Subtract the amount in box 8.2 from the amount in box 8.1. Continue with page CG3 unless any of the following applies:

- If the answer is £7,100 or less, you have no capital gains tax to pay in the tax year ending 5 April 2000. Enter the answer in box 8.3 and in box 8.7 on page CG8. Enter 0 in boxes 8.4, 8.5 and 8.6. Give any information needed on pages CG4 to CG6 and turn to page CG8.
- If the answer is more than £7,100 and you have enough losses brought forward from a previous year to reduce your gains to £7,100, you have no capital gains tax to pay. Enter in box 8.6 the amount of losses from previous years needed to achieve this and enter £7,100 in box 8.3 and in box 8.7 on page CG8. Enter 0 in boxes 8.4 and 8.5. Give any information needed on pages CG4 to CG6 and turn to page CG8.
- If the answer is a minus amount, your allowable losses are greater than your chargeable gains. You have no capital gains tax to pay – enter 0 in boxes 8.3, 8.4, 8.5 and 8.6 and box 8.7 on page CG8. Give any information needed on pages CG4 to CG6 and turn to page CG8.

Column I: Enter 'Bus' in this colum in the appropriate row if the asset was a business asset or used partly for business after 5 April 1998.

Column J: This column is for the taper rate on the disposal – the percentage of the net gain that is taxable after deducting taper relief. So if the rate of taper relief is 5 per cent, the taper rate is 95 per cent. Because taper relief only came in with the 1998 Budget, the taper rate will be 100 per cent for non-business assets (see p. 113).

Column K: This column is for entering any losses to be deducted from net gains – with three possible sources.

Column K1: Enter allowable losses from the tax year ending 5 April 2000. Allocate these against the gains on assets with the highest taper rates first. If you still have some losses unused after doing that, allocate the rest against the gains on the assets with the next highest taper rates.

Suppose, for example, you have a net gain of £10,000 with a taper rate of 100 per cent and another of £10,000 with a taper rate of 92.5 per cent. You have an allowable loss of £15,000. You should allocate £10,000 of the loss to the gain with a taper rate of 100 per cent, the highest taper rate. The remaining £5,000 of the loss should be allocated to the gain with the taper rate of 92.5 per cent. That leaves a net gain of £5,000 with a taper rate of 92.5 per cent. If you allocated the loss the other way – £10,000 to the gain with a taper rate of 92.5 per cent – you would be left with a net gain of £5,000 with a taper rate of 100 per cent, and a higher tax bill.

Note that you must deduct the losses so long as there are gains to deduct them from – you can't hold losses from the same tax year back even if your total gains are going to end up below the tax-free allowance of £7,100 for the tax year ending 5 April 2000.

Column K2 is for entering losses on several types of income you can deduct from a net chargeable gain if you haven't enough income to set them off against:

- any trading losses from self-employment (p. 247) or a partnership
- losses from furnished holiday lettings (p. 259)
- certain expenses incurred in the seven years after you have closed a business which would have been allowable against business income (post-cessation expenditure) – for example, bad debts, costs of rectifying faulty work (p. 185)
- certain expenses incurred by employees up to six years after they have left their jobs (post-employment deductions) – for example, insurance premiums for policies that pay out against claims of faulty work.

If you have such losses, you don't have to deduct them here – and you shouldn't deduct more than you need to reduce your total gains to the tax-free allowance of £7,100 for the tax year ending 5 April 2000.

Column K3 is for losses carried forward from earlier tax years. Again you shouldn't deduct more than you need to reduce your total gains to the tax-free allowance of £7,100 for the tax year ending 5 April 2000.

Add the losses claimed in column K2 and enter the total in box 8.5. Add the losses claimed in column K3 and enter the total in box 8.6.

Column L: For each asset, subtract the losses in Columns K1, K2 and K3 from the net gain in Column J and enter the result in Column L. This is the gain after losses.

Column M: For each asset, multiply the amount in Column L by the taper rate in Column J and enter the result in Column M. This is the tapered gain on the disposal.

So if the gain after losses is £10,000 and the taper rate is 92.5 per cent, the tapered gain on disposal would be:

$$£10,000 \times 92.5\% = £9,250$$

Add the gains in column M and enter the total in box 8.3.

11 Attributed gains from UK resident trusts *(enter the name of the Trust on Page CG7)*	£
12 Attributed gains from non UK resident trusts *(enter the name of the Trust on Page CG7)*	£

Enter any gains which are attributable to you as the person who put assets into a trust which is not resident in the UK or is a beneficiary of such a trust. This may also apply with a trust resident in the UK. If you think either of these applies to you, ask for Inland Revenue Help Sheet *IR299 Non-resident trusts and capital gains tax*. Give the name of the trust on page CG7 and details of how the gains have been attributed to you.

Total of attributed gains	**8.4**	£
		box 8.3 + box 8.4
Total taxable gains		£

Add the amounts of attributed gains and enter the total in box 8.4.

Add the amount in box 8.3 to the amount in box 8.4 to find your total taxable gains. Enter the answer in the box and copy it to box 8.7 on page CG8. Complete pages CG4, CG5 and CG6 for all disposals not involving quoted shares or securities.

You don't have to submit the calculations done to reach these figures – but you can if you want to. There's space on page CG7 to give details.

PAGES CG4 TO CG6: FURTHER INFORMATION

These pages are for giving extra details needed for any transactions in unquoted shares or securities, land and property or other assets. Each page has room for two such transactions – if you need more space, make copies.

PAGE CG7: ADDITIONAL INFORMATION

This page is for any extra details you need to give.

PAGE CG8: CHARGEABLE GAINS AND ALLOWABLE LOSSES

Start by completing the first few boxes which summarise what you have already filled in.

Chargeable gains and allowable losses

Once you have completed Page CG1, or Pages CG2 to CG6, fill in this Page.

Have you 'ticked' any row in Column B, 'Tick box if estimate or valuation used' on Pages CG1 or CG2? | NO | | YES | |

Have you given details in Column G on Pages CG2 and CG3 of any Capital Gains reliefs claimed or due? | NO | | YES | |

If you have used an estimate or valuation in listing any of your gains or losses, there will be a tick in column B on page CG1 or CG2. Tick YES in the first line if there are any ticks in column B, and NO if not.

If you have filled in pages CG2 and CG3 and have claimed any tax relief on a gain other than indexation allowance in column G, tick YES in the second line. Tick NO if you have not claimed any reliefs.

Enter the number of transactions from Page CG1 or column AA on Page CG2 for:

- transactions in quoted shares or securities | box Q | |
- transactions in unquoted shares or securities | box U | |
- transactions in land and property | box L | |
- other transactions | box O | |

Enter the number of transactions in the four main categories:

- Box Q – quoted shares and securities
- Box U – unquoted shares or securities
- Box L – land or property
- Box O – any other assets

If you have filled in page CG1, all the transactions should be 'Q' – quoted shares or securities. If you have filled in pages CG2 and CG3, each transaction is categorised in column AA.

• Total taxable gains (from page CG1 or page CG3)	8.7 £

Enter the total taxable gains from Box F7 on page CG1 or from the total taxable gains box on page CG3, bottom right.

	box 8.7 *minus* £7,100
• Your taxable gains *minus* the annual exempt amount	8.8 £

Subtract £7,100 from the amount in box 8.7 and enter the result in box 8.8. This is the net amount of chargeable capital gains you have to pay tax on in the tax year ending 5 April 2000.

• Additional liability in respect of non-resident or dual resident trusts (see Notes, page CGN6)	8.9 £

This is where you give details if you have benefited directly or indirectly from non-resident or dual resident trusts. You may be liable to capital gains tax on anything you receive from the trust – whether it be cash, a loan or an asset. You need to give details in box 8.9 of the amount of tax due on what you have received in the tax year ending 5 April 2000. To work this out, use the calculator on Help Sheet *IR301 Capital gains on benefits from non-resident and dual resident trusts*. Enter the name of the trust (and its tax reference if you know it) on page CG7.

CAPITAL LOSSES

This part of the Capital gains supplementary pages helps you keep track of your allowable losses. It summarises the losses you have made in the year ending 5 April 2000 and how you have used them. And it lists losses from previous years and whether these have been used. The information will be useful when you come to fill in next year's tax return.

There are some losses that can only be set against gains of certain types – called 'clogged losses'. These are losses on:

- Disposals to connected persons (see p. 112). These losses can only be set against gains on disposals to the same connected person
- Assets transferred to you after 15 June 1999 by trustees when you become absolutely entitled to settled property. These losses can only be set against gains on the same asset or an asset derived from that asset and have to be used before any other losses.

If you have clogged losses, make a copy of page CG8 for each one and keep separate records for each one. This will help you use them at the right time. Keep each copy until the clogged losses have been fully used up.

This year's losses

The first few boxes are for losses for the tax year ending 5 April 2000. Enter in box 8.10 the total allowable losses for the year – the figure from box F2 on page CG1 or box 8.2 on page CG3.

Used against gains (total of column K1 on Page CG3, or the smaller of boxes F1 and F2 on Page CG1)	8.11 £

Enter in box 8.11 the amount of the allowable losses for the tax year ending 5 April 2000 used to reduce your chargeable gains in that year. This is the total of the amounts entered in column K1 on Page CG3, or the smaller of boxes F1 and F2 on Page CG1.

Used against earlier years' gains (generally only available to personal representatives, see Notes, page CGN11)	8.12 £

Personal representatives clearing up the estate of someone who has died can carry unused losses back to earlier tax years and effectively claim a tax rebate for the estate (see p. 112). Enter any amount this applies to in box 8.12.

Used against income (only losses of the type described on page CGN9 can be used against income)	8.13A £	amount claimed against income of 1999-2000	box 8.13A + box 8.13B
	8.13B £	amount claimed against income of 1998-99	8.13 £

If you have made losses on shares in unquoted trading companies, you can set them off against income from the same tax year or the previous tax year. For more information, see Help Sheet *IR286 Income tax losses for new shares you have subscribed for in unlisted trading companies* and *IR297 Enterprise Investment Scheme and Capital Gains Tax.*

If you make such a claim, enter the amount claimed against income for the tax year ending 5 April 2000 in box 8.13A, and the amount against the previous tax year in box 8.13B. Add boxes 8.13A and 8.13B and enter the total in box 8.13.

	box 8.10 *minus* (boxes 8.11 + 8.12 + 8.13)
• This year's unused losses	8.14 £

Add the amounts in boxes 8.11, 8.12 and 8.13 and subtract the total from the amount in box 8.10. Enter the result in box 8.14 – this is the total unused losses for the tax year ending 5 April 2000 which can be carried forward to future tax years.

Earlier years' losses

■ *Earlier years' losses*	
• Unused losses of 1996-97 and later years	8.15 £

The next few boxes record what has happened to losses carried forward from previous tax years. Enter in box 8.15 the amount carried over from the tax year ending 5 April 1997 and later tax years. You can find the figures you need on last year's tax return – the one for the 1998-99 tax year. Add the figures in boxes 8.14 and 8.15 of that tax return to fill in box 8.15 on this year's tax return.

• Used this year (losses from box 8.15 are used in priority to losses from box 8.18) (column K3 on Page CG3 or box F6 on Page CG1)	8.16 £

Enter in box 8.16 the amount of the losses from box 8.15 used this year – these losses must be used before losses from earlier years. The figure is the amount in box F6 on page CG1 or the total in column K3 on page CG3 – if none of these losses have been used, put 0 in box 8.16.

	box 8.15 *minus* box 8.16
• Remaining unused losses of 1996-97 and later years	8.17 £

Subtract the amount in box 8.16 from the amount in box 8.15 and enter the result in box 8.17. This is the remaining unused losses from the tax year ending 5 April 1997 and later years.

• Unused losses of 1995-96 and earlier years	8.18 £

Enter in box 8.18 the total of any unused losses from the tax year ending 5 April 1996 and earlier tax years. You can find this figure in box 8.12 of last year's tax return – the one for the 1998-99 tax year.

<table>
<tr><td>• Used this year (losses from box 8.15 are used in priority to losses from box 8.18)
(column K3 on Page CG3 or box F6 on Page CG1)</td><td></td></tr>
</table>

Box 8.19 records the mount of losses from the tax year ending 5 April 1996 and earlier tax years used in the tax year ending 5 April 2000. It can be found by subtracting the amount in box 8.16 or box F6 from the amount in box 8.6. If box 8.6 and box F6 are blank, put 0 in this box.

Total of unused losses to carry forward

Finally, the tax return has space to note down the totals of losses you can carry forward to future tax years.

<table>
<tr><td>• Carried forward losses of 1996-97 and later years</td><td></td></tr>
</table>

Add the amounts in boxes 8.14 and 8.17 and enter the total in box 8.20. This is the amount of losses for the tax year ending 5 April 1997 and later tax years you can carry forward.

<table>
<tr><td>• Carried forward losses of 1995-96 and earlier years</td><td>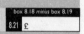</td></tr>
</table>

Subtract the amount in box 8.19 from the amount in box 8.18 and enter the result in box 8.21. This is the amount of losses for the tax year ending 5 April 1996 and earlier tax years you can carry forward.

NON-RESIDENCE

29 Are you claiming that you were not resident, or not ordinarily resident, or not domiciled, in the UK, or dual resident in the UK and another country, for all or part of the year?

 NO YES   NON-RESIDENCE ETC YES

If you are a resident of the UK, you are liable for UK tax on all your income whether it comes from within the UK or abroad. But, if you count as a non-resident, there is no UK tax on your income from abroad, only on any income which originates in the UK.

If you want to claim non-residence (or non-domicile) for the tax year ending 5 April 2000, you need to fill in the Non-residence Supplement which you can get through the Orderline (see p. 139). You are likely to need this if:

- you are normally a UK resident but you are working abroad for an extended period
- you have been a UK resident but you are going to live abroad permanently or indefinitely – for example because you are retiring abroad
- you have been resident elsewhere but you are based in the UK for now or you have returned for permanent residence.

This guide cannot give you all the detail you may need so you should consult a professional adviser.

Residency is not defined in the tax laws, but broadly it means the place where you usually live. Because different countries use different criteria to decide who is resident, it is possible to count as a resident of more than one country at the same time, in which case you could pay two lots of tax on the same income. However, the UK has double taxation agreements with many countries to avoid this situation.

In general, payment of UK taxes depends on whether or not you were resident during the particular tax year in question. Occasionally, it may hinge on where you are ordinarily resident. Again, there is no hard and fast definition, but basically your ordinary residence is the country you are resident in year after year, which you use as your base, returning to it for extended periods, and probably where you have an established home.

Your domicile can be the key to whether or not there is tax on foreign income and gains you receive and any inheritance tax to pay on your estate when you die. Your country of domicile is the place which you consider to be your permanent home and where you would intend to end your days. You can have only one country of domicile and it is not necessarily the country in which you are resident or ordinarily resident. Claims for foreign domicile should be made as soon as possible on form DOM1.

Note that even if you are non-resident for tax purposes, you might still be able to claim the UK personal tax allowances to set against your income from UK sources, for example, if you are a citizen of a Commonwealth country or a European country within the European Economic Area (this includes the UK), a Crown employee (or a widow or widower of someone who was a Crown employee) or employed by a UK missionary service.

If your intention is to be out of the country for less than four years, you could have continued to pay any mortgage on your UK home through MIRAS and so claim the tax relief on it (see p. 50) for the tax year ending 5 April 2000.

A word of warning: there are Inland Revenue concessions which might apply to you. You can claim the concessions, providing you don't use them simply as a means of avoiding tax. If the Inland Revenue suspects that tax avoidance is your main motive, it will refuse you the concession.

How do you count as being non-resident?
If you have generally been considered as a UK resident, to count as non-resident for tax purposes, you need to pass all four of the following tests:

- the motive test
- the absent for a whole tax year test
- the 183 days test
- the 91 days test.

The notes which accompany the Non-residence Supplement include a calculator which will help you to work out whether you pass all these tests.

The motive test
You will pass this test if you go abroad to work full-time, providing the other tests are also met. Whether or not your job is full-time is judged, first, by comparing your hours with the norm in the UK, but if your job is less struc-

tured it will be assessed on its own merits and in the light of what is normal for your type of work and the country you are going to. You could also count as working full-time if you have two or more part-time jobs.

By concession, if you count as non-resident because of your work abroad, your wife or husband, if they go with you, will also count as non-resident, providing they pass the other tests.

Another way to pass the test is if you go abroad to live permanently or at least indefinitely. The Inland Revenue will want evidence that this is your intention – for example, that you have bought a home abroad or you are going to marry someone in another country. If you still have a UK home, it wants to know how that fits with your plans to live overseas. Once you've lived abroad for three years, it will be accepted that you are non-resident.

If you can't pass this test at the time you go away, the situation can be reviewed later on, if new evidence of your motive becomes available or once you have been abroad for three years.

The absent for a whole tax year test
To count as non-resident for a tax year, if you work abroad, your job must last for at least a whole tax year and you must be out of the country for the whole tax year or longer, except for visits within the other rules (see below). Similarly, if you go to live abroad permanently or indefinitely, you must be out of the country for at least a whole tax year.

By concession, in the year you leave and the year you return, you can count as non-resident for just part of the year, provided that year is part of a longer period of non-residency. If you want to claim this split year treatment, you must give details of your date of arrival in or departure from the UK in box 9.25 or box 9.26 of the supplementary pages.

The 183 days test
You will always count as resident for the tax year if you spend 183 days or more in the UK. There are no exceptions to this rule. For example, if you make visits back home during a period working abroad, the total of your visits during any tax year must come to less than 183 days if you are not to lose your status as a non-resident. For the purposes of this rule and the next, the days on which you travel do not count as days spent in the UK.

The 91 days test
In addition to the 183 days test, the average time you spend in the UK must come to less than 91 days in a tax year. This is worked out over the period

since you left until you have been away for four tax years. After that it is worked out over the most recent four tax years. You are allowed to ignore periods you had to spend in the UK for reasons beyond your control – for example, because someone in your family was ill.

How do you count as being non-domiciled in the UK?

Your domicile is relevant only if it will affect the tax you must pay, so unless you fall into one of the following categories, you do not need to fill in boxes 9.27 to 9.31, and you should also leave box 9.5 blank. The tax areas which might be affected are where:

- you have income or gains from foreign investments which you will not be bringing in full into the UK
- you are claiming UK tax relief on contributions to a foreign pension scheme made out of earnings from a non-UK resident employer
- the costs of travelling between the UK and your normal home have been paid by your employer
- you worked abroad for a non-UK employer and have not brought all the earnings into the UK.

You can have only one domicile at a time and there are three ways in which it can be established: by birth, by dependency or by choice. From birth, you normally have the domicile of your father – that is not necessarily the same as the country in which you were born. If the domicile of the person on whom you are dependant changes, so will yours. Similarly, if you become dependant on someone else of a different domicile, your own domicile will fall into line with that. Women no longer acquire their husbands' domicile on marriage. Once you reach the age of 16, you have the right to choose a new domicile but the change is not easily made. You would need to show that you had settled in the new country of domicile with a view to staying there permanently. Your home, business interests, social and family ties, and the form of any will would all be relevant, but other factors could also be just as important.

> ## TAX-SAVING IDEAS
>
> If you go to work or live abroad, make sure your trips back home average less than 91 days a year and come to less than 183 days in any single tax year to avoid paying UK taxes on your overseas income.
>
> Taking a long lease of three years on a home abroad would help to show that you intended to live abroad permanently.
>
> If you are returning permanently to the UK after a period of non-residence abroad and you have been saving through an offshore roll-up fund, make sure you sell your investment before you become a UK resident again. If you don't, you will become liable for tax on the rolled-up income.

KEEPING AN EYE ON YOUR TAX AFFAIRS

The introduction of self-assessment means you can take control of your tax affairs, and make sure you don't pay a penny more than you should. But even if you do all the sums, there are several forms the Inland Revenue will send you that you need to check to make sure you aren't paying too much.

This chapter looks at three of the most important forms:

- the Tax Calculation which your tax inspector issues after you send in your tax return – correcting any mistakes and setting out his or her calculations of your tax bill
- the PAYE Coding Notice sent to people who work for someone else – this tells your employer how much tax to deduct from your pay
- the Statement of Account sent to taxpayers who have income from being self-employed, rent from letting out property or income from investments paid without deduction of tax.

TAX CALCULATION

Once you have sent in your tax return, the Inland Revenue checks through it for any obvious errors – such as arithmetical mistakes or failing to copy figures correctly from one part to another. If you have decided not to work out your own tax bill, it is calculated for you. And even if you have done the sums yourself, the Inland Revenue checks your answers by running the figures through its computers. The Tax Calculation form tells you the result of this process, the total tax the inspector thinks you owe and the amount of any payments on account you have to make. Check this carefully as soon as it arrives and challenge your tax inspector if you don't agree with the figures.

The first page of the Tax Calculation form summarises the figures:

- first it says if there are any corrections to your tax return – if there are, they will be listed on the back of the first page
- then it tells you the total amount of income tax plus capital gains tax owed for the tax year – the calculation will be set out on the second sheet

- lastly it says what the tax inspector calculates as the two payments on account you have to make towards the next year's tax bill (see p. 17).

If you have calculated your own tax bill, checking the Tax Calculation form is straightforward. It is simply a matter of comparing the figures you worked out on the Tax Calculation Guide with the inspector's calculation. If you have left it to the tax inspector to do the sums, you will need a copy of your tax return and a calculator to check the figures.

If there is anything you don't understand on the Tax Calculation form, write or phone your tax office for clarification. And if you disagree with the tax inspector's figures, do the same – otherwise you will be expected to pay up.

PAYE CODING NOTICE

This form sets out the calculations your tax inspector has made in setting your PAYE code for the tax year. Your employer will use the code to work out how much tax should be deducted from your pay. People with two jobs should have two PAYE codes – and two Coding Notices.

If you have retired, any pensions you get from an employer's pension scheme or personal pension will also have tax deducted from them before you receive the money. Again, you should have a PAYE code for each one if you have more than one substantial pension.

Your PAYE code reflects the amount of allowances your tax inspector estimates you can set against your earnings in the current tax year. It may also be adjusted to collect tax on fringe benefits and income such as freelance earnings, odd pensions and savings interest. The amounts are based on information given in your tax return, by your employer and by other organisations that send details of payments to the Inland Revenue.

If you have been given the correct code or codes, you will have paid the right amount of tax on your income by the end of the tax year. But if there has been a mistake, you may pay too much and have to wait for a rebate. And although paying too little tax may seem attractive, you will have to make up any underpayment in the following tax year – often in one go if it is more than £1,000. So it makes sense to check your PAYE code carefully whenever you receive a Coding Notice.

Checking a Coding Notice

The main figures on a PAYE Coding Notice are in two columns. The first lists the allowances that are to be set off against this income to reduce the tax bill on it. If this is your main source of income, the Coding Notice should normally list all your allowances unless they are specifically to be set off against other types of income (for example, against rents or freelance income).

The second column lists amounts that will be deducted from your allowances in order to collect extra tax. For example, if you have taxable fringe benefits, their taxable value will normally be in this column. So will other sources of untaxed income, such as freelance earnings, taxable state pensions and benefits and income from savings that have not been taxed.

Checking the entries is very straightforward – the Inland Revenue guide sent out with notices explains the headings. Start by making sure you have all the allowances and deductions you're entitled to in the first column. Some allowances and deductions won't be included for basic rate taxpayers where they get tax relief directly. For example, you get tax relief at the basic rate on contributions to a personal pension scheme by paying lower premiums (see p. 75). If you pay tax at the higher rates, there will be a entry on your Coding Notice to give you the extra relief, as the following example shows. Higher rate tax relief can also be given in this way on single gifts to charity – Gift Aid (see p. 184).

E X A M P L E

Gerry Walker makes £500 gross (before-tax relief) in personal pension payments in the tax year beginning 6 April 2000. Since the basic rate of tax for the tax year is 22 per cent, he gets basic rate tax relief of 22 per cent of £500 = £110. So he actually hands over £500 – £110 = £390.

But Gerry pays tax at the higher rate, so he is entitled to tax relief of 40 per cent of £500 = £200. The extra £90 (£200 – £110) is given by increasing his tax allowances by £225, since 40 per cent of £225 is £90.

Then check the amounts to be taken away from your tax allowances in the second column. These include the **Allowance restriction** for tax allowances restricted to tax relief at 10 per cent only – for example, married couple's allowance for people aged 65 and over and widow's bereavement allowance. You will have been given these allowances in the first column, but the PAYE system would then give you tax relief at your top rate of tax. This will be the right amount of tax relief if you pay tax at the 10 per cent lower rate of tax only. But if your top rate is the 22 per cent basic rate or the 40 per cent higher rate, you would get too much tax relief. The allowance restriction recovers the extra tax relief you would get if this happened.

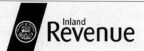

PAYE Coding Notice

This form shows your
tax code for the tax year   **2000/01**

*Please keep all your coding notices. You may need
to refer to them if you have to fill in a Tax Return.*

846

MR H SVENSEN
143 WENDOVER ROAD
LONDON

SW14 5NJ

HM INSPECTOR OF TAXES
LONDON PROVINCIAL 24
GRAYFIELD HOUSE
5 BANKHEAD AVENUE
SIGHTHILL
EDINBURGH   EH11 4AE

Tax Office telephone	Date of issue
0131 453 7200	12 JAN 2000

*Please quote your Tax reference
and National Insurance number
if you contact us*

Tax reference	National Insurance number
976/52425	YR 61 53 51 C

Your tax code for the year shown above is   **214T**

This tax code is used to deduct tax payable on your income
from

VIKING SHIPBUILDERS

If you move to another job, your new employer will normally
continue to use this tax code.
The tax code is worked out as follows:

The *'See note'* columns below refer to the numbered notes
in the guidance leaflet P3 *Understanding Your Tax Code.*
Leaflet P3 also tells you about the **letter part** of your
tax code.

Check that the details are correct. If you think they are
wrong, or you have any queries, contact your Tax Office
(details above).

This coding notice replaces any previous notice for the
year. You should pass it to your tax adviser if you have one.

See note	Your tax allowances	£
01	PERSONAL ALLOWANCE	4385
10	PROFESSIONAL SUBSCRIPTIONS	60
	Total allowances **A**	4445

See note	Amounts taken away from your total allowances	£
30	BENEFITS IN KIND	150
30	CAR BENEFIT	2146
	Total deductions **B**	2296

C Your tax free amount for the year is £ 2149 , making your Tax Code 214T

*See example
overleaf*

If necessary we will use this box to give you further information about your tax code

From 6 April 2000, the following are withdrawn:
- the Married Couple's allowance for couples aged under 65
- relief for maintenance payments for those born after
  5 April 1935
- the Additional Personal allowance.
From the same date, the Government plans to cut the basic
rate of tax to 22%. A new Children's Tax credit will also
be introduced from April 2001. For more information
please read the enclosed leaflet FS2.

EXAMPLE

Harold Svensen checks his Coding Notice for the 2000–01 tax year – the one beginning 6 April 2000. This is the code for his main job with Viking Shipbuilders.

He first sees that he has been given the right tax allowances for the year:

- £4,385 personal allowance
- £60 a year for his subscription to his professional body.

This makes total allowances of £4,445. The following amounts are deducted from this:

- £150 for Harold's membership of a local sports club paid by the company
- £2,146 for the benefit of his company car.

Thus Harold has total deductions of £2,296. Harold's tax-free amount for the year is £4,445 – £2,296 = £2,149. His tax code is found by dropping the last digit to get 214; the letter to be added is T, because he has a company car (see p. 305). So Harold's code is 214T.

If you expect your top rate of tax to have changed in this tax year, this restriction might be too large or too small. If so, tell your Tax Inspector so the right amount of tax is deducted through PAYE.

EXAMPLE

Betty Pinder gets widow's bereavement allowance – £1,970 at 10 per cent only for the tax year beginning 6 April 2000. This means she should get tax relief of 10 per cent of £1,970 = £197. But Betty pays tax at the higher rate of 40 per cent – so if the allowance of £1,970 is set against her income, the PAYE system would give her tax relief of 40 per cent of £1,970 = £788. This is £788 – £197 = £591 more tax relief than she should receive.

Betty's tax inspector corrects this with an allowance restriction of £1,478: by deducting this amount away from her allowances, the Inland Revenue recoups 40 per cent of £1,478 = £591.

Untaxed interest collects tax on interest you are expected to get during the tax year which will not have tax deducted from it first – for example, from National Savings Investment Account (see p. 151). If you are a basic rate taxpayer, the amount entered here will be less than you actually get. This is because you pay tax on interest at 20 per cent only (p. 62) but tax is deducted from your earnings at 22 per cent for the tax year which began on 6 April 2000. This entry will avoid collecting too much tax on it.

> ### EXAMPLE
> Gerry Walker gets £200 of interest from his National Savings Investment Account in the tax year beginning 6 April 2000. He should pay tax of 20 per cent of £200 = £40. But he is a basic rate taxpayer, so adding £200 to his taxable income would collect too much – 22 per cent of £200 = £44.
>
> Gerry's tax inspector adds £182 to Gerry's income with an untaxed income deduction from his PAYE code. This will collect the right amount, since 22 per cent of £182 = £40.

Higher rate tax adjustment collects extra higher rate tax due on interest, dividends and some other sorts of income which are paid after deduction of tax which covers any basic rate tax due.

> ### EXAMPLE
> Betty Pinder pays tax at the higher rate and receives £1,000 of interest. This is paid after deduction of tax at 20 per cent: 20 per cent of £1,000 is £200, so she receives £1,000 – £200 = £800 of savings income net.
>
> But Betty should have paid tax at 40 per cent on the gross amount – 40 per cent of £1,000 = £400. So she owes another £400 – £200 = £200. To collect this £200, a higher rate tax adjustment of £500 is made: by adding £500 to Betty's taxable income, she will pay 40 per cent of £500 = £200 on her income taxed under PAYE.

If you have underpaid up to £1,000 of tax in a previous tax year, the Inland Revenue will normally try to collect this by a **Tax underpaid** adjustment to your PAYE code. For example, if you owe £500 and pay tax at the basic rate of 22 per cent, your tax inspector will add £2,273 to your taxable income to collect it: 22 per cent of £2,273 = £500.

Calculating your PAYE code
Total deductions are subtracted from total allowances to find the amount of income covered by the PAYE code which can be tax-free during the tax year. This is then converted into a PAYE code – normally by knocking off the last figure and adding one of the following letters, depending on your allowances and tax rate:

L - personal allowance for those aged under 65 only
P - personal allowance for those aged 65-74 only
Y - personal allowance for the over-75s only

H - personal allowance for under-65s and married couple's allowance for those aged 65 and over, paying tax at the basic rate

A - personal allowance for under-65s and married couple's allowance for those aged 65 and over, paying tax at the higher rate

V - personal allowance and married couple's allowance for those aged 65-74, paying tax at the basic rate.

So if your only tax allowance is the single person's allowance for people under 65 of £4,385 and you have £160 deductions for fringe benefits, your total tax-free amount for the year will be £4,385 – £160 = £4,225. Your code is found by knocking off the last figure to give you 422, and adding L because you get only the single person's allowance. Your PAYE code will be 422L.

When it comes to deducting tax from your pay, the employer's tax tables will say that an employee with a code of 422 was entitled to tax-free pay during the tax year of £4,229 – divided equally over the year.

The letters after the number mean that if the main allowances change, your PAYE code can be adjusted by your employer or pension provider. So when the single person's allowance was increased from £4,335 to £4,385 in the 2000 budget, everyone with an L code automatically got an extra £50 of tax-free pay.

If the code ends in the letter T, your tax position is more complicated – you may be getting other allowances, for example, blind person's allowance or allowances for people aged 75 and over. You could also get it if you have fringe benefits such as a company car, or have asked for it because you don't want your employer to know what allowances you are entitled to. Changes cannot be made automatically if you have this sort of code and you will have to wait longer for the tax office to make the adjustments.

K codes
If the amount of deductions is more than your allowances, you will have a PAYE code that begins with a K. This is calculated as follows:

- subtract the deductions from the allowances – the answer will be a negative number
- take the last figure off the number
- reduce that number by one
- put a K in front of the answer to give a PAYE code.

K codes have to be recalculated every time the tax allowances change or there is some alteration in your circumstances.

EXAMPLE

Sanjay Patel is a single man, and his only tax allowance is the personal allowance of £4,385. However, he has a company car with a taxable value of £4,650, so his tax-free amount for the year is £4,385 – £4,650 = – £265.

His PAYE code is therefore found by dropping the last digit to get 26. Then he subtracts 1 to get 25 – giving a code of K25. With a PAYE code of K25, Sanjay would have £259 added to his pay for the year before the tax was worked out (instead of having some allowances deducted).

PAYE codes with more than one source of income

There are special PAYE codes which don't have numbers or which have numbers which don't stand for tax allowances. These are mainly used for deducting tax from second or third sources of income:

- BR – this income is all to be taxed at the basic rate. This is where other sources of income have had all your allowances set against them and used up the amount of income which is taxed at the lower rate
- D – this income is all to be taxed at the higher rate. This is where other sources of income have had all your allowances set against them and used up the amount of income which is taxed at the lower and basic rates
- DT – you are not entitled to any tax-free pay, but this source of income is to be taxed first at the lower rate, then the basic rate and perhaps eventually the higher rate
- NT – this income should be paid without any tax being deducted, perhaps because it is less than your tax-free allowances.

STATEMENT OF ACCOUNT

If you have income of £500 or more in a tax year from being self-employed, from letting out property or from investments which pay out income without deduction of tax, you will normally have to make two payments of tax on account against your final tax bill for the year. However, there will be no need to make such payments if most of your tax – 80 per cent or more – is deducted from your income at source.

If you do have to make payments on account, the first is due on 31 January during the tax year, the second by 31 July after it has finished. The amounts are based on the income you got in the previous tax year.

If you are calculating your own tax bill (see p. 16), it is up to you to work out the amounts. But if you ask your tax inspector to do the calculations, the amounts will be notified to you in two Statements of Account sent out by the

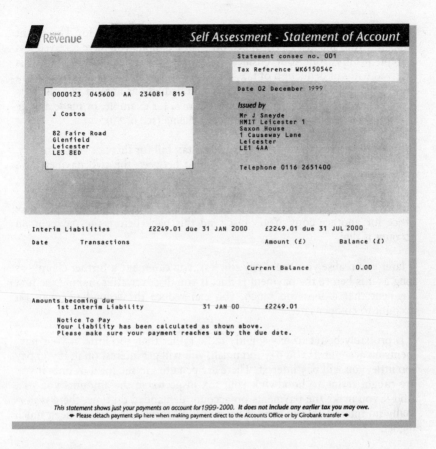

Inland Revenue: one around December during the tax year; the other around the end of the tax year.

Unless you appeal against a Statement of Account, you must pay the tax requested on it by the right date – paying late could mean an interest charge (see p. 18). So it is vital to check the statement. If it demands more than you should pay in the current tax year, you can ask for the payments to be reduced. But you must do this before the date the payment is due. This section of the guide tells you how to check a statement and how to claim a reduction.

How to reduce your payments on account
If you think your tax bills for the types of income covered by a Statement of Account will be lower than in the previous year, you can claim to make a

lower payment on account than the Inland Revenue is asking for. This might happen if your income has dropped off – for example, you have received less in rent, profits from your business or on the investment income which is received without deduction of tax. Or your tax bill might be less because you are entitled to claim higher allowances and deductions against your income – if you have paid large pension contributions, for example, or made a large investment in the Enterprise Investment Scheme (see p. 80).

If this is the case, work out your expected tax bill for this tax year carefully. Then calculate how this should be divided between the two payments on account. If you should be paying less than the Inland Revenue is asking for, make your claim to pay less on Inland Revenue form SA303. A copy is sent out with every Statement of Account – if you have lost yours, ask your tax office for another copy. You must send this back before the payment on account is due.

If later you realise you could pay still less, you can make a further claim – as long as it is before the payment is due. If you discover after making the first payment that it was too much, you can reduce the second payment on account to compensate.

It is probably better to pay slightly more rather than too little in your payments on account. If you pay too much, you will get interest on it; if you pay too little, you will pay interest. There are penalties in the form of fines if you are caught trying to hoodwink your tax inspector in the amounts you pay. And if you make the payments on account demanded on time, there is normally no interest to pay even if your tax bill turns out to have been much higher.

TAX-FREE INCOME

Income from a job
Check with your employer if you are uncertain about whether any of these forms of income is taxable

- work-related expenses you are reimbursed for by your employer covered by an agreement with the Inland Revenue that they do not need to be declared (see p. 202)
- some fringe benefits, such as canteen meals and Christmas parties provided for all staff, special clothes for the job and subscriptions to approved professional societies (see p. 83)
- foreign service allowances paid to diplomats and other servants of the Crown
- the first 15p a day of luncheon vouchers
- goods and services your employer lets you have cheaply (see p. 83)
- miners' free coal or cash allowances in lieu of coal
- long-service awards so long as they are not in cash and are within set limits (see p. 85)
- awards from approved suggestions schemes (see p. 200)
- payments for moving to higher-cost housing areas, within set limits (see p. 85)
- genuine personal gifts – for example, wedding presents
- pay received under a registered profit-related pay scheme on or before 31 December 1999 – within limits (see p. 200)

Income on leaving a job
Check with your ex-employer

- statutory redundancy payments
- wages in lieu of notice
- gratuities from the armed forces
- lump-sum compensation for an injury or disability that means you can no longer do the job
- tax-free lump sum instead of part of a pension and certain other ex gratia payments on retirement or death

- up to £30,000 of other compensation on leaving a job, including counselling and outplacement services (see p. 207)

Pensions and benefits
Check with the organisation paying the pension or benefit

- state pension Christmas bonus
- war widows' and orphans' pensions and equivalent overseas pensions
- widow's payment
- certain compensation payments and pensions paid to victims of Nazi persecution
- war disablement pensions
- additional pensions paid to holders of some bravery awards such as the Victoria Cross
- the part of a pension paid to a former employee who retires because of a disability caused by injury at work or a work-related illness which is in excess of the pension paid to an employee who retires on normal ill-health grounds
- income support paid to people aged 60 or over, single parents with a child under 16 and those staying at home to look after a severely disabled person. Part of income support paid to unemployed people may be tax-free – see your statement of taxable benefits (p. 159)
- jobfinder's grant, most youth training scheme allowances, employment rehabilitation and training allowances, back to work bonus
- family credit and its successor, working families tax credit
- housing benefit and council tax benefit
- improvement and renovation grants for your home
- payments from the social fund
- maternity allowance (but statutory maternity pay is taxable)
- child benefit, one-parent benefit, school uniform grants
- additions for dependent children paid with a state pension or social security benefit
- guardian's allowance
- student grants and educational maintenance allowance
- incapacity benefit for first 28 weeks (and if paid to replace invalidity benefit)
- industrial disablement benefits
- disability living allowance, disability working allowance
- attendance allowance

Investment income
If in doubt, check with the organisation paying the income

- interest on National Savings Certificates (and Ulster Savings Certificates if you normally live in Northern Ireland), National Savings Children's

Bonus Bonds
- interest and terminal bonuses on bank and building society Save-As-You-Earn (SAYE) schemes
- first £70 of interest each year from National Savings Ordinary Account (£140 for married couples with a joint account)
- dividends and other income from a personal equity plan (PEP), so long as no more than £180 is drawn out in interest (see p. 79)
- interest on a tax-exempt special savings account (TESSA) kept open for the full five years – provided some of it is reinvested for the term of the account (see p. 80)
- income from an individual savings account (ISA) – see p. 76
- dividends on ordinary shares in a venture capital trust (see p. 82)
- part of the income paid by an annuity
- amount paid out by a regular-premium life insurance policy such as an endowment policy or a unit-linked one – including money paid out on the death of the policyholder (see p. 67)
- loan interest paid to members of a credit union

Other tax-free income
If in doubt, check with the organisation paying out the money

- what you receive under maintenance agreements from 6 April 2000 (previously payments under agreements made before 15 March 1988 were taxable) – see p. 47.
- up to £4,250 a year of income from letting out a furnished room in your only or main home – the rent a room scheme (p. 253)
- gambling winnings (as long as it is not your business)
- lottery winnings
- premium bond prizes
- income from qualifying life insurance policies that pay out on death – for example, mortgage protection policies, family income benefit policies (see p. 164)
- income from insurance policies to cover mortgage payments if you are sick or unemployed
- income from a permanent health insurance policy, creditor insurance and some long-term care policies
- pay-outs under some accident insurance policies (usually group ones)
- interest on a delayed settlement for damages for personal injury or death
- compensation for being wrongly sold a personal pension (paid following the review ordered by the Securities and Investments Board)
- interest on a tax rebate

GROSSING-UP TABLES

Some forms of income are paid net – after some tax has been deducted from them. For example, 20 per cent tax is normally deducted from the interest on savings accounts in banks and building societies before it is paid out to you or added to your account (unless it is a tax-exempt special savings account or individual savings account). In working out your tax bill, you may need to know how much the income was before the tax was deducted – the gross income.

You can find the gross income by grossing-up the net income using the ready reckoners below. With most forms of investment income, tax will have been deducted at 20 per cent, so that is the rate in the first ready reckoner. The second is for grossing-up income where tax has been deducted at the basic rate of 23 per cent. The third is for grossing-up income which comes with a tax credit of 10 per cent – share dividends and unit trust distributions.

If the tax rates change, you can use the following formula to work out the grossed-up income:

$$\text{Amount paid to you net} \times \left(\frac{100}{100 - \text{rate of tax}} \right)$$

So when the basic rate fell to 22 per cent on 6 April 2000, £50 received after tax would be grossed up to:

$$£50 \times \left(\frac{100}{100 - 22} \right)$$
$$= £50 \times \frac{100}{78}$$
$$= £64.10$$

Grossing-up at 20 per cent

Net amount £	Gross amount £	Net amount £	Gross amount £	Net amount £	Gross amount £
1	1.25	10	12.50	100	125.00
2	2.50	20	25.00	200	250.00
3	3.75	30	37.50	300	375.00
4	5.00	40	50.00	400	500.00
5	6.25	50	62.50	500	625.00
6	7.50	60	75.00	600	750.00
7	8.75	70	87.50	700	875.00
8	10.00	80	100.00	800	1,000.00
9	11.25	90	112.50	900	1,125.00
				1,000	1,250.00

EXAMPLE

Gary Loudon receives building society interest of £1,793 in the tax year ending 5 April 2000. He must gross up this net interest at 20 per cent as follows:

	Net income	Gross income
	£1,000	£1,250.00
	£700	£875.00
	£90	£112.50
	£3	£3.75
TOTAL	£1,793	£2,241.25

Grossing-up at 23 per cent

Net amount £	Gross amount £	Net amount £	Gross amount £	Net amount £	Gross amount £
1	1.30	10	12.99	100	129.87
2	2.60	20	25.97	200	259.74
3	3.90	30	38.96	300	389.61
4	5.19	40	51.95	400	519.48
5	6.49	50	64.94	500	649.35
6	7.79	60	77.92	600	779.22
7	9.09	70	90.91	700	909.09
8	10.39	80	103.90	800	1,038.96
9	11.69	90	116.88	900	1,168.83
				1,000	1,298.70

Grossing-up at 10 per cent

Net amount	Gross amount	Net amount	Gross amount	Net amount	Gross amount
£	£	£	£	£	£
1	1.11	10	11.11	100	111.11
2	2.22	20	22.22	200	222.22
3	3.33	30	33.33	300	333.33
4	4.44	40	44.44	400	444.44
5	5.56	50	55.56	500	555.56
6	6.67	60	66.67	600	666.67
7	7.78	70	77.78	700	777.78
8	8.89	80	88.89	800	888.89
9	10.00	90	100.00	900	1,000.00
				1,000	1,111.11

USEFUL LEAFLETS

You can get all these leaflets free from your tax office.

Introductions to self-assessment

SA/BK3 Self-assessment – a guide to keeping records for the self-employed
SA/BK4 Self-assessment – a general guide to keeping records
SA/BK5 Self-assessment – electronic version of the tax return
SA/BK6 Self-assessment – penalties for late tax returns
SA/BK7 Self-assessment – surcharges for late payment of tax
SA/BK8 Self-assessment – your guide

General guides to the Inland Revenue

IR37   Appeals against tax
IR73   Inland Revenue investigations: how settlements are negotiated
IR120   You and the Inland Revenue
IR141   Open government
IR160   Inland Revenue enquiries under self-assessment
IR167   Charter for Inland Revenue taxpayers
SVD1   Shares Valuation Division – an introduction
AO1   How to complain about the Inland Revenue
COP1   Mistakes by the Inland Revenue
COP2   Investigations
COP10   Information and advice
COP11   Enquiries into tax returns by local tax offices
COP17   Enquiries into applications for Working Families' Tax Credit or
        Disabled Person's Tax Credit

Income tax for particular groups

IR33   Income tax and school leavers
IR41   Income tax and job seekers

IR60	Income tax and students
IR90	Tax allowances and reliefs
IR121	Income tax and pensioners
IR170	Blind person's allowance
IR171	Income tax: A guide for people with children

Income tax and international issues

IR20	Residents and non-residents – liability to tax in the UK
IR138	Living or retiring abroad – a guide to tax on your UK income and pension
IR139	Income from abroad? A guide to UK tax on overseas income
IR140	Non-resident landlords, their agents and tenants

Income tax – general

IR1	Extra-statutory concessions (plus supplement with latest concessions)
IR45	What to do about tax when someone dies
IR46	Clubs, societies and associations
IR65	Giving to charity – how individuals can get tax relief
IR87	Letting and your home
IR93	Separation, divorce and maintenance payments
IR113	Gift Aid
IR115	Tax and childcare
IR119	Tax relief for vocational training
IR122	Volunteer drivers
IR123	Mortgage interest relief: buying your home
IR125	Using your own car for work
IR144	Income tax and incapacity benefit
IR163	Millennium Gift Aid

Savings and investments

IR78	Personal pensions
IR89	Personal Equity Plans (PEPs)
IR110	A guide for people with savings
IR114	TESSA – tax-free interest for taxpayers
IR129	Occupational pension schemes – an introduction
IR137	The Enterprise Investment Scheme
IR150	Taxation of rents – a guide to property income
IR152	Trusts – an introduction
IR153	Tax-exemption for sickness or unemployment insurance payments
IR169	Venture Capital Trusts
ISA1	The answers on ISAs. Your Guide

Employees

480	Expenses and benefits – a guide for tax
IR16	Share acquisitions by directors and employees – explanatory notes
IR34	PAYE. Pay As You Earn
IR69	Expenses payments and benefits in kind – how to save yourself work
IR95	Approved profit-sharing schemes – an outline for employees
IR97	Approved save as you earn share option schemes – an outline for employees
IR101	Approved company share option plans – an outline for employees
IR134	Income tax and relocation packages
IR136	Income tax and company vans
IR145	Low-interest loans provided by employers
IR161	Tax relief for employees' business travel
IR172	Income tax and company cars

Self-employed

CWL1	Starting your own business?
CWL2	National Insurance Contributions for self-employed people
IR56	Employed or self-employed? A guide for tax and National Insurance
IR72	Investigations: business accounts

Income tax – construction industry

IR14/15	Construction industry tax deduction scheme
IR40	Construction industry: conditions for getting a sub-contractor's tax certificate
IR116	Guide for sub-contractors with tax certificates
IR117	A sub-contractor's guide to the deduction scheme
IR148	Are your workers employed or self-employed – a guide to tax and National Insurance for contractors in the construction industry

Employers

480	Expenses and benefits – tax guide
490	Employee travel – a tax and NICs guide for employers
IR64	Giving to charity – how businesses can get tax relief
IR109	Employer compliance reviews and negotiations
IR132	The taxation of company cars from 6 April 1994: employers' guide
IR136	Income tax and company vans
IR155	PAYE settlement agreements
IR173	Tax credits – a summary for employers

Capital gains tax

CGT1	Capital gains tax – an introduction

Inheritance tax

IHT2   Inheritance tax on lifetime gifts
IHT3   Inheritance tax – an introduction
IHT8*   Alterations to an inheritance following a death
IHT11* Payment of inheritance tax from National Savings or British Government Stock
IHT13* Inheritance tax and penalties
IHT14* Inheritance tax – the personal representative's responsibilities
IHT15* Inheritance tax – how to calculate the liability
IHT16* Inheritance tax – settled property
IHT17* Inheritance tax – businesses, farms and woodlands
IHT18* Inheritance tax – foreign aspects

*Available from the three Capital Taxes Offices:
England and Wales: Ferrers House, PO Box 38, Castle Meadow Road, Nottingham, NG2 1BB (0115 974 2400)
Scotland: Mulberry House, 16 Picardy Place, Edinburgh EH1 3NB (0131 556 8511)
Northern Ireland: Dorchester House, 52-58 Great Victoria Street, Belfast BT2 7QL (028 9050 5353)

Business Economic Notes

These give information on how tax inspectors approach particular businesses such as travel agents, road hauliers, hairdressers and funeral directors. You can get them from:

Inland Revenue Reference Library
Room G9
South West Wing
Bush House
Strand
London WC2B 4RD

They cost £2 each (cheques payable to INLAND REVENUE).

INDEX

as income 8
industrial disablement benefits
157, 310
jobfinder's grant 157, 310
jobseeker's allowance 157, 159
maternity allowance 157, 310
one-parent benefit 310
renovation grants 310
school uniform grants 310
Social Fund payments 157, 310
student grants 157, 310
tax return 156–62
widow's bereavement allowance
11, 49, 193
bereavement allowance 11, 49, 193
widow's 303
betting winnings 7, 101, 311
bicycles, encouraged use of 34
blind person's allowance 11, 33,
187–8, 194, 305
bravery awards and decorations 101,
310
bridging loans 52
British Museum 130
Budget 2000 changes
allowances 26–7
businesses 29–30
capital gains tax 29
employees 30–1
income tax rates 26
inheritance tax 28
National Insurance 30, 31
reliefs 27–8
savings and investments 28
spending plans 26
stamp duty 29
tax credits 26, 27
tax return 31
value added tax 30
building societies
interest 8, 36, 149–51
grossing up 62
non-taxpayer 65

in tax return 147
without deduction of tax 65
mutuals becoming PLCs 120
permanent interest bearing shares
153
Business Economic Notes 318
business expansion scheme 82, 101
Business Links 240
businesses
Budget 2000 changes 29–30
business relief 134
information and communication
technology expenses 30
canteen meals 83, 309

C

capital allowances
adjustments 244–6
amount claimable 241–4
buying and selling capital items
243–4
claiming 244
furnished holiday lettings 259
information technology and
computer equipment 35
property 264
scrapping short life asset 244
self-employment 35
writing-down allowance 241–2
capital gains tax 1
accumulation unit trusts 119–20
antiques 39
Budget 2000 changes 29
businesses 29–30, 124–5
calculation of bill 115
calculation of gain 102–15
allowable expenses 106–8
assets owned on or before
31 March 1982 109–10
capital losses 111–12
chattels 111
gifts 106
indexation allowance 108–9

grossing-up
  interest 62
  tables 312–14
guardian's allowance 156, 310

H
heritage property 130
hold-over relief 281
holiday pay 199
home improvement loans 54
home income schemes 10, 52
homeowners
  absences 58–9
  capital gains tax 56–60
  dependents 54, 57
  gardens 57
  home improvement loans 54
  home income schemes 10, 52
  improvement grants 310
  inheritance tax 132–3
  joint tenancy 132–3
  lettings 60
  mortgages *see* mortgage interest
    relief
  private residence relief 38, 56, 57,
    58, 59
  property dealings 60
  renovation and repair grants 156
  rent a room scheme 38, 253–5,
    311
  second homes 38, 56, 57–8
  separation and divorce 48
  tax savings 38–9
  tenancy in common 133
  working from home 55, 58
houseboats 51, 57, 88
housing associations 101, 130
housing benefit 156, 310

I
improvement grants 310
incapacity benefit 156, 157, 160, 310
incentive awards 199–200

income
  asset sales 7
  casual earnings 6, 167
  filling in return 146–69
  freelance earnings 167
  furnished holiday lettings 256
  inherited 277–8
  leasing equipment 167
  losses unable to be set against 167
  notification of new sources 14
  payments that are not 6–7
  pensions and benefits 156–62
  permanent health insurance 167
  rent from letting 6
  salary as 6
  savings 3
  self-employment 231–4
  shares unit trusts 3
  tax-free 7
    benefits 310
    from job 309
    on leaving work 309–10
    pensions 310
  taxable 2–3, 4
  total 2–3, 4
  trusts 6
  types 8
  see also fringe benefits
income support 27, 157
income tax 1–5
  construction industry 317
  filling in return 146–69
  information leaflets 315–16, 317
  paid by employer 98
  rates 4–5, 26
indexation allowance 99, 108–9
individual learning accounts 27
individual savings accounts (ISAs) 28,
    37, 76–9, 101
  CAT standards 78
  choosing 78–9
  investments 77–8
  life assurance policies within 166

electronic payment discounts 30
threshold rate 30
vans 95–6, 205
Venture Capital Trusts 101
Budget 2000 changes 27, 30
dividends 149, 311
income relief 171, 181–2
minimum holding time 28
saving and investing 82
Victoria Cross 310
vocational training 27
costs 171, 177–8
vouchers 87–8, 203–4
luncheon vouchers 83, 309
wages in lieu of notice 309

W

war disablement
benefits 157
pensions 310
war orphans benefit 157
war widows pension 157, 310
wasting assets 100

wear and tear 39, 262, 264
wedding presents 40, 130, 309
widows
bereavement allowance 11, 49,
193, 303
abolition 49
payment 157
pension 157, 159
war widows pension 157, 310
widowed mother's allowance 157,
159
wills 40
winnings 7, 101, 311
work buses 85
working families tax credit 12, 14,
26, 27, 310
working from home 55, 58
workplace nurseries *see* childcare
writing-down allowances 241–2

Y

youth training scheme allowance 157,
310